Dynamic Drive

Dynamic Drive

The Purpose-Fueled Formula for
Sustainable Success

Molly Fletcher

hachette
BOOKS

NEW YORK

Hachette Go, an imprint of Hachette Books
Hachette Book Group
1290 Avenue of the Americas
New York, NY 10104
HachetteGo.com
Facebook.com/HachetteGo
Instagram.com/HachetteGo

First Edition: September 2024

Published by Hachette Go, an imprint of Hachette Book Group, Inc. The Hachette Go name and logo is a trademark of the Hachette Book Group. The Hachette Speakers Bureau provides a wide range of authors for speaking events. To find out more, go to hachettespeakersbureau.com or email HachetteSpeakers@hbgusa.com.

Hachette Go books may be purchased in bulk for business, educational, or promotional use. For information, please contact your local bookseller or Hachette Book Group Special Markets Department at: special.markets@hbgusa.com.

The publisher is not responsible for websites (or their content) that are not owned by the publisher.

Print book interior design by Sheryl Kober.

Library of Congress Cataloging-in-Publication Data has been applied for.
ISBNs: 978-0-306-83419-6 (hardcover); 978-0-306-83421-9 (ebook)

Printed in Canada

MRQ

Printing 1, 2024

To my daughters Emma, Meg, and Kate, who are central to my purpose.

And to all of you who seek the joyful pursuit of a better life.

Contents

Contents

Dynamic Drive

Introduction

One Point Away

My heart pounded as I gripped the phone while it rang. When my social science professor answered, I took a deep breath and said, "Sir, this is Molly, I think there's been a mistake. I just received my grade from your class. I got a 'D.'"

He responded fast and firmly, almost as if he were expecting my call, "You were one point away from failing the entire class, so you might want to hang up the phone and be grateful."

I hung up in shock. My GPA for the fall term at Michigan State was a 1.8, which meant that not only had I been one point away from failing my social science class, I was one point away from getting kicked off the tennis team. That would have been a disaster, after years of training and yearning to play college tennis. As a walk-on—I held the last spot—I had been thrilled to squeak onto the team at my mother's alma mater. That day I felt the pang of disappointment, the cold chill of fear wash over me. It was far too close to no court time.

When my mom saw my first semester grades, she looked at me in a way I hadn't seen before and said, "You can do better, Molly." My heart sank. She was my fiercest supporter, but she was also never one to hold her tongue. "Molly," she continued, "you can be great."

I don't know if you've ever had someone speak that kind of truth into your life, but knowing that my mom loved me enough to confront me with those two realities really hit home. *I can do better. I can be great.* I nodded reluctantly as she added calmly, "Something has to give. What's it going to be? Partying or tennis?" Then she placed my anemic grade transcript on the dining room table and walked away.

As she walked away, I started to mentally review the events of my first term at Michigan State. I had fought my way onto the tennis team, but I was struggling with my confidence as a player. I felt like I was still playing catch-up compared with most of the girls who had started playing as soon as they could grip a racket.

During my freshman year I periodically contributed as the fifth singles line (that's the last spot) and consistently contributed in doubles (two girls got injured, which plugged me in). It wasn't lost on me that I would have missed the opportunities for advancement that arose as the result of a few injuries if my GPA had been one point lower. My mom was right: I knew I could do better. I knew I had to do better.

The year before, when I was training in hopes of making a college team, my junior tennis coach had imparted wise words that resonated with me: "You need to get inside the baseline and look for opportunities to attack the ball—to close in, cut off the angle, and take the ball early. You've settled back at the baseline, gotten comfortable there, waiting for the ball to come to you. That isn't going to get it done at the next level."

I had been a good tennis player in junior tennis, in part due to talent and effort, less so due to strategy or tennis acumen. His advice to attack the ball, to run toward the opportunity and seize it with every fiber, began to seem like advice that would serve me well off the court, too. My goals outweighed the discomfort. I had made it to Michigan State and onto the tennis team. Now it was time to give it my all to make sure I stayed there. I needed a mindset of "going for it." So, I made a decision. I was going to be better—a better student and a better athlete. I had to dig deep inside myself and unlock the drive within. No one else could.

On campus, I lived across the street from the student-athlete weight room and began to plan my schedule around getting in extra workouts. I was getting stronger and quicker on the court. The extra workouts, the ball machine, and the wall drills were paying off. I slept well, I ate well, I cut back on the parties. I lived at the library, making the back corner of the second floor into my second home.

Anytime I felt my discipline slip or woke up without the motivation to hit the gym, I pushed forward anyway. I reminded myself of my goal of competing at my highest level, my desire to contribute to the team. My reasons for training, for sacrificing, for grinding that I threaded through everything I did. I showed up when I was tired and when I didn't feel like it. I asked questions of my professors, coaches, and parents to learn more about the "why" at the heart of the lesson. I failed often, too, and in the face of that failure, I began again, each and every time. I connected to other athletes and to my classmates who were in the same pursuit.

I didn't know it then, but I was tapping into something that would power me throughout the rest of my life—drive. The drive to make oneself better is attached to our greatest desires. I wanted to play tennis. I wanted to be better at it. At eighteen, I was about to learn just how far I could go with drive.

My freshman year, I played more than expected, in part due to team-mates' injuries and my resilience.

By my sophomore year, I was contributing in both singles and doubles consistently. The other walk-on whom I battled to secure court time our freshman year quit the team. I traded nights at the bars with my friends for a second workout or an early bedtime. Before big tennis matches, I'd drive two miles home to sleep at my childhood home instead of my sorority house with fifty girls. That year, my hard work paid off and I earned a partial scholarship. (Very partial.)

By junior year I earned a half scholarship. I was playing the number-one doubles spot as well as singles, and I was voted team captain by my teammates. My commitment was paying off in the classroom, too. I was Academic All-Big Ten my sophomore, junior, and senior seasons, a recognition given to varsity athletes who maintain a high academic standard.

Senior year, I was on a full scholarship and I was again voted team captain by my teammates. I graduated with honors and I felt confident in my skills as a leader.

My drive had paid off, and it was so much fun to reap the rewards I had worked so hard to attain.

I remember like it was yesterday: walking into the house where I grew up, telling my two hard-working, loving parents that I had earned a full scholarship. College was expensive for a teacher and a sales rep, and I knew that saving a year of tuition was a bigger deal than they let on. Both of my older brothers were on scholarships—one was attending the Air Force Academy on full scholarship and the other was in the ROTC program at Auburn. I was the third and final kid they were helping through college, and I knew the bills were substantial.

It's easy to imagine that the time I was spending improving my tennis game would distract from my studies, or vice versa, but it was the opposite. After my near-disastrous first semester, I 4.0'd seven terms in a row after that 1.8. There was something powerful in learning how to optimize my performance on and off the court, and this kind of drive, I was learning, was transferable. It wasn't just about what I was achieving; it was who I was becoming.

We're all one point away from failing when we live in complacency. When you're not willing to step into hard, to push yourself into discomfort, or to take on the very real, tedious work of self-improvement, then you can never reach your potential.

I would have survived being cut from the tennis team. I would have beaten myself up some, and then gone through the rest of my college experience struggling through classes and longing for the one goal I had always dreamed of: being a Division I athlete. I would have settled for average grades, for playing tennis casually with friends or family. I would have spent a lot more time partying with my friends, which was fun but didn't really add up to anything substantial. I would have gotten comfortable with the feeling of "good enough" as I started my career. But I would have never known what I was capable of, and that would have been the real loss.

Instead, I learned that if I wanted to improve, it was up to me. I would need to be all gas, no brakes. I would need to strive, get uncomfortable, put in the hours of work, and sometimes ask for directions. Hit a few speed bumps, scratch the paint, heck maybe change my tires—it was all part of the journey. One thing was for sure: it was not going to stop me from getting to my destination.

How I Learned About Dynamic Drive

Throughout my life, I've been gathering experiential data around peak performance, both personally and professionally. I have observed and studied the risks and the benefits of drive and its enemy, complacency. How one could unlock more than you ever envisioned for yourself, while the other could lull you into a fall sense of security.

I've had a front-row seat to a master class in drive for almost two decades as a sports agent, representing some of the biggest names in sports—the most accomplished athletes and coaches in the world, Hall of Famers, national and world champions, Olympians, All-Stars. The world sees the achievement, the trophy, the tears of joy, the fame. I see everything before and after that moment, what it takes to get there and what happens next if you want to do it again and again.

After I transitioned from my career as an agent and entered the more traditional business world, I saw a reality that I hadn't experienced before. I thought everyone woke up every day and strived to get better. I thought building resilience and mindset, setting goals, and embracing the grueling work to achieve them was the norm. I couldn't shake the curiosity about what drives top performers in every field, not just sports. In sports, if you don't perform, you lose your job. Drive is essential for survival. Period. I found that the sports world offers so much wisdom and inspiration that all of us can learn from.

I began to envision bringing the tools I'd seen athletes use day in and day out in improving their performance to more people across different fields.

I launched my podcast *Game Changers with Molly Fletcher* in hopes of getting to the bottom of what drive truly is. Over the course of nearly two hundred episodes, I've had the chance to ask accomplished CEOs, entertainers, entrepreneurs, and thought leaders questions about their stories, overcoming obstacles, facing failure, and so much more. Through these candid and inspiring conversations, I began to piece together the commonalities at the core of their success. I then built a methodology that enables everyone to harness this same high level of drive.

In 2021, I took everything I had learned and put it into a TED Talk—"Secrets of a Champion Mindset"—where I spent seventeen minutes outlining the importance and power of drive, and, most importantly, expanding on how it could help people. When the video went viral and was viewed by millions, I knew that there was an audience ready and eager for concrete steps on how to achieve high-level drive in their own lives.

This book is about what I've learned in some of the most privileged perches in sports, business, and beyond. My work on Dynamic Drive is built on the decades I've spent working and learning from top professional athletes and coaches and the hundreds of thought leaders, innovators, business leaders, and entrepreneurs I've interviewed for my podcast. I've synthesized hundreds of hours of conversation and observations over the last thirty-plus years into this book. I will offer you a lens into my experiences and research while tapping into neuroscience, philosophy, psychology, and more. I will act as your guide through the path to building the kind of relentless, unshakable drive that put a man on the moon, built the Great Pyramids, discovered penicillin, and created Artificial Intelligence.

Dynamic Drive is the formula for sustained high performance in all areas of your life. It is the consistent and joyful pursuit of a better you. A better life. One of fulfillment. One without burnout. A version of you that becomes a magnet to people you know and don't know. Dynamic Drive is the way to push yourself to reach your greatest potential and learn how to make your success sustainable, despite the inevitable ebbs and flows we all experience professionally and personally.

Dynamic Drive is by your design and created on purpose.

How to Use This Book to Find Your Dynamic Drive

It is my deepest desire that this book will change your life, personally and professionally, forever. I offer you a new definition of drive and expose its enemy, complacency.

But while I've cited the research and science here, this book is not an academic research paper. It's better. It's a real story. Full of real people. It's an operating manual. My contribution is to pull together ideas that matter most and connect them in a way that is highly actionable for you. You'll find wisdom and practical application. Let this book be your guide. Something you reference constantly as you live into Dynamic Drive.

Dynamic Drive promises lasting principles that bring joy, meaning, and a life without regrets. It offers a framework around which you can build your days, your relationships, and your work. It is about constantly evolving into the best version of yourself.

The strategies I cover are relevant to anyone looking for an approach to living their life in a way that aligns with their deepest values. This isn't about achievement for achievement's sake or doing more, more, more. It's about figuring out whether there are parts of your life where you are playing small or safe or are dissatisfied. Maybe you're burned out, but feel forced to grind it out. Maybe you're wildly successful, but feel alone. Maybe you're climbing the ladder at work, but it isn't fun anymore. Maybe you're feeling disconnected from the relationships in your life that matter most, but you don't know how to reengage. Maybe your couch-to-5K program is looking a lot more like just a couch program. If you're stuck in some area of your life—whether it's personally, professionally, physically, relationally, emotionally, or mentally—the tools I've developed will help you reignite your purpose, renew your energy, and engage in the pursuit of your dreams.

Imagine a world in which people engage their Dynamic Drive at a high level, where people are finding their purpose, getting clear on what they're chasing, and pursuing it every day. A world where aspirations are rooted in values, not achievement.

Imagine a world where every obstacle is viewed as an opportunity because it's seen as a vessel for growth. A world where people respond with curiosity, not judgment.

Imagine a world where the desire to learn and grow is valued more than the desire to be right. Where we have never arrived, but are always becoming.

Imagine a world where you have the energy for the people and activities in your life that matter most. Where the choices you make create alignment, not disconnect.

Imagine a world where connection with others is core. Where stepping toward, not away, is how we solve problems and serve one another.

This imagined reality is not out of our reach. The key is learning to ignite Dynamic Drive. It lies within each of us. Even if it has never been cultivated or has been allowed to go dormant, it can be tapped into and harnessed to finally realize those dreams. It's for the fighters, the seekers, the believers, the doers who know there is more out there for them but need a push to get the traction on the journey.

This book might have a beginning and an end; but Dynamic Drive doesn't. What you are about to embark on is a journey of a better life. Along the way, every day you have a choice: to unlock your drive or stay in your comfort zone. To strive or settle. To change or stay put. To compromise your deepest values, or live into them. To grow or stagnate. To step into the game, or stand on the sideline.

It's inside of you and it's up to you.

Part 1

The Truth About Drive

Chapter 1

The Road to a Better Life

I spent most of the spring of 1995 at the baseball fields at Georgia Tech. The campus is located just north of downtown Atlanta, and by the middle of baseball season the temperature is a very humid eighty degrees. Day after day, I would lean on the fence along the home-team dugout and watch the players right alongside all the scouts with stopwatches around their necks and clipboards in their hands. All these guys (and yes, they were all men) knew each other. Here I was, a twenty-four-year-old woman elbowing my way into the middle of an old boys' club whose members sported chewing tobacco in one cheek and a wad of bubble gum in the other.

How exactly did I find myself there? I had built on the skills discovered on the Michigan State tennis courts to move to Atlanta. I wanted to break into the sports business, and it seemed an almost-impossible feat for a young woman with no connections in the field (literally). I had gotten my foot in the door with a sports marketing agency in Atlanta and I was eager to go for more.

Six months into my tenure at the agency, I found myself sorting free merchandise and making piles of high-end sunglasses on my desk when I was hit with the feeling that I was capable of so much more. My duties had begun to feel mindless. I served as a driver to Olympic events for Lenny Wilkens, I picked Chuck Daly up at the Atlanta airport, I delivered Mike Fratello his dry cleaning. Legendary NBA coaches, no doubt—but I wanted to be more than their gofer. I could feel myself starting to settle, just doing the next small task that landed on my desk. But in that moment—up to my elbows in sunglasses—I knew that the only way I would get the chance to do more would be to ask for it.

So, with a sense of youthful confidence and a good bit of naïveté, I popped my head into my boss's office and said, "Hey! Quick question."

"Yes?" He half-spun his chair around to acknowledge me. "What's up?"

"What's our growth plan?" I apparently didn't believe in asking easy questions. As he turned to fully face me, I took it as permission and stepped into his office.

"What do you mean?" His face showed a mix of surprise and amusement, but not annoyance. That was good. I could work with that.

"Well, for example. What's our plan to sign more coaches and players?"

"Referrals," he assured me. "That's how we got here. Our clients love us, and they refer clients to us." I nodded and slipped into the chair in front of his desk. He didn't protest, so I continued.

"Got it. Love it. But—" I paused and smiled "—what if we got a little bit more aggressive?" He cocked an eyebrow and leaned forward as I continued. "I mean, we're here in Atlanta. Baseball's a big deal here. The Braves are here. Minor league teams are close. There are strong college programs right here. What if we went out and recruited players instead of just waiting for referrals?"

He stared at me for what seemed like ages. I sat uncomfortably awaiting his reply, my heart now racing. My excitement and confidence were starting to give way. I figured he was probably assessing if I even had a clue as to what I was talking about. Finally, I swallowed my nerves and went for it.

"What if I put a business plan together to show you how we could start with baseball?" I said.

He looked at me and then half-turned to look out the window for what felt like another eternity. Turning back to me, he shrugged. "If you can figure it out, go for it."

I thanked him and backed out of his office. As I walked back to my desk and sat down, the adrenaline cleared and I thought: *Oh, wow . . . Now what?* I didn't know anything about baseball. I never followed baseball growing up; I didn't know the players or the intricacies of the game. But I knew I could learn.

I don't know if he actually believed I could do it or if he just wanted me to stop coming into his office uninvited. All I know is that he gave me a shot. And I ran with it.

I remember that conversation like it was yesterday. I can picture the office, my boss sitting at his big desk, and the way I felt walking out having earned my chance to prove myself. I remember it because of what it ended up becoming for me. It changed my life.

Slowly but surely, I built relationships with the coaches, the scouts, the players, and even the parents. I showed up to the fields every day to learn everything about the players and the game, knowing that the insider perspective would give me the edge I needed. Before long, I was using the lingo, talking about going deep, sitting on a curveball, roping it to first. I loved the process and—get this—I loved the grind of pushing to get better every single day, to connect, to uncover the opportunity.

More than anything, I really loved the idea of helping an athlete capitalize on such a remarkably unique window of time in their lives. Imagine the boy in the backyard dreaming of playing in the big leagues. Draft day is the moment those childhood dreams become reality. It can be life-changing. I signed a couple guys out of Georgia Tech that first year and a few more the next year. I expanded my relationships to other college programs, other minor league teams, and even into other markets. From baseball, we expanded to other sports, like golf, and then to representing college coaches.

When our coaches would get fired (which inevitably happens when you make a lot of money and don't win enough), we'd find them broadcasting jobs. Thus, a broadcaster division was born.

By the time I left the agency more than fifteen years later, I'd grown our client representation division to over three hundred athletes, coaches, and broadcasters. By my mid-thirties, CNN dubbed me "the female Jerry Maguire" for forging new ground as one of the first top female sports agents.

I look back to that day in my early twenties, with more big ideas and bravado than actual know-how, and I see the crossroads that I was facing. I had a choice to stay in my lane, continue working hard and completing the tasks assigned to me—or to disrupt the status quo, put myself out there, and push for more. I had an instinct that company growth would come only through expanding our talent representation division, serving our clients in a holistic way. And I was willing to bet on myself.

The deck was stacked against me. For starters, there was no visible representation of women pursuing this career path and many people—often thinking they had my own best interest at heart—discouraged me. It would have been easy to believe that I didn't belong there. I was different, yes. But I was able to unlock the gift and the value in that. It forced me to figure out how to be better than the challenges that stood in my way. I had to find a way to be so good that prospects couldn't say no. And if they did, I had to learn that "no" was simply feedback I could use to improve and get better.

It didn't happen overnight. Far from it. It was years of pushing boundaries, testing my confidence, and strengthening my purpose that allowed me to succeed and find fulfillment. That is what I've distilled into the **Seven Keys to Unlock Your Dynamic Drive.**

The New Definition of Drive

Drive is commonly defined as "the energy and determination to achieve things." It plays a significant role in achieving both short-term and long-term objectives. Drive is finite. You work toward your goal and when you achieve it, you stop the work. You train for a marathon, run your race, and hang up your sneakers. You double-down on sales calls, hit your quota, and then coast. Dynamic Drive is more. It's a vision for your life fueled by your purpose. It's an unending pursuit of better.

Dynamic Drive is the spark that ignites and fuels the joyful pursuit of a better life.

It's a way of life. A mindset. A daily commitment to live in a way that aligns with your soul. It's not the linear pursuit of a singular goal. Achievement is just a part of the journey, not the end goal.

Dynamic is defined as "constant change, activity, or progress; a force that stimulates change or progress within a system or process." Key word: progress, not a single moment.

Dynamic Drive combines the goal-directed, pressing urgency of the typical definition of drive with a purpose-driven evolving nature. Our lives are changing constantly. We can either hide our head in the sand or we can learn to be flexible and step toward the opportunities offered to us. Dynamic Drive is a choice. It's about becoming a person who embraces the fluidity of life and the positive energy it can unlock in us. Dynamic Drive recognizes that we are always a work in progress—that our goals change, our purpose evolves, and so do we.

Dynamic Drive is the process by which we implement and sustain intentional change. It is an approach to life that roots success in creating deep alignment with your values and priorities. Dynamic Drive is sustainable because it's fueled by purpose. Instead of depleting your energy, it renews it.

Dynamic Drive is healthy livin'. It's not a diet. It permeates every aspect of your life. It has no goal line. It's unending. It's stacking days on days of putting in the work to get better. It's a muscle you strengthen daily with intention. Dynamic Drive doesn't wait for confidence; it establishes it. Dynamic Drive is about seeing challenges as opportunities, change as a gift.

Dynamic Drive needs human connection because it's empty without it. It's available to introverts and extroverts, leaders and non-leaders. It's a belief system that the "yeses" will come if we stay the course, and the "nos" along the way are just feedback.

Dynamic Drive isn't about achievement but rather fulfillment. It isn't about fame or money. It isn't about winning. It's about who you become as a result of the journey and the lives you change along the way. Dynamic Drive is not the candle on top of the cake; it is the layers underneath.

Now, don't miss this: drive isn't just about motivation. Motivation is a part of Dynamic Drive, but motivation is fleeting. It comes and goes. One morning you're motivated for an early run, and the next you want to hit snooze. Dynamic Drive is a guarantee you'll never hit the snooze button again. That you'll wake up from a life of autopilot.

It doesn't matter whether your dream is to play pro ball, become the best sales manager, cultivate a happy and loving family, or run the best bakery on the East Coast. Dynamic Drive is the secret sauce to make it happen. No matter who you are, what you want, or what you've accomplished (or not accomplished), you can unlock and harness Dynamic Drive to realize your wildest dreams and enjoy the journey while doing it. You see, Dynamic Drive is not about what you achieve, it's about who you become.

What Are You Chasing?

The Dynamic Drive lifestyle begins with understanding your values and priorities. Get clear on what's most important to you, what excites and challenges you, and where you're going.

To fully embrace your Dynamic Drive, you must begin to get a sense of who you want to be. The legacy you want to leave. We'll go deeper into your purpose soon, but for now, I'd like you to begin thinking broadly about what you want your life to look like.

Intentionality about where you put your time and energy is essential to finding fulfillment, which is the real goal. It's not about more, more, more. Because more money, more trophies, and more promotions won't bring fulfillment. I have personally seen miserable millionaires, empty souls with more trophies than friends and corner offices that no one wants to walk into. It's about finding meaning and enjoyment in your intentional efforts anchored in your values.

Every day you will be presented with distractions from your mission. Keep your purpose front and center. You will need it. There will be moments, big and small, when you have choices to make. To ask yourself: "Is the story I'm telling myself taking me where I want to go, or do I need to shift my mindset?" Or, "Is this where I should put my energy?"

Too often, I've seen smart, talented people jump onto that hamster wheel, focusing on speed with no real sense of direction. When you're going so hard, you pick up speed, for sure. But you also stop paying close attention to where you're going, and that's never a good sign for long-term success.

Intentionality in your efforts is more important than speed. When you go too fast, the view out of the window is blurry. You might get somewhere faster, but is that somewhere where you wanted to end up? It feels easier to hold on tight to the wheel, keep the gas down; it's what you know.

Maybe you like the speed because it's distracting. It becomes your sole focus, and it feels good most of the time.

Or maybe professionally, you are killing it. Promotions, money, you name it; but something feels off. "What is it?" you ask yourself, but then the calendar dings and you are off to your next meeting.

Or maybe you've poured everything into your kids and now they're off to college, building their own lives, and you want more. Something that feels as purposeful as raising your miracles.

Knowing the why behind your efforts can bolster resilience during challenging times. When you face obstacles or setbacks, your clear intentions can help you stay motivated and focused as you overcome them.

Whatever your circumstances, if they are not ideal, what's at risk to change? What's at risk to opt into a better life? The life that you want most. What's at risk to close the gap between where you are and where you want to be?

Maybe the gap you feel between your current state and your ideal state feels too vast. Just too big to undertake. Too hard, and no fun.

When we get busy, distracted, frustrated, or overwhelmed, we rarely pause to reorient ourselves. But you need to reflect, to check in with your internal GPS to make sure wherever you're heading is taking you to where—and who—you want to be.

Start by considering:

What am I chasing? And why?

With all of this demand, what is being compromised? And, am I okay with that?

Do my values align with where I put my energy?

Or, the bigger questions, like:

What do I want my legacy to be?

How do I want people to describe me?

Who will be at my eightieth birthday party?

You will be faced with endless opportunities to reinforce your Dynamic Drive and to practice the tools you'll learn here. Each day you can choose to do what you want most, to live into your highest purpose and ignite all cylinders of your Dynamic Drive.

The Heartbeat of Dynamic Drive Is Purpose

Dynamic Drive is about aligning our goals with our purpose and our values. A focus on achievement is a one-way street to . . . well, achieving something. What happens *after* you achieve that thing? You must remain consistently curious about what's possible in your life. You have a purpose threaded through the daily effort. Purpose is your North Star that is rooted in your core beliefs and core values. People who find meaning in their efforts report higher life satisfaction.[1] When you devote yourself to meaningful pursuit, you tap into a deeper sense of purpose that fuels a feeling of fulfillment.

Along the way, there will be detours to navigate and exits offered often. If you want off the path of Dynamic Drive, you will have plenty of opportunities to cruise off into the sunset of complacency. But with a wider lens, you can see and embrace the path. That's normal.

Navy SEALs are some of the toughest people on the planet. They embody the tenets of Dynamic Drive, and they've embraced the grind, particularly through their training. Before becoming SEALs, candidates are put through some of the most mentally challenging and physically demanding training in the world. As part of that training, they must graduate from a twenty-four-week program called Basic Underwater Demolition/SEAL training, or BUDS. The first seven-week phase is a grueling test of physical endurance and mental fortitude that consists of running, swimming, and calisthenics performed in the blazing sun on Coronado Beach, California, that gets progressively more challenging each week.

It's no surprise that candidates often begin questioning their decision to continue on in this training, with a significant number dropping out. The Navy knows that. To weed out those who aren't fully committed, to make it easy for those who want out to get out, they put a large brass ship's bell on a pole easy for candidates to access during their training. At any time, a participant in the program can ring the bell. The bell is visible during their training, making it remarkably easy for them to ring it, as they endure extremely uncomfortable circumstances. It's very easy to leave, making it even harder to stay. Ringing the bell stops the pain, the exertion, and it's a mental test as much as physical to embrace that grind in the face of the bell. Dynamic Drive is a choice. You can tap out anytime you want.

Purpose will help you to stay aligned with the work, even when it's painful or uncomfortable and feels never ending. The importance of purpose is beautifully underscored in the parable about three bricklayers. After the great fire of 1666 that leveled London, the world's most famous architect, Christopher Wren, was commissioned to rebuild St Paul's

Cathedral. One day, he observed three bricklayers working very hard and fast. To the first bricklayer, Wren asked the question, "What are you doing?" to which the bricklayer replied, "I'm a bricklayer. I'm working hard laying bricks to feed my family." The second bricklayer responded, "I'm a builder. I'm building a wall." But the third bricklayer, the most productive of the three and the future leader of the group, when asked the question, "What are you doing?" replied with a gleam in his eye, "I'm a cathedral builder. I'm building a great cathedral for The Almighty."[2]

Purpose is what sets them apart. It's one thing to work hard to earn for your family, it's another to be engaged in building a wall or a building, and it's even more meaningful to be building a cathedral to worship in. Imagine the difference in focus and commitment among the three mindsets. There is no doubt that when you are laying that brick down with the vision of the people on the other side—the baptisms, the weddings, the funerals that will all take place within the walls you're building—you will take every chance to do your best work, to fix the alignment when needed, to go the extra mile to ensure the highest standard of work.

I'm not building a cathedral, but I do connect with large groups of people and try to inspire them as a keynote speaker. There are times when I have to snap myself into "go mode." I deliver almost one hundred keynotes a year. Some days I feel better than other days, more rested, mentally sharper, emotionally more engaged. Like all of us, right? Over the years, I've learned to optimize my energy and strengthen my mindset through the tools I outline in this book. I've trained in a way that ensures moments of complacency or distraction are just that—moments. But when that moment hits, I reconnect to my purpose quickly, dialing back into why I speak and the opportunity to transform lives.

How do I do this tactically? I step out from backstage and look at all of the people walking in. Each one has their own story, which I try to envision—the longtime leader tasked with inspiring her team, the new sales team member brimming with excitement, and the newly promoted manager trying to find his lane. I see how hard they work and the level of demand on their time and energy. A guy trying to get an email out before my speech starts. Two people talking and laughing. Then I look at the leaders in charge of the event who have trusted me with their people. They're trusting me to stand up on a stage in front of thousands of people and connect with them in a meaningful way. In that moment, I refocus on my purpose: to lead, inspire, and connect with courage and optimism. As soon as I focus in on that, any feelings of nerves, tiredness, or distraction quickly fade away.

Purpose is the key. I recently gave a keynote to ADP, a company that provides payroll solutions for businesses of all sizes. The leader kicked off the event by talking about how they help people get paid. Then he took it a step further: if people don't get paid, they don't have a house, they don't have a car, and they don't have food on the table. I could see the people in the audience nodding their heads, connecting *what* they do to *why* they do it. When you frame it that way, you can find deep purpose in the work being done at ADP. So, you might wonder how to find purpose inside of your job and your company, but I promise you there is.

How to Use Dynamic Drive

The road to a better life is open to anyone with the desire. If you feel stuck, if you find yourself wondering, *Is this all there is?*, or if you find inspiration but are unable to stick with it, there is hope. You can train yourself to unlock your Dynamic Drive and to live a life aligned with your deepest values.

Recently I was working with a group of about twenty-five leaders who were going through an exercise I teach called the Alignment Audit, where participants evaluate how aligned their values are with their actions. One of the gentlemen in attendance (I'll call him Dave) was a big, burly, long-tenured company man, who'd selected the last seat in the back and was visibly skeptical of the experience he was embarking on. However, within an hour he was in, leaning forward almost as if regretting his choice of the back row. After a break, Dave moved to a table in the front of the room. He was all in!

I asked the group to consider the top five most important things in their lives. I observed him as he concentrated on his list, slowly writing on each line.

I gently directed the group to then rate how important each one is to them on a scale of 1 to 10. No problem. Next, I said, "Now, I'd like you to rank how much time, attention, and energy you invest in each." This is when it gets real, real fast.

Dave, the 6-foot-2-inch guy with biceps the size of my thighs, started to cry. He stayed focused on the paper, but tears were beginning to drop slowly, creating a pattern of wet patches on the audit. I quietly walked over and handed him some Kleenex. This wasn't uncommon at all. Dave clearly saw the significant misalignment with what he holds most dear in his life and how much time and energy he gives it.

Here were Dave's answers:

What's Important?		Rate on a scale of 1 to 10 (1 being not important; 10 extremely important)		
Write down what's most important in your life. Consider the categories of physical, emotional, mental, relational, and spiritual.		How important is each to you?	How much time, attention, and energy have you invested in each?	Calculate the difference.
1.	**Health.** (Dave is thirty pounds overweight.)	10	5	5
2.	**Faith.** (He is skipping Mass, only going on holidays now and feeling spiritually disconnected.)	10	4	6

3.	**My son.** (He misses about half of his son's baseball games.)	10	5	5
4.	**My work team.** (He is well respected and has solid relationships with both his peers and direct reports, but could benefit from more focus.)	8	6	2
5.	**My aging parents.** (He recently canceled a trip to visit them because of a last-minute client meeting.)	9	3	6

This exercise illuminated a huge disconnect for Dave in the things that he valued versus how much time he was investing in those things. Living with such discord is not only a source of angst and frustration, it's also a drain on your energy. But most of us aren't even aware of this misalignment in our own lives. Seeing the difference between what we value and where we spend our time is the first step in making necessary shifts.

After the group completed the audit, I asked for volunteers to share what they discovered through the exercise. To my surprise, Dave raised his hand.

"Sorry guys, this one got me . . . but I'm sure it got a bunch of us in here. . . ." He looked around. People were nodding. You could hear a pin drop.

Dave shared, "My son, man I love that little man . . . But I'm screwing this one up. I've got a problem here, a misalignment . . ." The tears were significant at this point.

I handed him more tissue and then asked: "Are you clear that your son is a 10 in importance for you?"

"Yes, yes, yes," Dave said with a shaky voice.

"Are you committed to making his games a priority?" I asked in an empathetic tone. "Are you committed to the other adjustments to align your time and energy output with what you are saying matters deeply to you: your son?"

"Yes!"

I looked around and scanned the room. "Does anyone else have some gaps in what they say matters most and the energy and attention they give to it?"

Every hand but two went up.

"Okay, then. This will help you too. Dave, what needs to change for you to give your son the time, attention, and energy you want to give him?"

I worked with Dave to develop concrete strategies in each area of his life. We first focused on how he can show up as a better father. These were the strategies we came up with:

- **Mental:** I will stay clear on my purpose—my role as a father—and remind myself I can't get this time back. I need to shift my mindset to know that he needs me more than he might let on. I am going to write my purpose and values on a whiteboard in my office to keep this visible.
- **Physical:** I can adjust my travel schedule for work to accommodate my time with him. (Dave was divorced and shared custody.) I need to make his room at my place his own. I need to say no to extracurriculars and trips so that I can be at his baseball games. I need to prioritize exercising at least three days a week and make better food choices, so I feel good enough to stay active with my son.
- **Emotional:** I am committed to modeling my ability to regulate my emotions so that he can see a male role model who is self-aware and intentional, and who has the courage to set boundaries and stick to them.
- **Spiritual:** On the weekends I have him, I will prioritize attending church together, joining in prayer before meals, and helping him to embrace his personal faith journey as he grows up.

- **Relational:** I will put my phone down and be present with him when we are together. He is a teenager with his own interests. I want to engage with him in what he likes to do and talk to him more about girls and dating. I need to always say yes when he wants to play catch in the yard.

He had a plan to execute, but did he have the skills to sustain this kind of large-scale change for the long haul? Well, I'm proud to tell you that he did. It's a constant work in progress, but today Dave is down thirteen pounds and is training for a 5K. His son is a junior in high school and Dave is planning their college tour this spring. At work, he's added three more people to his team and was tasked with leading a new company-wide initiative. With his parents facing new health issues, Dave moved them closer to him so that he can be more involved in getting them the right care. He still misses church occasionally, but when he does, it's usually because he's at his son's tournaments.

Now, it's your turn to try the Alignment Audit exercise.

Consider the top five most important things in your life. Then, on a scale of 1 to 10, ask yourself: "How important is each to you?" (Again, not ranking them in order, just on an individual scale for each one.)

Next, think about the past six months. On a scale of 1 to 10, how much of your energy and resources have you dedicated to this important area of your life? How well have you prioritized and protected it?

What's Important?	Rate on a scale of 1 to 10 (1 being not important; 10 extremely important)		
Write down what's most important in your life. Consider the categories of physical, emotional, mental, relational, and spiritual.	How important is each to you?	How much time, attention, and energy have you invested in each?	Calculate the difference.
1.			
2.			
3.			
4.			
5.			

In the far right column, subtract the number in column three from the one in column two. That's your gap. In general, when you have a difference of two or more, it's a sign of misalignment that also results in less optimized energy. You have to decide if that gap is okay, or if it's an opportunity for you to "train" to move your energy more toward what is most important. If someone could only see your actions, and not hear your words, what would they say are your top priorities?

Sustaining substantial changes like these are a challenge for anyone. It begins with your mindset, combining your desire for change with a clear sense of purpose. Clarity on your purpose is key to making change in your life, and starting is often as simple as getting clear on your priorities.

Chapter 2

The Complacency Epidemic

Golfer Matt Kuchar was the can't-miss kid out of Georgia Tech, where he was a two-time first-team All-American and winner of the US Amateur. He turned pro in 2000 and won the Honda Classic in 2002. Winning in the PGA Tour guarantees a player a Tour card for the next two years. Now what? Like a salesperson who lands a huge deal and hits their quota for the year, the motivation to keep performing often dries up.

After that win, he started to struggle. It appeared that his motivation was challenged. For so long, he had worked toward the goal of playing professionally but now that he had made it, he didn't know how to sustain that drive. His status as a player on tour was also now secure. With that job security, he didn't *have* to work as hard to keep his job on the tour. So, he didn't. His mindset slipped from striving, working, grinding to one that throttled back his efforts and accepted the status quo. Over the next several years, he missed more than half of the tournament cut lines each year.

It became clear that complacency had set in. In 2005, he finished ranked 159th, outside of the top 125 players, which meant he lost his PGA

Tour card. The next year, he competed on the mini-tour, the equivalent of minor leagues in golf.

Instead of seeing it as a career-ending demotion, Kuchar began to see it as the place he belonged at that point—but not for long. Matt later told me that he embraced the idea of treating his golf career like a business and acting as the CEO of his own company. He needed the right team around him and he needed to be laser-focused on his mission. He reevaluated everything from his golf swing to his support system. He surrounded himself with former teammates from Georgia Tech to spark confidence and authentic feedback. He dug deep on who he gave his energy to and who he didn't, was disciplined with his schedule, and worked consistently to shift his mindset to one of belief and possibility, not doubt and negativity. Slowly his confidence starting coming back. It worked. He finished in the Top 10 on the mini-tour, and regained his PGA Tour status.

Today, Kuchar is known as one of the most consistent players on the Tour. To date, he has earned more than $50 million in his career and nine PGA Tour victories. Golf is such a mental game, and Kuchar was able to rebuild his career when he learned to view his disappointments as learning experiences and opportunities for growth. He rediscovered his love for the game and owned that he needed to make changes if he wanted to get back to competing at the highest level.

Our natural state is to remain in comfortable territory, not to seek out the unknown. It's a biological safety feature left over from the days when a new path could mean life-threatening danger. One recent study showed that "every human being's brain will be inclined to rest in habit mode and avoid activating its executive functions whenever possible."[1] Our brains prefer the familiar, the people, places, and things that we've seen before over the new and novel—and certainly the challenging. It keeps us safe, and it maximizes brain efficiency. So when complacency becomes a habit, like it did briefly for Kuchar, it can be a challenge to overcome.

Complacency is the byproduct of habit. It's just how the brain is designed, not an indictment.[2] That said, it represents the most pervasive and most damaging roadblock to progress, and to a fulfilled, engaged, and abundant life.

The Danger of Complacency

Complacency is a feeling of self-satisfaction that keeps you from reaching your potential.

Drive and complacency battle each other inside each of us all day. And because complacency has the competitive edge, without awareness and a proven arsenal to beat it, it usually wins. If we're not actively defending against it, we're probably slipping into it. Like an invasive weed, complacency covertly penetrates our lives to surface when and where we least expect it.

Complacency indicates a lack of progress. This silent dream killer seeks to invade our souls and steal our dreams, causing us to live a life of regret. It can even disguise itself, lure us into its trap, and suffocate our hopes of a better life. There is a time and a place to recharge, reflect, and restore, of course. Drive need not be exhausting; recharging and reflecting are critical to maintain drive instead of creating burnout.

But when we stay stuck in the eddies of life, all hopes of success simply pass us by. Our lives become regretful tales of would've, could've, should've.

For all too many, complacency becomes the default life setting.

Maybe you used to have dreams that you once pursued, but now they've slipped into the gap of what's easiest, what's most convenient, what's guaranteed. You still physically show up every day, but inside you wonder, *Shouldn't I feel more engaged in my own life? Shouldn't there be something more?*

From time to time, you might consider making a change, but change gets hard quickly. And when the path forward feels unclear, complacency smiles and invites you back in. Complacency is like quicksand; before we know it, we have sunk down to our knees. Moving feels harder because it is. We have to get more aggressive to break free. At some point your mental chatter tells you it's okay just to stick it out until you're sixty-five, until the kids leave for college, until your boss changes, until you get promoted and make more money, until . . . until . . . until. Complacency becomes a lifestyle, and you've lost the urge to go for more. Most tragically, you've lost your sense of self.

But what if we can detect complacency and keep it at bay? As I share here, through several poignant stories from my life in sports and business, complacency must be acknowledged and combated to fully realize success and avoid dream-derailing disaster.

Myths	Truths
Complacency isn't such a bad thing. I'm happy and content.	Complacency suffocates your potential. It will leave you stuck and unfulfilled.
Complacency isn't a choice. My environment gives me no other option.	You can't choose your circumstances, but complacency is always a choice.
I'm highly successful and have achieved so much; there's no way I'm complacent.	Achievement often leads to complacency. You can't revel in a win for long.

Complacency is like a virus that takes root inside of you and can spread without awareness. The antidote is Dynamic Drive, and it's transferable to the physical, mental, emotional, relational, and spiritual roles in our lives. Complacency lulls you into a false sense of security, an "I can do it later" mindset. Time is a precious, finite commodity. So we miss opportunities and we accept the status quo.

I have a friend, Diane, who is struggling with fear of failure and embarrassment when it comes to her health. It keeps her stuck and complacent in a life that's not as full and vibrant as she's capable of. She's about twenty pounds overweight and I've seen it affect every single area of her life. She isn't confident walking into a social setting, she doesn't feel strong and capable professionally, and she isn't eager to maintain the intimacy in her marriage. I'm friendly with Diane's husband, too, and I've noticed that he's piled on some weight as he follows her lead at mealtimes and together they've slipped into a slow-energy, inactive lifestyle.

I've seen firsthand that one person's complacency can drag down somebody else; complacency spreads like a virus from its patient zero to the rest of the family, or even a company. Complacency is not just an individual issue. At a corporate level, it means a lack of innovation, a resistance to change, and a very low risk tolerance.

Let's look at the example of Blockbuster. At its peak in 2004, Blockbuster had 9,094 stores and employed approximately 84,300 people globally. Blockbuster seemed to be on top of the world as their name became synonymous with movies and home entertainment. But the company filed for bankruptcy just six years later. So, what happened?

There were many factors that contributed, of course, but they all add up to complacency at the highest levels.

In the bankruptcy filings, Jeffery Stegenga, chief restructuring officer of Blockbuster, attributed Blockbuster's declining revenue to five main events: (1) increased competition in the media entertainment industry, (2) technological advances that changed the landscape of the industry, (3) changing consumer preferences, (4) the rapid growth of disruptive new competitors, and (5) the general economic environment.[3]

It doesn't surprise anyone to hear that the greatest challenge for Blockbuster was the rapid rise of new competitors utilizing alternative distribution methods. The big competitor on the market was Netflix, whose early business model included mail-order DVDs. (Let's not forget: Netflix didn't start creating original programming until much later in the game, once they'd already established a foothold.) Blockbuster wasn't able to adapt quickly and actually declined an opportunity to buy Netflix for $50 million.[4] These competitors acquired substantial market share and eroded the size of Blockbuster's traditional, store-based customer market. Even though Blockbuster eventually created a mail-order DVD service, it was too little, too late. They couldn't compensate for the declining revenue from the reduced traffic in stores. There was simply no longer a robust market for the rental and sale of physical DVDs. The landscape had changed, and Blockbuster remained complacent.[5]

I spoke to Patty McCord, who served as chief talent officer of Netflix for fourteen years and helped create the lauded Netflix Culture Deck. She attributes a lot of the early success of Netflix to a super-focused and lean team. When you're in survival mode, she told me, you get clear on your objectives. Netflix was able to adapt their own business model quickly and effectively as they launched their streaming service in 2007 and moved away from the DVD mail-order model. Blockbuster, meanwhile, never pivoted. They remained fixated and stuck on physical stores and video rentals, even as that industry collapsed around them.

Complacency affects businesses of all sizes, just as it affects individuals. A business may begin to experience a little success and then start taking it easy. They may ignore competitors, a changing marketplace, or evolving consumer behaviors, just like Blockbuster did. And then, it's too late. The business collapses.

The Path of Complacency

Understanding the stages of complacency can help you identify where you might be in the process and take appropriate action to prevent or reverse the negative effects of complacency and decline. Without that awareness, it's all too easy to slip from Drift to Decline to Despair without consciously choosing to do so.

Once you slip into complacency, the first stage is Drift. It's the place you coast into. You didn't set out to get there, but you didn't really plan to go anywhere else either. It almost happens accidentally. This is the easiest stage of complacency to mistake for a more positive place because it can look an awful lot like comfort. Drift feels like a lack of intention and acceptance of the status quo.

However, it's not about all-out effort all the time without balance. Along the journey of Dynamic Drive you must seek out opportunities to rest and recover. The key here is that rest and recovery are calculated. Beware: sitting too long in the comfort of success can often lead to drifting toward complacency. That's when the throttle's off, when you've stopped pushing your perceived limits, when you've stopped driving toward a better life. Often after success, people get comfortable. You earn first chair in the orchestra and pull back on your practice time. Landing the big sale at work and sitting back at the next sales meeting. You should absolutely celebrate your wins—but don't rest on laurels. I'd often remind my athletes, "You're only as good as your last game."

Let's go back to my friend Diane. How did she find herself twenty pounds overweight, feeling heavy, tired, and disconnected from her life? It started how most downward spirals start—slowly, one day at a time. First, she let her gym membership lapse and quit her running group when she had a big project at work taking up her time. Then, a few nights of takeout and Netflix on the couch after a long day made it tough to get up early, ahead of her family, and start her day.

If you don't recognize the gravitational pull of complacency and reverse course, you won't stay in the Drift stage forever. Things will get worse—first gradually, then all at once. You'll slide into the second stage of complacency, which is Decline.

Diane, for example, might start to avoid social settings where she could feel self-conscious. She'll stop playing with her weekly tennis group, and let a few friendships slip. In Decline, she might not present her idea in a meeting at work effectively—or at all—and get passed over for the next promotion.

In this stage, you see different areas of your life getting noticeably worse. Skills you didn't maintain start failing you. Your health starts slipping because you haven't actually put in the effort to stay fit. Relationships may start to sour because you haven't been intentional about growing them in a healthy way. Your career could begin to flounder as others perceive you just aren't as engaged as you used to be. However it expresses itself, you are in Decline, and others can tell. You probably can too. But as you slip further down the negative slope, you also gain momentum. It becomes easier and easier to slide deeper and deeper into the complacency abyss and harder and harder to pull yourself back up.

The inevitable result of the sliding leaves you in a nasty place: Despair. No optimism for a better future. No hope. No spark. Not because it isn't there, but because it's been buried so deep within that it becomes little more than a faint memory of a time when life could be, should be, would be more. Often when people reach this stage, relationships disintegrate, careers collapse, and health deteriorates. It is a very bad place to be—one I wouldn't wish on anyone. The further down you go, the harder it is to lift yourself up and out of it. Complacency breeds more complacency.

Part of awareness includes recognizing and addressing the triggers that can push you into complacency in the first place.

Fear is often a key ingredient in complacency. Too often, people don't try or don't put themselves out there because of fear. Fear of change, fear of the unknown, and fear of discomfort can cause you to feel stuck.

The same is true after success. When you've accomplished something significant and reached a new level of performance in any area of your life, you may find yourself faced with fear again. Success can be as crippling as failure. The stakes are higher, and you're likely more visible and have more pressure on you. Fear of failure or embarrassment too often prevents people from even trying.

But fear will not kill you. Staying stuck, meanwhile, will dim your light, prevent you from connecting to your Dynamic Drive and finding out what you're capable of.

How Do You Know If You're Complacent?

During many of my speaking engagements, I pose this question to the audience: "Do you feel **stuck** in life, personally or professionally? Stuck mentally, physically, emotionally, relationally, spiritually?"

I've asked thousands of people this question, for decades, one-on-one and to audiences around the world at my keynotes. Here is what I get: "Yes!" or "I do at work," or "I do physically," or "In my marriage, yes." I consistently see well over half the room raise their hand.

But sometimes, I ask a similar question with one slight adjustment: "Do you feel **complacent** in life, personally or professionally—mentally, physically, emotionally, relationally, spiritually?"

Here is the response I often get: "Ah, no . . . I mean . . . I don't think so," or "What do you mean?" or "A little maybe . . . yes, but . . ."

Feeling stuck is normal, and it's an expected pitstop on the road of life. The key is to identify that you're stuck and to do something to change it. Complacency happens when you don't recognize that you're stuck or when you aren't willing to do anything about it, when you let yourself stay motionless—and that is when you begin to drift. Most people aren't aware of or don't want to admit to this.

In order to make change, you first have to recognize the gaps and own them, so you can live your best life. If you, too, raised your hand in response to my question, then you might also recognize yourself in some of the following classic demonstrations of complacency.

To catch yourself before you start to drift, be aware of the most common triggers. These physical, mental, emotional, relational, and spiritual triggers can be internal (limiting beliefs, negative self-talk, low confidence and no clear purpose) and external (environment and relationships). When someone understands the rhythms of life needed to sustain Dynamic Drive, they discover the place where potential and opportunity thrive. It is there, when awareness moves people to make the decision to engage Dynamic Drive, that pain gives way to hope and breakthroughs become the norm.

Do You Recognize Yourself in These Habits and Thought Patterns?

These triggers can be both internal and external.

Internal triggers might include physical, mental, emotional, relational, financial, and spiritual trip wires such as:

- Limiting beliefs
- Negative self-talk
- Complaining and blaming
- Low confidence or overconfidence
- Fear
- Feeling unmotivated
- Inability to focus
- Failure to follow through
- Not taking initiative
- Low standards and expectations
- Lack of curiosity
- Taking shortcuts
- Playing it safe
- Operating on autopilot

On the other side, **external complacency triggers** can also cover a wide range:

- Upbringing
- Environment
- No support network

- Lack of resources
- Doubters and criticizers
- Distractions

Recognizing some of these triggers in yourself can also help you start to discover the root of the complacency. These triggers often sneak up on us before we're even realizing the effects they have, so as we take this journey together, I'll call them out to help you identify those things that might cause you to stumble. Because once you have the awareness of what triggers the problem, you can make the conscious decision to respond differently.

Complacency is a threat no doubt, but it's a controllable threat. Some threats are easier to spot than others. Complacency is invisible early on its journey. It can be hard to pinpoint and even harder to admit to. It manifests itself in a variety of ways.

Below is a list of some of the common ways complacency manifests itself in our lives and what Dynamic Drive says instead.

	Complacency says . . .	Dynamic Drive says . . .
I don't like my job.	I am close to retirement, so stick it out.	I am going to pursue my purpose in my work and take action now.
I am overweight.	I only live once, so I am going to eat what I want.	I am committing to a healthy lifestyle and making better food choices so I live a long, vibrant life.
I am burned out.	I'll just keep grinding it out, I have no choice. I can't lose my job.	I need to evaluate why I am burned out and pinpoint what I need to change, then figure out how to ask for that or create boundaries.

I'm unhappy in my marriage.	I'm comfortable and don't want to rock the boat.	This is my most important relationship, and we need to be aligned and connected even if it means getting uncomfortable.
A big opportunity opened up at work.	I'm not qualified and I'm afraid to put myself out there by demonstrating interest because I probably won't get it.	I'm capable, experienced, and willing to learn, and I would rather strive for the position than not.
I want to learn a new hobby.	I don't have enough time to learn something new.	I'm going to prioritize curiosity and learning in my life.

While there isn't one silver bullet to pull you out of complacency, once you identify that you're struggling with it, you can begin to lift yourself up out of the uninspired, compromised state of being and into the empowered, energized, and intentional pursuit of better.

Drive is living life in full, vibrant color, while complacency is living in grayscale. Complacency dims the light slowly, often making it difficult to recognize until you're standing in the dark. When you embrace the Dynamic Drive mentality, the lights come back on, the color returns.

Don't Wait for Your Wake-Up Call

On August 30, 2010, I took my family to an Atlanta Braves game. The Braves were hosting the Mets, which meant I could see a few clients play at the same time. I preferred to maximize my time when I could. We were seated right behind the visitors' dugout—me, my husband, and our three daughters, Emma, Kate, and Meg. A perfect line of the four most important people in my life. It was a perk of my job to be able to share this with my family. Even my husband had gotten used to walking into stadiums and walking toward the field, never up and away from it. My clients would wave to my girls and throw them balls when they would come in in between innings.

In the fourth inning, a Braves outfielder drilled a foul ball that struck my six-year-old daughter in the front right side of her head, fracturing her skull in thirty places and causing traumatic brain injury. Immediate panic. A rushed ambulance ride to the hospital. Emergency brain surgery. Fear, hope, helplessness, faith.

The following morning, I curled up in the hospital bed with my daughter, her head wrapped in gauze like a helmet to keep the stitches and plates stable, and I felt the tears rolling down my face. That moment of despair pushed me to see what was most important in my life. It pushed me to see how I was prioritizing my life. She would survive, and she would eventually make a miraculous full recovery and become a remarkable and poised young woman.

But in those horrifying moments, and the hours and weeks of recovery that followed, a shift was occurring inside me.

I left the business three months later. It's almost as if God said, "I am not sure how clear I need to make this for you, but you need to change."

The irony isn't lost on me that the sports agent's child got hit in the head with a baseball and that led to the end of her career. The very thing that had taken so much of my time and attention away from my family was now threatening its very existence.

Change is hard; it's uncomfortable particularly when you have been in a current state for a long time. For me, I was closing in on twenty years as a sports agent. I was good at it. I had great relationships, I knew the process, the key players. I'd achieved a high level of success, and the work was rewarding. Even still, I found myself running on autopilot and occasionally losing sight of purpose.

On the side, I had started dabbling in motivational speaking. I wrote two books that were leading to requests to come speak. And if I was being honest with myself, I was finding it more fulfilling. I had more control of my schedule and I was changing lives in a different way, at a broader scale. There was a tug that was pulling at me that had begun to build, but I'd been pushing it to the side. When my daughter got injured, I could no longer ignore what I had been feeling. It was clear I needed to make the leap, but, man, it's hard.

I had embraced my drive wholeheartedly and pushed full-throttle into my career. I was beginning to see that I wanted to utilize this same drive in other areas of my life. Despite my success, I had let complacency creep in. There was more inside of me, a renewed sense of purpose tugging at me, if only I made the move.

It took a traumatic, life-changing moment for me to make the change I'd been avoiding. But it doesn't have to. Don't wait to be fired. Don't wait for the heart attack. Don't wait for life to hit you over the head. Change now. Change because you know you can do better, be better. Want more for your life. Change before you have to.

Chapter 3

The Power of Dynamic Drive

I worked with Coach Tom Izzo during his fifth year as head coach of men's basketball at Michigan State University—yes, it was a full-circle moment for me after my own formative experiences as a student-athlete—during the exciting 1999–2000 season. He had moved rapidly from grad assistant to head coach and had coached his team to the school's first appearance in the NCAA Elite Eight since 1979 and their first Final Four appearance in twenty years during the previous season. They had lost a heartbreaker to number-one Duke but had set a school record for wins in that season.

But great coaches, like all people who leave a mark in this world, are rarely content to settle on past successes. Coach Izzo certainly wasn't. In the 1999–2000 season, the Spartans encountered their share of challenges: Their starting point guard suffered a stress fracture and they lost to lower-ranked teams a few times. Yet they still managed to break their twenty-one-game conference winning streak. Then they bounced back from every hit and finished the season as the number-two seed in the Big Ten tournament.

They won that tournament for the second year in a row and made their way to the NCAA tournament. MSU won every game by double digits despite playing the best possible seed in each round. They got past the Sweet Sixteen, the Elite Eight, and back to the Final Four where their season had ended the previous year. After a hard-fought win in the semifinals over fellow Big Ten foe Wisconsin, their starting point guard injured his ankle again halfway through the championship game against Florida. Still, the team pushed through and finally won the elusive National Championship 89–76. The win marked the school's second-ever national championship—and the very first for Coach Izzo.

After the game, the Spartans celebrated while fans spilled onto the court. They cheered and embraced, grinned through post-game interviews, climbed the ladder, cut down the net—all the traditional celebratory traditions. Coach Izzo beamed as he received the national championship trophy while his team and fans chanted behind him. Like a true champion, he credited his team with working just as hard as he had for the win, especially his seniors he had coached for four years "like family." He thanked his staff and the fans back home.

After the ceremonies, he celebrated some more with his team and staff in the locker room. It was the biggest moment of Izzo's career, and he enjoyed every minute of it. It had to have been super late by the time the team made it back to Lansing. I don't know when he got to sleep that night, if at all. He told me later, just hours after hoisting a trophy, he was back at it. You'd think he might chill a bit, right?

That's what most people would do, but Coach Izzo wasn't (and still isn't) like most people. Less than twelve hours after his first National Championship win, he was talking to a recruit about coming to play basketball for him at Michigan State next season.

Think about the message he sent to everyone around him: his staff, his team, the kid on the phone. That recruit had just seen him cut a net down the night before on national television. And then the winning coach calls him to say, "Hey, it was amazing, but this is how much you mean to me—I want you to come here and be part of the next one." Imagine the recruit's realization at that moment. "Wow, Coach Izzo wants me. He just won it all and he's talking to me!"

He sent a message to his staff too. I can imagine the talk on the plane on the way home, "Okay, who are all our A-list guys? Let's get on the phone with these kids. Let's remind them this is a great place to be, a great team, a great coaching staff."

The message to his existing team was the same: "We had an unbelievable season, but buckle up, because getting the next one starts now!" Imagine how motivated they would feel to get right back at it because that's what their coach was doing.

Tom Izzo knows the importance of focusing on the process, on the push to be better every single day. It's not about the singular achievement or the trophy. It's about pursuing excellence each and every day, about falling in love with the work. His first priority was to continue to drive forward. There would be time to refresh and reset, but he knew that he needed to send a message to his inner circle—they weren't finished.

The best of the best know the desire to achieve might get them there, but the desire to get better will keep them there. Like Coach Izzo, they choose to keep getting better.

The view from the summit is nice, but it's the climb that makes it all worthwhile.

The Magic Is In the Pursuit

"The illusion is that the finish line is the destination, but the act itself is the destination."

—PHIL KNIGHT

University of Connecticut women's basketball coach Geno Auriemma is incredibly successful and a tremendous leader. He's won eleven national championships, coached six undefeated seasons, and earned more than one thousand career wins. He's an eight-time Naismith National Coach of the Year. He's been to twenty-two Final Fours, including a streak of fourteen consecutive tournaments. Let that sink in. That level of sustained success is insane. That's the tell of Dynamic Drive—sustained success, not just getting there, but staying there.

So I had to ask him—how do you do it? After all these years, with so much changing in the college sports landscape, with different teams and different players every year? With injuries, with transfers, with all the unknowns? With the competition circling their calendars and coming for you every game?

He told me, "My biggest fear is that it becomes boring and monotonous and that winning just for the sake of winning becomes the goal. There's no excitement to it anymore. There's no challenge to it anymore. And then even winning isn't fun anymore."

I love what he said because he talked about how it's not just about winning. What gets him up every day is the journey. The different obstacles every year. The challenges he gets to figure out.

In other words, it's not just about the drive to achieve; it's about the drive to get better. The road in and of itself is dynamic, just as life is. We need to be dynamic in order to thrive.

True satisfaction in life is about a consistent and sustainable journey toward being better. Fulfillment is prolonged satisfaction. It's the real win and will mean more for your quality of life—and prolonged success—than any singular trophy.

When you focus on the win, on the work product instead of the work, you lose focus over the process. Focusing solely on the goals, the trophies, and the accolades minimizes the journey itself and sets you up for the hollow pang of disappointment or disorienting lack of continued focus.

If it is only about achievement and not about who people become in the process, it won't be sustainable. It's about the daily work, not the trophy.

The traditional definition of drive is one anchored solely in achievement. The problem is, focusing on achievement alone isn't sustainable. The happiness around achievement is fleeting. We've been led to believe that achievement is the goal. We worship the awards, the celebrations, the finish lines. Then what? Picture your favorite athletes holding their trophies, crying tears of joy. We see that image and equate it to happiness. But what we are missing is that those tears of joy are coming because they know what they put into it—all those moments we aren't privy to when no one is watching. The early mornings, the late nights, the daily grind of sustained effort, the hours of watching film. If they were just handed that trophy, without everything behind it, it wouldn't bring them happiness. It wouldn't mean anything.

Emory University scientists studied regions of the brain during decision-making to weigh the costs versus the benefits of making a physical effort. Neuroimaging shows that the ventral striatum, a brain region that plays a key role in processing rewarding outcomes, is more strongly activated when we achieve something through higher effort than lower effort.[1]

The more effort something takes, the more we tend to value it. People are willing to pay more for an object they built themselves than the same object built by experts—a phenomenon aptly named the IKEA effect.[2] Labor alone is sufficient to increase a sense of value.

Researchers found that rewarding effort—and not the outcome—prompted people to seek out more difficult tasks later, even if they didn't get additional rewards.[3]

This is all proof positive we can learn to enjoy the journey, regardless of the destination: that effort itself can be rewarding.

Magic happens in the day-to-day, especially when fueled by a higher purpose. Rather than waiting for lightning to strike, or for the opportunity to achieve the "big goal," the person who embraces Dynamic Drive knows the secret lies in embracing the day-to-day journey that powers incremental improvement—and the byproduct is achievement.

It may start with a goal or outcome in mind (winning a National Championship, becoming the number-one golfer in the world, getting promoted to VP, raising millions of dollars for a cause), and that's still a legitimate part of drive, but it can't be the sole focus. As a sports agent, I saw firsthand the ones who only focused on the trophy, the win, the number-one ranking, without wrapping it with a love for the journey, and those athletes didn't stay in the sport or at the top long.

I saw inside the moments of achievement for two decades in real time. And here is what I know: if the sole focus is achievement, what comes next are dark, empty, lonely moments. I witnessed what happened after a first PGA Tour win or a national championship, and if that moment was the sole focus of their journey, what happens next is heartbreaking. Or think about when an athlete gets drafted and embarks on their professional career. There have been so many kids who get drafted, handed a lot of money, a ton of praise and attention around them, and a huge opportunity. Then, they can get complacent and take it all for granted. They party too much, get distracted from training, buy toys, and goof off. They assume the talent that got them drafted will carry them in the big leagues. But the truth is, when you get into that next level, even if you're a top draft pick, you're just like everybody else. You're playing with the best players in the world. You're guaranteed nothing. This isn't the pinnacle, this is just the start.

The Dopamine Effect

Working hard at something for the sake of the reward at the end can make the hard work much more challenging—*and* it makes you less likely to lean into hard work in the future.

There was a classic experiment done at Stanford many years ago in which children in nursery school and kindergarten drew pictures. The researchers took the kids that liked to draw and gave them a reward for drawing, such as a gold star or some other small token that they enjoyed. This was an activity that prior to the reward, the children intrinsically enjoyed and chose to do independently. The kids who received the award didn't want to continue drawing.[4] The study found that relying on extrinsic rewards for engaging in an activity proved to undermine a child's intrinsic interest in that activity.[5]

When we receive rewards—even if we give ourselves the reward—we tend to associate less pleasure with the activity itself. The cognitive takeaway is that you didn't do the activity because you loved the activity—you did it for the reward.[6]

Striving to be better is itself the end goal. This is the definition of Carol Dweck's growth mindset, which we'll discuss in the next chapter. Learn to access the rewards from effort and doing by telling yourself that the effort is pleasurable. Over time, you can start to evoke a dopamine release from the friction and the challenge.

Andrew Huberman, associate professor of neurobiology at Stanford University School of Medicine and host of the *Huberman Lab* podcast, has been studying dopamine and its correlation to motivation and drive for years. Dopamine is a neuromodulator that is closely linked to our sense of motivation. Huberman says that the ability to access pleasure from effort within our dopaminergic circuitry is without question the most powerful aspect of our biology. And it's accessible to all of us.[7]

There is always a baseline level of dopamine in our bodies. When you feel motivated, there are tonic and phasic releases: tonic, or your baseline, is always there circulating in the brain, and phasic are the peaks above the baseline. These two things interact, and our goal is to keep our dopamine at the right levels consistently.[8]

Dopamine levels affect how capable we perceive ourselves to be—when dopamine levels are low, we feel unmotivated, derive less pleasure from pursuits, and feel physically tired.

Dopamine is involved in the pursuit of rewards, which is what makes the challenges we feel en route to success purposeful. When we set goals and work toward achieving them, the brain's reward system kicks in, releasing dopamine as we make progress or reach milestones. This dopamine release helps to reinforce the behavior, making us more likely to continue pursuing similar goals and engaging in activities that lead to success.

The key is to pause for a moment after every milestone and tell yourself: *I'm heading in the right direction.* Every time we take a moment to acknowledge our effort, we realize we are laying the foundation toward achieving a bigger goal, and the next action will lay another foundation on top of it.

This is what produces dopamine at the right time. When we reward ourselves by valuing our efforts, we are constantly generating little pulses of dopamine. And this is what keeps us from depletion. We feel replenished. Our neural bank account stays healthy.

If we don't acknowledge our effort and constantly remind ourselves that we are heading in the right direction, we will end up depleting our energy. That's the cost of solely focusing on achievement. Our brain gets tired. We get tired. The neural bank account gets smaller and smaller because the dopamine is wearing out.

Our baseline dopamine levels are influenced by many factors, including genetics, behaviors, sleep, nutrition, and the level of dopamine you experienced on previous days.[9] It is critically important to maintain sufficient levels of baseline dopamine to sustain day-to-day motivation. We don't want the baseline too low or too high. Because our brains are wired to restore balance, peak levels of dopamine can be followed by painful crashes, marked by cravings for more thrills.[10] Low levels of dopamine can make you feel tired, moody, unmotivated and—crucial for us as we engage our Dynamic Drive—it can lessen the feelings of pleasure you experience from your pursuits.[11] That's the starting point for complacency, which can lead to depleted levels of dopamine.

My friend Russ Rausch, the founder of Vision Pursue, has improved the mindset and performance of thousands of corporate leaders and employees, as well as professional athletes and coaches, through his training programs.

He developed the concept of "expect the expected," which is a great mindset tool to keep dopamine levels from spiking. Everyone deals with bad traffic, difficult people, and other predictable challenges, yet we act surprised when they happen. Training the mind to align expectation with reality is one way to reduce stress, increase performance, and enhance life experience.[12]

The concept of "expecting the expected" is intended to help manage dopamine levels both in moments that are positive (spikes) and tough moments where one could be disappointed (drops). It's about creating a consistent optimal internal state for sustained drive. For example, a basketball player has to expect a bad call from a ref in a game so when it happens, the player is already prepared for it mentally, which minimizes dopamine fluctuation and supports the "next play" mindset, which is a focus on the immediate future instead of dwelling on past mistakes or successes.

There are many ways to maintain consistent levels of dopamine, and they're accessible and under your control. Telling yourself you are moving toward your goals is a huge stimulator of dopamine release. Try engaging in regular exercise, eating the right food,[13] and avoiding things that cause a spike, such as alcohol and nicotine. When we maintain a healthy baseline, research supports that when we engage in things that make it spike the result of the spikes is that the dopamine levels return to a lower level.

Dynamic Drive Shows Commitment

Dynamic Drive often looks selfish. When you're highly focused, you begin to exclude the distractions, sometimes turning down invitations, saying no to activities and relationships that pull too much time or energy away from your path of Dynamic Drive. When your purpose—and the work to fulfill it—is so meaningful to you, you won't hesitate to occasionally prioritize it above all else. Dynamic Drive requires you to be what others might view as selfish, to focus on your highest priorities above fun, pleasure, and the expectations of others.

Declining an invitation or not volunteering to bake brownies for your kid's school can come with some guilt. Here is the shift: I am saying "no" now because I am saying "yes" to what I've already aligned on matters most. Is that selfish or is that focus? Is it selfish or clarity? Is it selfish or committed?

This is actually commitment.

Commitment is at the core of what Dynamic Drive requires. Commitment to the daily pursuit of your best self. The consistent and unwavering focus on what you must do, regardless of the doubters and the questioners. Of which there will be tons. Filter it all through your lens of drive. With clarity and alignment anchored in a lifestyle of Dynamic Drive, this gets easier. Trust me, because your action is connected to your values, doing work that matters to you based on the legacy you want to leave. Sometimes this requires you to embrace a laser focus, push aside other pursuits, or even ask friends and family for space. Or, you may need to set firmer boundaries at work or say no to a new potential client or opportunity in order to reserve your focus for pursuits in other areas of your life.

The best athletes in the world didn't get there without behaving in ways the world would say is selfish. But if you look closer, it's actually a commitment to self and your goals. When you are spending hours on the field, court, or course, you aren't somewhere else where people might want you to be. There are countless examples of athletes who honor their commitment to their purpose at the highest level. Often, they distance themselves from their relationships and personal responsibilities before key games. They prioritize their physical training and health above the fleeting pleasures. Dynamic Drive says this is a clear and intentional decision, with a long view, wrapped with intention.

NFL running back Austin Ekeler knows that sometimes you have to lean into your commitment and shut everything else out. Ekeler played Division II football at Western State (now Western Colorado University) and blossomed into an elite player. But undersized and overlooked, he was also very realistic about his future. The NFL wasn't on Austin's radar until his senior year of college, when an NFL scout began to show up on campus and the possibility of a different future began to open up.

It was then that Austin decided to go all in. After his final season, he left college and moved to Denver to train with other prospects. He went undrafted in 2017 but he was invited to training camp by the Chargers. That opportunity was all he needed. He told me that the moment when he entered the training camp for the Chargers was one of the most defining moments of his life. He dove all the way into the mindset and focus required to make this long shot a reality.

He says he told his family, "I know you're excited but don't call me. I do not want to be distracted. I have everything to prove. I cannot mess up."

Austin was sixth string on the depth chart. There are virtually no sixth stringers that make it (his coach at the time didn't even know his name!). There are five guys ahead of him in his position vying for a spot on the team. It also means that in practice he's getting very few reps or very few opportunities to prove himself. Each one mattered. He kept his head down, and went hard each and every time as if a Super Bowl ring was on the line. He studied the playbook, too, wanting to be prepared in any scenario in case he was called in.

It worked. The tunnel vision Austin adopted, along with the hard work and resilience, helped land a roster spot. After earning a role on special teams and then as the backup running back, Austin took over the starting role and became one of the best players in the league at his position.

People might judge you. Question your choices. Let it go. Dynamic Drive is uniquely yours. It doesn't abide by the expectations of others. You'll achieve your dreams and end up inspiring those same people. If you believe in the pursuit of better, the outcome of your effort will likely produce fruit for all the people who questioned your commitment. Don't apologize for putting your goal and your grind first.

During the early days in my sports agent journey, I worked tirelessly, putting in long days in the office, spending my evenings and weekends going to baseball games to recruit young players. I was focused and I was driven. It was certainly easier with fewer demands in my life at the time—No husband. No kids. I often said no to the things that didn't align with the very focused journey I was on to build my clientele, over deliver consistently to the growing roster of clients, and hire agents to support the mission. My husband jokes that the only way I had time to date him was if he moved in next door to me in my apartment complex. And he did. We married two years later. Had three daughters in twelve and a half months (a singleton and then twins). Dynamic Drive at play here too, one might joke. Becoming a mother actually intensified my Dynamic Drive. I was more intentional in my decisions and more confident in saying no to things that weren't aligned with my purpose and priorities.

Selfish has a bad rap, but often that judgment is rooted in other people's opinions and expectations for your life.

Sports psychologist Dr. Michael Gervais calls our fear of people's opinions "the single greatest constrictor of human potential." Our concern about what others think about us can be a significant barrier to reaching our full potential. When we are overly preoccupied with seeking approval or avoiding criticism, we may hold ourselves back from taking risks, expressing our true selves, and pursuing our goals with confidence. This fear of judgment can create self-doubt, anxiety, and a reluctance to step outside our comfort zones. Just as sometimes you must block out the distractions and invitations to focus on your most pressing pursuits, you must also block out the opinions of others. Dr. Gervais says that if "you start paying less and less attention to what makes you *you*—your talents, beliefs, and values—and start conforming to what others may or *may not* think, you'll dramatically limit your potential."[14]

When you are engaged in Dynamic Drive, it requires you to prioritize your pursuits above pleasures. It requires you to choose your aspirations over the approval of others, and to put your desires above the criticism of others. What I learned as an agent is that greatness—becoming the best version of yourself—requires you to be selfish at times. The result of this singular focus? You show up as a better version of yourself.

Drive Has No Opponent

In my line of work, I've been privileged to be surrounded by some of the most incredible athletes and coaches in the world. What I learned from them is that you must set the bar *internally*, not externally. When you do that, the drive to achieve or win gets replaced by something more sustainable: the drive to get better.

I've seen this reality play out firsthand climbing the ranks as a young agent. Apparently, there are more agents than athletes to represent—not a great business model. To say it's competitive is an understatement. Unless you sign an athlete straight out of high school or college, the only way to land a new client is to persuade them to switch agents. It would have been easy for me to focus on competing with other agents. And sometimes I did.

I would ask a prospective client, "What other agents are you considering?" This information is helpful, but can't be the sole focus of the pursuit. The minute I started focusing on the external, I began to lose perspective on what mattered most: positioning myself as the best and only solution for the prospect. I would forget to focus on anticipating the gaps in the life of the prospect, adding value, acting like I had the business before I had the business, and behaving in a way that sent the prospect a message that this relationship matters to me. That, in fact, it matters so much I am going to start adding value to your life right now with endorsement deals, appearances, or training support. When I would catch myself watching the "other guy," I'd blur my lens on running my own race, which meant keeping the head and heart of the prospect as my primary focus.

When I kept the focus on the internal, I could over deliver for my clients and prospective clients. In other words, when I competed with myself, I got better and better every day, repped more and more players, and received more and more referrals from my existing clients. When I focused on the other agents, scrutinizing their every move and comparing myself with them, I was quickly distracted from upping my own game. I didn't ignore them, but I didn't focus on them.

When we focus on the opponent instead of running our own race, we allow the measuring stick to be our competition instead of ourselves. We are distracted by something uncontrollable.

Drive is internal. Drive needs no external motivation because it is ignited by fuel within you. Being competitive uses someone or something else as the benchmark for success or the motivator to keep moving forward. This limits what we are capable of and who we might become.

The best athletes know how to stop focusing solely on the competition and start focusing on themselves. Golfers won't focus on the scoreboard, because they can only control their play. Tennis players don't look out in the draw and future matches, because they want to stay focused on the present moment. They control what they can control. The rest is just noise.

Opponents on the field, or in life, are like the side mirrors on your car. You glance at them for a quick reference point, but you can't focus on them while you're driving or you'll crash.

It's clear that when you focus on your competition, you can lose focus on your own work. Author and speaker Simon Sinek has a great take on perceived competition in business. Simon explains that competitors only exist in finite games. You can't beat another player in an infinite game because there's no finish line and there's no agreed upon way in which we keep score. If you're number one, you're only number one for now. So the whole thing is arbitrary.

Simon also shared with me a story of getting caught up in a rivalry when he published his book. There's another author who treads in some of the same waters as Simon, speaking and writing books. While Simon respects his work, he also felt immensely competitive with him. Simon would regularly go online to check his book's ranking on Amazon and found himself immediately checking his so-called competitor's ranking as well. Simon admits, "If I was ahead, I was smug. And if he was ahead, I would be sort of unnerved and angry."

Well, Simon and the other author were invited to speak at the same conference together and were actually interviewed together. They were asked to introduce each other at the top of the program. Simon remembers that he looked at the author in question and said, "You make me extremely uncomfortable. All of your strengths are all of my weaknesses." A strange thing happened. The author looked at Simon and said that he felt the same way. That's when Simon realized that his feelings of competition have nothing to do with anyone else. It was much easier for him to take all those feelings of discomfort and channel them against a competitor than to do the hard work of seeing where he can improve. Since this realization, Simon has never checked his book rankings or anyone else's.

Healthy competition can increase motivation, improve productivity and performance, and provide accountability and validation.[15] Competition can work in the short term or as a reference point from time to time, but it is not sustainable as the reason for the daily grind. Like animals that can't focus solely on their predators, they must also source their own food and find shelter to ensure their survival. This is a competitive world, with multiple people battling for promotions or job openings, start-ups vying for venture capital infusions, or competitors beating your personal best at your favorite workout class. There's a role for all of that in Dynamic Drive; you don't want to remove competition entirely but you do want to manage the level of attention you give it. Studies suggest that competition can motivate employees, increase their efforts and results.[16] Largely, competition enables higher performance by stimulating physiological and psychological activation, which prepares body and mind for amplified effort.[17]

Competition isn't without its downsides. Competitive stress can hinder performance as well. Researchers Po Bronson and Ashley Merryman conducted an experiment in which they gave 124 Princeton University undergraduates a test. For some of the students, the investigators presented the test differently to add to the psychological stress. First, the students were asked to report which high school they'd attended and how many of their high school classmates were also at Princeton. "This was intended to make most test-takers feel as if they were alone at Princeton, that they were lucky to be at Princeton, and that they had barely made the bar for admittance," Bronson and Merryman explain.

Second, researchers further labeled the test "Intellectual Ability Questionnaire." Bronson and Merryman created the title "to be threatening to the students, to make the students fear that, if they did poorly, the test would reveal they lacked the true ability to be at Princeton." The other group of students answered the questions about high school only *after* taking the test, when it could no longer affect their performance, and their exam went by the less-threatening name "Intellectual Challenge Questionnaire."

Students in the first group answered 72 percent of the questions correctly; those in the second group got 90 percent of their answers right. By subtly manipulating the competitive stress felt by the participants, Bronson and Merryman note, the researchers "were able to engineer an 18% difference in their test scores."[18]

In studying mergers between competing corporations, finance professor Paolo Fulghieri found that these mergers may have an adverse effect on employee incentives to innovate and can destroy value because they can reduce the incentive for employees to push their creative thinking. In industries where innovative intellectual property (IP) is critical to the company's success—pharmaceuticals, telecommunications, and other high-tech markets—competition tends to stimulate innovation.

Fulghieri explains: "Take away that competition and an employee would feel like he was working for a corporate bureaucracy. If he feels stuck and has nowhere else to go, his motivation to keep working hard at producing innovative IP erodes."[19]

The key is to consider how we're using competition. Research shows that competition leads to higher physical effort and motivation. However, in cognitive performance involving memory and tasks requiring sustained attention, competition may be a distraction.[20] So ask yourself:

"Is competition fueling me in a healthy way to pursue the best version of myself? Or is it distracting me from what I'm truly capable of?"

Ignoring the competition entirely may not seem possible for you, and I want to reassure you that complete ignorance is not the goal. The best do glance at the competition to level set, recognize, and drive themselves to be better. A competitive environment often leads to better performance, if you can manage how focused on the competition you become.

Dynamic Drive is about not focusing on the competition as your measuring stick. You set the bar for yourself and you work to build your own Dynamic Drive, engage in the process of betterment, and ultimately hit many goals on your list.

While it's not always healthy to solely measure your success based on how you compare with others, competition can serve as a valuable motivator and catalyst for improvement. There's no doubt that competition can help raise the level of play, too. Think about the great athletes locked in epic battles for the top spot in their fields: Tiger and Phil, Federer and Nadal, or Tara Lipinski and Michelle Kwan.

I had the chance to speak with Tara on my podcast, and I heard her perspective on the role competition played in one of the most high pressure sports out there, figure skating. Tara catapulted onto the world stage at the 1998 Winter Olympics at age fifteen, becoming the youngest individual gold medalist ever. Tara had been training her whole life for the Olympics, and at the age of thirteen she began competing against the world champion, Michelle Kwan. In the lead-up to the Olympics, both Tara and eighteen-year-old Michelle Kwan were favored for the gold medal, though many assumed the older and more experienced Kwan would take the medal. Their performances were both best in class and nearly flawless. Tara won the gold, perhaps because of the level of difficulty in her program, and Michelle took home a silver.

Tara is a naturally competitive person, and she said she'd keep tabs on what the best skaters in the world were doing because it motivated her. It gave her that spark to push a little bit harder. She began to compete on the national team at thirteen years old, sometimes holding the last spot on the team while Michelle Kwan took home the top medal. Tara tracked what the top competitors were doing on the ice, so she knew where the bar was set technically. She had to know what skills are required to compete at the highest level, so she could push herself to achieve them.

Tara says: "It definitely fueled me to keep an eye on what was happening. But without focusing on it completely because truthfully, at the end of the day, you could be thinking about your competitor all day long, but you still have to do your job. You can mess up three times and it doesn't mean you've won. The hardest part is landing on a quarter-inch blade. So you do have to focus on yourself. First and foremost."

Tara says she thrives under pressure. Looking back on her athletic career, she performed her best when everything was on the line.

A Drive Like No Other

Dynamic Drive goes beyond any of the traditional definitions of drive. It's not a means to an end. It's not about setting goals and checking them off the list. Dynamic Drive is a philosophy and an approach to life that unlocks more joy, more fulfillment, more purpose-fueled satisfaction.

Dynamic Drive is a practice, a muscle that can be strengthened through regular engagement with the Seven Keys coming in this book.

My Dynamic Drive model on page 59 shows the path of the Seven Keys, how each one builds on the last until you're summiting the mountain of Dynamic Drive and enjoying the view from the peak.

It's a way of living that becomes part of who you are and how you show up in every aspect of your life. Dynamic Drive kicks in to keep you doing the daily work required to experience breakthrough—even when (maybe especially when) you don't feel like it. Dynamic Drive transforms every area of your life.

It's not about perfection. Dynamic Drive means you've never arrived. You're constantly seeking to improve. You're responsible for locking into

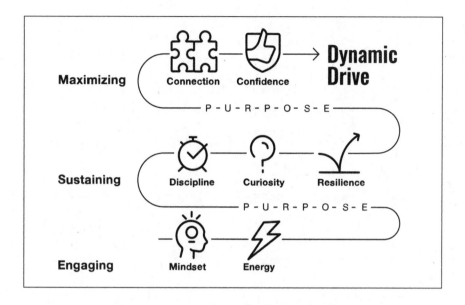

your purpose and using the tools of Dynamic Drive to engage and reengage your motivation throughout your life to continue to get better in all pursuits.

It's not about going from point A to point B. It's about who you become along the way.

Dynamic Drive is a never-ending journey. You're never done improving your drive. You will occasionally find the need to circle to the Seven Keys and use them to improve and push yourself to your greatest potential. For example, you might be nailing it professionally but need a mindset shift physically or you might be in a good spot relationally, in business, but could benefit from more connection at home. What is the ultimate goal? To continue to strive, connect with deep motivation and purpose, practice lifelong discipline, and show up each day hungry for better.

It all begins with discovering what is possible for you.

Part 2

The Seven Keys to Unlock Your Dynamic Drive

Stage 1

Engaging Your Dynamic Drive

The journey of Dynamic Drive unfolds in stages. The first stage is learning how to engage your drive, which you'll do next.

If you're a Marvel Comics fan, think of it like Dr. Strange having to learn how to master the mystic arts for the first time. He had to first discover the power possible for him and how to ignite it before he could make any attempts toward mastery. (If you're not a comics fan, don't worry. Just think of anything you've ever tried to master before—tennis, cooking, parenting, riding a bike, running a business, etc.)

In this initial stage, we'll unlock the first two keys: Mindset and Energy. These forces shape our attitudes, drive our actions, and ultimately determine our ability to drive toward success. Don't underestimate the transformative power of mindset and energy. They can be harnessed to unlock your full potential and propel you toward their goals.

At the outset of any journey, you'll need to first establish the right mindset. By shifting from negative, critical, or limiting mental chatter to a proactive, optimistic, and limitless mentality, you'll begin to see the possibilities inside of obstacles.

Once you have your mindset locked in, you'll next need to evaluate how you're managing your energy. Energy provides the necessary fuel to overcome challenges and to embrace the discipline required in your journey. Without the right focus and clarity on your priorities, you can end up distracted, pulled in too many directions, and ultimately burned out.

Through the tenets of Dynamic Drive, you'll learn to cultivate a limitless mindset, foster positive thinking, and unlock your potential. Likewise, managing and nurturing your energy levels can be the difference between stagnation and progress, despair and fulfillment. They work hand-in-hand to set you on the path of Dynamic Drive.

Chapter 4

First Key: Mindset

mind·set \mīn(d)-set\: a set of attitudes or ideas that shape your life

Carli Lloyd is one of the most accomplished soccer players to ever step foot on the field. She's a two-time FIFA World Cup champion, two-time FIFA Player of the Year, four-time Olympian, and two-time Olympic gold medalist. She's got the trophies and the medals—not to mention the street cred—to be called a champion. She had an incredible natural ability, but she almost lost her way because of her mindset.

She had undeniable raw talent at a young age, but she didn't have the discipline or the mindset in place to play at the highest levels. Her raw talent only took her so far. The turning point for Carli came when she was cut from the Under-21 National Team in 2003 and almost quit soccer. The coach gave her a number of reasons why she wasn't making the team, but the one that stood out above all else: she didn't work hard enough.

Carli told me: "I was a player who from the outside looking in, may have looked comfortable. But inside I was actually struggling with the fact that I didn't believe in myself."

Carli knew she had to do a lot of work in order to play at that elite level—and most of the work was inside her head. Carli took stock: She struggled with negative self-talk stemming from perfectionism and an all-or-nothing approach, which prevented her from developing new skills. She had adverse reactions to criticism. She knew she had to learn to face her weaknesses head on, to work on them over and over again until they became her strengths. As she continued with this approach, her discipline grew.

Carli says she began to read the books of other best-in-class athletes like Michael Jordan, Muhammad Ali, Wayne Gretzky, and Diego Maradona. She immersed herself in new ideas around positive self-talk and letting go of ego.[1] She learned to meditate before big games and practiced visualization to see exactly what she needed to do on the field.[2]

Through her mindset work, Carli began to build the discipline and positive self-talk required, and in turn, she was able to level up with increased endurance, athleticism, and skills. Her mantra became: "Empty The Tank." Giving 100 percent effort, 100 percent of the time, never leaving anything to chance.

Carli's mindset has been a crucial tool in her outstanding performance on the field. When Carli first met her coach on the US Women's National Team ahead of the 2007 World Cup, he asked her about her goals. Despite not yet having proven herself on an international stage, being young, inexperienced, and often a bench player—she responded boldly. She said, "I want to become the best player in the world."[3]

These lessons in mindset helped her achieve incredible feats and have continued to serve her well after retirement. Carli's story illustrates how a mental reset broke her out of complacency and led to increased performance.

Your mindset is a set of beliefs that shape how you see the world and yourself. It's not enough to simply think positively; our mindset must move beyond positivity and into action if it's going to lead to real, lasting success. Does your mental chatter or running script sound like it's hurting more than it's helping? Are your "buts" getting in the way of your dream? You can make a conscious choice to change your self-talk and change your mindset. When you do the work to train your mindset, learn how to create constructive and positive internal dialogue, and practice reframing challenges as opportunities, you'll begin to unlock a greater level of possibility.

As Ethan Kross, award-winning psychologist and author of the book *Chatter*, puts it, "Our inner voice can be both a liability and an asset. The words streaming through our heads can unravel us, but they can also drive us toward meaningful accomplishments . . . if we know how to control them."[4]

Why Mindset Matters

Our beliefs have immense power. They dictate where success begins and ends. Research shows that "beliefs determine how people feel, think, motivate themselves, and behave."[5] Beliefs shape our attitudes, behaviors, and decisions, which influence how fulfilled we can be in life—however you define success. Ruthlessly exterminating any limiting beliefs will keep us out of complacency and poise us to make the most of every opportunity we face. Dynamic Drive starts with our mindset.

Athletes who work on strengthening the mental side of their game are more likely to achieve success—*the research says 80 percent more*—as they take on challenges, navigate difficult situations, and ultimately achieve their goals.[6] You can implement these same tools to strengthen your mindset as you navigate opportunities and challenges in your own life.

A limitless mindset is how I define a commitment to what's possible for yourself. It's the willingness to step into the next thing with the conviction that good will come as a result of taking action. By focusing on what's possible, and harnessing the power of your purpose, you can accomplish what you set out to do. A limitless mindset is a crucial first step toward developing your Dynamic Drive. It will lead you to use your curiosity, discipline, resilience, and confidence to execute on your goal in your own unique way.

The flip side is a limited mindset, in which doubt, restriction, and weakness seep into everything you do. It's believing that the worst will happen, that failure is likely at every turn. A limited mindset is also believing that there is one way to do something, and if you can't do it "the right way," then you've failed. It inhibits progress; it steals the joy from the pursuit of better; it prevents big thinking and big goals. The result of a limited mindset is, of course, complacency.

Your beliefs can often shape your reality without you even recognizing it. When you have such a powerful, unseen tool at your disposal, you want it working with you, not against you.

Self-talk is the stream-of-consciousness thoughts running through your head as you engage in various tasks throughout your day.

In fact, positive self-talk can be a motivating and effective tool for peak performance. It's associated with a significant reduction in the perception of effort.[7]

Here's the incredible thing about mindset: you're in control. The view you adopt for yourself profoundly affects the way you lead your life.[8] The belief that you have the power to make changes and reach your goals is foundational to developing a limitless mindset. It's deeply correlated with confidence, resilience, and motivation, as well as other positive behaviors like qualitative risk-taking, curiosity, and problem-solving.

With consistent effort, you can develop a strong belief in yourself that will help you reach your goals and live with a limitless belief system. Let's consider a few of my favorite examples of athletes who took believing in themselves to the next level.

NFL quarterback Tom Brady is generally considered to be one of the best to ever play the position and the game of football. Tom wasn't a first-round draft pick. Nor was he chosen in the second, third, fourth, or even the fifth round. For some players, being the 199th player chosen would curb their confidence and unlock limiting beliefs. "I'll probably just be a bench guy," or "No one thinks I am good enough to start." But not Tom. He joined the team as a backup, yes—but he kept tapping into his drive. And when star quarterback Drew Bledsoe went down with an injury, Brady stepped in behind that center and never gave the starting position back. The rest, my friends, is history.

Tennis legend Serena Williams didn't secure twenty-three Grand Slam titles or fourteen Grand Slam Doubles titles or three Olympic gold medals in doubles with her sister, Venus, without an ability to see obstacles as opportunities. As a Black woman in a predominately white sport, she and her sister became role models for young female athletes worldwide.[9]

You don't have to be an elite athlete to have this kind of self-belief. It's submitting your résumé for the job even when you don't check all the criteria. It's training for a marathon when you've only ever completed a 5K. The key is to not defeat yourself before you even start—which is exactly what a limited mindset does.

Renowned developmental psychologist Carol Dweck of Stanford University has spent her career studying mindsets and her work has illuminated where limitless mindset comes from. Through her work, she's defined two types of mindset—*growth* and *fixed*—which align and support the limitless and limited mindsets inherent in Dynamic Drive. A growth mindset is one in which you believe your basic qualities can be cultivated through your efforts, while a fixed mindset means that you believe these qualities are fixed—so, if you're not good at something, you'll never improve.[10] These definitions are aligned with Dynamic Drive's limitless and limited mindsets, though they're not entirely the same. A limitless mindset goes beyond believing that your qualities can be improved to a bigger vision that your potential is unclear until you believe that you have untapped potential that only you can tap. There is no telling what you're capable of until you try wholeheartedly and with the right Dynamic Drive tools.

Dweck highlights the importance of feedback in understanding where mindsets come from. Feedback that focuses on the person, i.e., their talent or ability, leads to a fixed mindset; whereas feedback that focuses on the process, i.e., effort or learning, fosters a growth mindset.[11] Consider the difference between telling someone "You tried your best" instead of "You're very smart." The first praises the effort, and, according to Dweck, leads to the desire to improve, to display similar efforts in the future. The second response is focused on identity, creating the binary idea that you're either smart or you're not. "You tried your best" tracks with contemporary parenting advice that promotes praising experience or effort above all else.

The key here, as Dweck points out in her research, is that improvement is possible with a growth mindset, and not with a fixed mindset. If you don't believe that you can change your intelligence, then why would you try to? Why would you take on increasingly difficult tasks to push yourself? You wouldn't. Dweck studied people with a fixed mindset and found that when they were presented with information that could help them learn after they'd gotten an answer wrong, they just weren't interested.[12] This limited mindset prevents you from engaging your Dynamic Drive.

In my own life, I think back to what my mom said to me after my 1.8 GPA freshman year of college. She didn't tell me I was a bad student or not smart. She told me that I was capable of doing much better, which made me very focused on the process of improvement.

A growth mindset is essential to engage your limitless mindset. When it's lacking, complacency abounds. A fixed mindset impedes improvement, the ability to overcome adversity and challenges, and inhibits risk taking—all necessary to embrace your Dynamic Drive.

As a sports agent, I had a front-row seat to peak performance as I helped the best shift their mindsets on a world stage. Ninety percent of my time was spent helping them navigate their careers, on and off the field, and 10 percent of my time was spent negotiating contracts. I was part mental coach and part agent through the processes of getting hired, fired, released, or traded, and navigating through slumps.

I have seen many performance problems that were rooted in a mindset gap. You'd be surprised at how many incredible athletes haven't invested in mindset work. They spend hours each day in the gym, working with trainers on high-level skills, developing strategies with coaches, but only some—the best of the best—bring this same work ethic to their mindset. They simply can't get to the next level of achievement without developing a limitless mindset.

Let's take Major League baseball player Jeff Francoeur as an example. He was drafted out of high school as a first-round pick by the Atlanta Braves in 2004 after he turned down college football scholarships for pro baseball. He made his way through the Braves minor league system quickly and was called up to the majors during the 2005 season. The right fielder had an incredible start to his big-league career after a mid-season call-up, finishing with a .300 batting average, in the running for Rookie of the Year and earning him the nickname "The Natural" by *Sports Illustrated*. But the following season, his first full big-league season, his performance dipped, finishing the season with a .260 batting average and 132 strikeouts, more than any other player on the Braves roster that season. Over the next two seasons, he was inconsistent—clearly talented, but his batting average, on-base percentage, and RBIs all dropped.[13]

Francoeur had always been praised for his natural athletic abilities, but he didn't know how to deal with failure and setbacks when he got to the major leagues.

"I just was going off raw talent," he said. "But after a while, you have to be able to hone it in and do something, and at that point, I wasn't able to. For two to three years, it was great and it all worked, and then I didn't know how to handle the failure when it happened."[14]

He was known for his aggressive attitude at the plate, never one to take a strike and look at a pitch.[15] At the high school level, that works. But not in the big leagues. His fixed mindset was rooted in the years of being told that he was incredibly talented.

"There were signs that I needed to work on some things at the plate . . .

but . . . When you're having success to that extent, it's tough to tell someone they really have to change."

Prior to his big-league struggles, Francoeur didn't have a lot of experience recovering from setbacks. He was beloved, thanks to his highly touted athletic frame and his hometown-hero persona. And the coaching wasn't sinking in.

By comparison, let's look at Francoeur's friend and Braves teammate catcher Brian McCann. He was drafted in the second round the same year as Francoeur and followed a similar path. Both graduated from Georgia high schools, were drafted as nineteen-year-olds, and made their MLB debut by the age of twenty-one.[16] While they were both impact players on the team, Francoeur was making headlines and McCann was playing a little in his shadow for a variety of reasons, starting with Francoeur being picked in the first round of the MLB draft and McCann the second. McCann was a catcher, masked up behind the plate, whereas Francoeur had a smile as big as his personality, outgoing and charismatic.

In 2007, in an unprecedented move, the Braves pulled both Francoeur and McCann into the front office together and offered them almost identical deals: $26 million for six years. This was unheard of. In fact, in my experience it has never happened before and won't happen again. Francoeur turned it down, confident he would work the process of arbitration and then free agency and earn way more. McCann took the deal.

I signed Francoeur the year after, in 2008. I saw firsthand that while he was a standout player who was passionate about the sport, he didn't make the mental adjustments to show up with the kind of mindset he needed to be the player the world thought he would be in the big leagues. Unfortunately for him, that played out through his on-field earnings. During their respective careers, Francoeur's on-field earnings totaled a little over $30 million, and McCann earned about $150 million in big-league contracts. Francoeur won one Gold Glove, and McCann won six Silver Slugger Awards and appeared in seven All Star game and won the 2017 World Series with the Houston Astros.

Francoeur's limited mindset kept him stuck, believing that his inherent talents would be enough. They weren't; it never is at the highest level. Whereas McCann's limitless mindset was anchored in a curiosity that is required as you keep leveling up. These figures don't just represent their career earnings, length of stay in the big leagues, or their respective awards. They represent the distinct difference between their baseball careers. They represent a tangible measurement of Dynamic Drive, proof that a limitless mindset is the basis for higher performance.

A limited mindset will make you feel physically exhausted and drained. It short-circuits your creativity, which is crucial to going for more in your life. When your own mind is locked up, you can't even muster the energy to envision yourself attaining your goal. Instead of feeling excited or exhilarated about opportunities, you focus on everything that can't and inevitably won't work. You're defeated before you even start.

Do you see evidence of a limited mindset in your own life? Do you hear yourself saying things, like:

- I can't do that.
- If only I was more like . . .
- I'm not good enough for that . . .
- I am not smart enough . . .
- It doesn't matter how hard I try . . . it's not going to work.

Do you put yourself in the place of a victim, blaming others or even outside forces for your inability to move forward? Do you complain about all the things that have gone wrong—or that could go wrong? Do you regretfully accept situations instead of trying to change them? Do you take your name out of the hat for promotions or opportunities because it's safer to avoid your self-inflicted anticipated rejection?

Or, as in Francoeur's case, did you struggle with leveling up beyond your natural ability? Just as a limited mindset can keep you stuck when you don't believe in your own talents, it can keep you stuck when you believe your natural abilities will be enough. When competing at higher levels or facing setbacks, you need more than just talent. You need the resources, like mindset, discipline, and resilience to dig in and do the hard work to improve. You need Dynamic Drive.

If any of this sounds familiar to you, I have to share some tough love. You're living with a limited mindset. You're stuck in complacency, which you now know is the killer of dreams. The first step to get out of complacency is to change your beliefs so that you can tap into your drive. You have to close the gap between what you think is possible and what actually *is* possible.

As the famous science-fiction writer Arthur C. Clarke said, "The only way to discover the limits of the possible is to go beyond them into the impossible." When you see obstacles as opportunities, you will start living into your vision of what is possible instead of into your current circumstances. Believing in yourself will give you 20/20 vision for your goals and a new lens for what you can achieve.

Reframing Obstacles as Opportunities

If you want a limitless mindset, you have to flip the narrative to see opportunities instead of obstacles. What might become possible for you, even at the subconscious level, if your mind could fuel—not derail—your dreams?

After growing up in East Lansing and graduating from Michigan State University, I decided to move to Atlanta. I knew I wanted to work in sports in some capacity, and Atlanta was about to host the Olympics and the Super Bowl. And with the local pro teams, it seemed like the city would offer me plenty of opportunities. But how would I get the money to fund this dream? I didn't even have a job yet! While I had their emotional support, my parents let me know I had to figure out a way to pay for my excursion to Atlanta. I could have let that obstacle derail me, but I decided to look at the financial barrier as an opportunity. I let it fuel my drive.

For the entire summer, I taught tennis lessons at a nearby club in

East Lansing, and I saved $2,000 for the big move. I packed up my Honda Accord and pulled out of the driveway of the home I had grown up in as the seasons changed. I was leaving home with no job, only a couch to crash on at a friend's place until I found my way. As you can imagine, my parents were more than a little concerned as they waved goodbye to me. Mom's eyes welled up with tears as Dad told her, "She'll be back in two weeks."

My college tennis coach gave me the names of three people in Atlanta who taught tennis full time. When I called them, I learned that tennis was very popular in Atlanta, so I knew I could leverage my tennis-teaching skills to make my $2,000 stretch even further while I was figuring everything out.

> **Where some people see obstacles, others see opportunities.**

I heard that there was an apartment complex in need of a tennis pro, so I stopped over there to introduce myself. But the news of the current pro's departure hadn't traveled as quickly as I had. "Oh no, we have a pro who teaches tennis to our residents," was the response I got from the apartment manager. "We love him!"

Knowing what I knew of his imminent departure, I politely handed her my homemade, unprofessional business card and asked her to call me if anything changed. I smiled and walked out.

Across the street from the apartment complex was a strip mall with a restaurant called Pero's Pizza. I wondered if they sold pizza at the apartments right across the street. It was a big complex, with lots of young people. I popped into Pero's on my way out. I was desperate, but I believed I had a great idea brewing.

"Do you sell a lot of pizza to that apartment complex right there?"

Mr. Pero replied, "Maybe a little bit. Not a ton."

Perfect. I pitched my idea: "If you give me fifteen pizzas for free once a month, I can give them to the residents at the apartment complex who come to the tennis clinics. And I could add a coupon from Pero's to the newsletter to help drive traffic back to Pero's."

He lit up. "I love it!" I had fifteen free pizzas every month to share with residents who came to my (as-yet-nonexistent) tennis clinic!

Next, I called my buddy at Wilson's Sporting Goods, whom I knew from my time on the Michigan State tennis team. He agreed to send me water bottles, key chains, T-shirts—the works. Then I went to Kinko's and printed tennis tips that I had previously written for a free local paper in Michigan, which I thought we could also add to the newsletter for the residents.

A few days later, I returned to see the manager of the apartment complex. As I walked back into the office, opening with, "Hi, I am Mol—," she interrupted me excitedly. "You won't believe this! Our tennis pro is leaving. This is amazing timing!"

Imagine that! Now, on to the logistics. I asked her how she worked with the pro previously.

"The rent is $850, so we gave him $500 off every month," she replied. "He only paid $350."

Then I laid out my ideas for the Wilson's merchandise, tennis tips for the newsletter, and the pizza deal. Boom! She loved it. "The pro we had was amazing, but—wow, he didn't do this! Free gear, tennis tips, and free pizza!"

I smiled. "You know the $850/$500/$350 thing? What if we just waive it?" Full stop. She just stared at me, so I added, "It's cleaner." She walked back to her office to call her boss. My unemployed self was happy to wait. And it worked. I lived in that apartment complex rent-free and taught tennis one night a week for nine years.

I could have told myself, "I'm in a new city, I know no one, and I have very little money—and nowhere to live. This will never work." But I didn't allow myself to hold onto a limited mindset. I couldn't dwell on what wasn't happening. I held tight to what could be possible. It would have been so easy to allow negative thoughts to dominate my thinking, but those thoughts would only have held me back from discovering what was really possible.

Rewriting Your Mental Script

My journey to make it on my own in Atlanta and to break into sports didn't stop with a clever living arrangement. I had to fight tooth-and-nail to prove to everyone around me that I had what it takes to compete at the highest level. And sometimes, while experiencing all sorts of moments of negative thinking (things like, *I don't belong here. No one will ever take me seriously as a female in a male-dominated industry. I didn't compete in the big leagues or coach at the D1 level*), I had to convince myself of that.

Friends, I could have wallpapered my seven-hundred-square-foot, rent-free apartment with those comments back in the day.

I still remember being behind home plate, talking to big-league ball players during batting practice. The managers would look me up and down warily and yell over to their players, "Dude! What are you doing talking to that chick?" Later, my players would comment that their manager couldn't believe that I was their agent. I was jamming up their old boy network script.

Later in my career, basketball legend Isaiah Thomas came into the office for a meeting to discuss his next move after a less-than-ideal exit from the Raptors. There was a broadcast deal on the table plus other coaching opportunities and endorsement deals to discuss. It was my first time meeting him in person. I was in the boardroom along with my male boss. After a few minutes of small talk, we all sat down. Isaiah looked at my boss and said, "She probably should leave. She shouldn't hear this." I was surprised—unfortunately, this is the type of thing that I heard on the sidelines and outside of locker rooms regularly—but my boss didn't miss a beat. He looked at Isaiah and said, "Molly leads our client rep side of the business. She knows everything. She's not going anywhere."

I think about that meeting from time to time still, more than fifteen years later. My boss's message that day—"You belong at this table, Molly!"—was the invitation I needed to take up space, to speak confidently and make my presence known in meetings with men who felt I didn't belong there. It informed my own self-talk as I would repeat the message that *I'm not going anywhere.*

Time after time, I'd hear those not-so-subtle comments. And I could have engaged in some serious negative self-talk. Of course, that narrative played in my mind and tried to take root. And sometimes it did, for a moment. But what I knew to do from my days as an athlete, and what I later helped my clients do, was remind myself that if I believed that narrative, if I allowed it to settle in, I would fail. I knew even then about the power of the mind and its impact on what we can achieve. I knew that this negative narrative would take me down if I let it persist. So, instead, I would focus on the fact that I am different, and that's a good thing. I held tight to the positive feedback I'd received from coaches and scouts who knew I could make an impact. I paid closer attention to the athletes and families who said, "You are refreshing and different. Thank you for doing what you do." My goals were too important to me to let people's misconceptions keep me from doing something that I loved. Yes, I didn't fit the typical mold of a sports agent. But no, I didn't need to believe the self-talk that would hinder what was possible.

I had to shift my mindset in order to become one of the top sports agents and one of the first female agents. Fifteen years and three hundred athletes and coaches later, I know that shifting my mindset and maintaining positive self-talk works. I know it can work for you, too.

You are the narrator of your life story. The old story is usually tied to something that's holding you back. The way you're talking to yourself isn't serving you. What you tell yourself matters, and it's time to take control of that messaging.

A mindset is like software: it runs on a script. If you want to change your performance, you have to change the script running inside your head. You need to replace the words that say, "You either have it or you don't." The creativity script says, "You have the ability to make yourself into anything you want. Your natural talent is important, but how much you work is even more important. If you can imagine it, you can do it." You effectively are issuing a challenge to yourself to do the work only you can do—using your unique talents, one small decision at a time.

For me, it would have been easier to stay on the sidelines. I understand the self-defeating attitudes and self-imposed hurdles that can hold you back from your true potential, but when I defeated my "playing small" thinking, I was able to get into the game.

Switching how you talk to yourself is only the first step. It's an easy one to do here and now. But this kind of mindset shift needs to become your default, as a consistent ritual. A new habit. Every day, you need to purposefully choose *possibility* over *limits*. The more you practice this shift, the better you will get.

Instead of feeling like you don't know your next steps, deploy creative thinking around what you desire and how to get it. It challenges you to shift your perspective and do the next right thing.

When people saw me as just "some chick" recruiting athletes, I needed to ask myself, "What if I could sign these guys, make their lives better, maximize their window of time on this unbelievably unique stage, and open the door for the next female agent who comes after me?" When I shifted into that mindset, I was able to see the opportunities, to establish myself, to sign players, coaches, more players, and even broadcasters until I had signed and served over three hundred.

You will want to take whatever it is that you are struggling with and reframe it to create the outcome you want most. You will be *thrilled* to tell yourself a new, more exciting story over and over again. You will carve your own path to your version of gold medals and your version of world records.

The Total Mindset Reset

The best way to rewrite your mental script and strengthen your default mindset is what I call a Total Mindset Reset, or TMR. With a Total Mindset Reset, you shift into Dynamic Drive and tap into your limitless potential.

This is not about what you do, but who you are. It will give you a completely new lens on the world, your obstacles, and your goals.

TMR helps you shift your thinking from destructive chatter to a constructive mental script. The human brain processes about seventy thousand thoughts *every single day*.[17] That's seventy thousand chances to reframe our internal narrative and tell ourselves a new story. Every single day, you have seventy thousand opportunities to shift your self-talk and step into a better life.

Does that sound hard? It's not as difficult as you think. Think back to one of the last setbacks or obstacles you experienced. Do you remember how you reacted? Maybe it derailed your progress. Now imagine looking that obstacle in the face and asking yourself, "What if? What's possible?" instead of "Why me? I can't."

What would have happened? Would the outcome have been different? You bet it would have been.

Small, powerful shifts in thinking can change everything.

TMR: Total Mindset Reset

Think about an area in your life where you are feeling stuck or where you've identified a performance problem. Let's explore how TMR can get you back on track.

1. Recognize: Dig deep into your self-talk. Anytime you say something about yourself, that's self-talk—and you decide which way it will go. Negative self-talk will keep you stuck where you are. The first step is to recognize where your limiting beliefs are showing up, and the nearest place to start looking is your negative self-talk. What is your limiting belief? Does it include phrases like:

I can't....

I won't....

I don't...

This isn't....

Why me...

If an athlete of mine was struggling at the plate, I'd ask them about their mental chatter. What are you telling yourself when you're getting loose on deck? As you approach the plate? When you step into the batter's box? It might be: *If I don't get a hit this at bat, I'm 0–3 on the night.* Recognizing your negative self-talk and how it is limiting your performance is step one.

2. Replace: Once you're aware of negative self-talk, challenge those thoughts. Ask yourself if there's evidence to support these negative beliefs. Are they based on facts or assumptions? Try to objectively evaluate the truth behind these thoughts and, more often than not, you'll see that they're not true. Then you can replace the negative self-talk. Ask yourself: "What would a person with a limitless mindset tell themselves? What should I tell myself to support the behavior and, in turn, the outcome I want most?" This is where you replace negative self-talk with positive self-talk and literally write a new mental script.

I can...

I will...

I am...

I've prepared...

I want...

For the athlete in the example above, the new script would be: *I got this. I've gotten hits off this pitcher before.*

3. Reinforce: Find ways to reinforce the positive script you've created.

Put a one-word reminder in a visible place, like on your bedside table, your bathroom mirror, or your phone screen saver. Create mantras and repeat them aloud or in your head at regular intervals throughout the day.

Through TMR, you'll gain insight into negative thought patterns that are keeping you stuck and replace them with new empowering scripts. Remember that replacing negative scripts with positive self-talk is an ongoing process, and you'll need to continue practicing over time.

At one of our recent training experiences, we worked with a group of executives in commercial real estate. It was a small session, with about twenty of the company's department heads gathered in a large conference room. From the moment our facilitator walked in, she noticed one group member who clearly needed some help.

Kevin walked into the conference room eight minutes late, holding a stack of loose papers on top of two notebooks, and a coffee mug. He smiled an apology to the facilitator, and took a seat off to the side. She then observed him sort and try to organize the papers while half-listening. When she got to the first part of the exercise, she asked the group to think about an intention or a goal that they were hoping to fix by engaging in the TMR. She asked them to write it down. Then she instructed them to begin listing their thoughts around the subject, asking themselves: "Why haven't I achieved it? What am I most afraid of?"

Kevin sat quietly, thinking, before finally beginning to write. When the facilitator connected with him in the small-group breakouts, she learned he wrote:

Goal: To transition to operations team and begin leading the company's key growth initiatives

Recognize: Why haven't I achieved my goal?

- I'm not organized enough.
- I'm not a competent public speaker who can lead meetings.
- I'm not a good boss who can manage many people.

- I spend too much time in the day-to-day and not enough time on future projections.

Replace: Next, Kevin answered: What would a person with a limitless mindset tell themselves? What should I tell myself to achieve the outcome I want most?

- I will develop new organizational practices to align with my vision.
- I am capable of inspiring others.
- I am empathetic, open-minded, and committed to my team's success.
- I can lead our company into its next growth phase.

Reinforce: Kevin needed to reinforce his goal through his behaviors. He wrote down his plan.

- Eliminate the physical clutter at my work office and create a dedicated home office; implement a bullet-journaling system.
- Sign up for public-speaking training programs to become more comfortable speaking.
- Request a management training or work with a coach.
- Protect time in my calendar each week to create the space to innovate, collaborate, and be more strategic.

We followed up with Kevin a few months after his training to see the progress he'd made. He implemented a new approach to his calendar, clearing thirty minutes each morning and thirty minutes at the end of each day to organize his files and desk, and to clear his inbox. He took on the new role within his company and he was thriving as he prepared to launch the first new initiative. While speaking in front of large groups still leads to some nerves, he has learned new skills to manage his anxiety around it and he continues to practice with a public-speaking group.

Now you try. Identify a goal that is most important and get honest with yourself. Easier said than done, right? Check out these examples below.

Recognize, Replace, Reinforce

Goal: To get a promotion to vice president of sales

Recognize: I will never get the promotion because I don't have the experience required.

Replace: A promotion means growth. Skills can be learned on the job. This is the next step for me to contribute and make a bigger impact, and I'm perfectly capable of growing into this role!

Reinforce: Get the job description of a vice president of sales and make it your screen saver on your computer.

Recognize, Replace, Reinforce

Goal: To get back into shape

Recognize: Between work and family demands, I don't have time to work out.

Replace: Working out and prioritizing my health will allow me to show up at my best at work and at home.

Reinforce: Find a picture of you when you physically felt your best and post it on your bathroom mirror.

Recognize, Replace, Reinforce

Goal: To eat at home more versus going out to eat

Recognize: I hate cooking, I'm horrible at it, and I don't have time. It's just easier to go out or order in.

Replace: Eating at home saves money, is healthier, and gives us a family ritual we look forward to. It's worth the little bit of extra effort!

Reinforce: Get a weekly meal planner calendar for your fridge so that you have a visible reminder of your plan and can prepare accordingly.

Recognize, Replace, Reinforce

Goal: To be able to pay for 50 percent of each of my kids' college education

Recognize: I don't make enough money and I never will.

Replace: I have almost two decades to save, and with a clear plan professionally and financially, I can achieve this goal.

Reinforce: Schedule monthly automatic investments into college savings accounts that support the estimated amount to reach or exceed your goal of 50 percent.

Your mindset is the first key to unlocking Dynamic Drive. Until you own your mind, you will always be limiting your potential. Focus on turning obstacles into opportunities *every single moment of every single day*. When you do this and are intentional about rewriting your mental chatter, you'll find yourself on the limitless mindset path. Remember, it's not a sprint. It can be a marathon to master a limitless mindset, but once you do, that's the gold medal.

Remember, drive exists in each of us. But it needs to be cultivated and, in this case, liberated from the captivity of a limited mindset. You have to intentionally craft a mental environment that serves you. You have to reframe and reshape your mental chatter over time with practice and intentionality. I promise that you have the capacity to unlock your drive and accelerate yourself on your journey to more success and more fulfillment.

Key Takeaways

- A limitless mindset is the willingness to step into the next thing with the conviction that good will come as a result of taking action. It will lead you to use your curiosity, discipline, resilience, and confidence to execute on your goal in your own unique way.

- By learning how to reframe obstacles as opportunities, focusing on what's possible, and harnessing the power of your purpose, you can accomplish what you set out to do.

- Check your mental script. If you want to change your performance, you have to change the script running inside your head.

- By following the three stages of the Total Mindset Reset—recognize, replace, and reinforce—you'll uncover detrimental thought patterns impeding your progress and learn to substitute them with empowering beliefs. Keep in mind that replacing negative self-talk with positive affirmations is a continuous journey requiring consistent practice over time.

Chapter 5

Second Key: Energy

en•er•gy \e-nər-jē \: the fuel that allows you to engage fully in life's demands

We have an energy crisis in our country, and I'm not talking about fossil fuels. Rather, the data tells us that people feel worn out, exhausted, and depleted, pulled in so many directions by increased demands on their time and more distractions than any previous generation. We're a multitasking workforce, juggling more than ever.

Have you ever noticed how most of us are obsessed with managing our time, with little thought to where we invest our energy? We fill our schedules to the max, and we measure our productivity by our level of activity. We misdirect our energy toward the wrong priorities and risk chasing the wrong things. Yet, some people prioritize consistently showing up with the kind of energy they want *when* and *where* they want it most. How? They look at their time through the lens of energy.

Time isn't the problem. The problem is the lack of intention around how you're spending this limited resource. It's a challenge to reframe the passage of time as an investment of energy. Recognizing this shift is the key to unlocking a new level of control over your efforts, increasing your effectiveness. Nothing will ever truly move forward if you are not investing meaning into how you spend your time.

Energy is crucial for Dynamic Drive. When we don't have enough energy, what gets compromised is our best life, our goals, visions, and aspirations because we operate in survival mode. We aren't pushing for more or better, we are simply surviving. Don't give that away.

Can you lead, sell, solve, love, empathize, connect, and recover if you don't have enough energy? Absolutely not.

If we don't decide where our energy goes, the world and everyone else will decide for us. When you allow yourself to fall prey to the constant dinging of your phone, interruptions when you're engaged in head-down work, and the allure of multitasking, your productivity, effectiveness, and mental acuity plummets.

The concept of "time famine," a feeling of having too much to do and not enough time to do it,[1] was introduced nearly twenty years ago by researchers, and yet it's never more essential than it is today. The study concluded that it's not the number of hours you work that leads to time famine; it's a frantic mindset of having too much to do and not enough time to do it. Working more effectively—changing the way you think about and use your energy—is key to the joyful pursuit of your goals. It's about the holistic view of your life and legacy.

Even with more time, we wouldn't necessarily use it for our highest priorities if the distractions are still present. We need to switch from a time-focused schedule to an energy-focused schedule. Stop complaining about not having enough hours in the day and start looking at your energy outputs instead. You must choose where your energy goes before others choose for you.

Consider the moments in your life when you need to show up fully—the biggest meetings and pitches at work, the race you've been training for all year, the performance of a lifetime, or when your aging parents have health issues. These are the focal points for your schedule and, therefore, should be the focal points of your energy spend. When you build your life around performing at the highest level, you'll engage your energy with intentionality. Dynamic Drive requires this level of intentionality and a shift in focus from time to energy for peak performance.

I learned about the importance of intentionality around energy when working with golfers. Professional golf is comprised of tournaments held around the world, some more prestigious and visible than others, with larger or smaller prizes depending. Yes, pro golfers have the time to play in almost every single one of these tournaments, but not the energy. To maximize their effectiveness, I would identify the big-picture goals for each of my players and assess when they need to perform their best. Then we'd map out their tournament schedule to ensure they perform at their best in the tournaments that matter most. This usually involves saying no to some tournaments so they're rested for the ones that have the most impact. This often means leaving potential prize money on the table or turning down a paid appearance to rest or train before a big tournament.

What I tell them—and what I urge you to consider in your own life—is that being fully prepared for their most important tournaments is the best way to ensure sustained success. Every great athlete operates like this. But outside of sports is a very different story.

When I left my career as an agent and entered the more traditional business world, it was apparent to me that businesspeople were not thinking about how to best utilize their energy. I saw so many top executives give little regard to the importance of each item on the schedule. They might spend an hour on a routine internal call, right before jumping into a high-level sales pitch or client presentation, without time to prepare or focus. Treating each scheduled meeting the same, with the same importance, is a significant mistake in the corporate sector.

I saw this firsthand at a recent speaking engagement in Phoenix when I addressed about fifteen hundred employees at a financial technology company. A woman came up to me with the realization that she had a schedule that routinely included back-to-back meetings and she rarely accounted for the most important of them. This meant she would walk into her crucial client meeting or sales pitch no differently and with no further preparation than when she walked into her weekly staff meeting. It was causing her to spend so much energy on less important meetings and managing such a tight schedule that she had little left to perform at her best. Imagine if a starting big-league pitcher couldn't throw a fastball because he was worn out from a backyard game with his buddies? It would never happen.

Take Control of Your Energy

We can make our greatest impact not just by showing up but by showing up prepared and ready to engage. But that can only happen if we have enough energy for those moments.

Dynamic Drive challenges us to assess who and what deserve our energy and why. We must ensure we are aligning what is meaningful to us with our energy outputs, and in doing so, we likely avoid waking up one day and realizing we are way off course.

Energy is defined in physics as the capacity to work. Energy can be systematically expanded and regularly renewed by establishing specific rituals—behaviors that are intentionally practiced and precisely scheduled, with the goal of making them unconscious and automatic as quickly as possible.[2] We need to recognize the costs of energy-depleting behaviors and then take initiative to change them.

World-renowned performance psychologist Dr. Jim Loehr is known for his groundbreaking science-based energy management training system. As cofounder of the Human Performance Institute, he works with top athletes and Olympians, Fortune 500 executives, and Army Special

Forces on training ways to maximize energy for peak performance. Not long after I began regular speaking engagements, I took Loehr's course, called Corporate Athlete, at the Human Performance Institute in Orlando. In just two and a half days, I learned more about leaning into my highest purpose and engaging my full energy toward that purpose. I had already figured out what I wanted to be doing that aligned with my purpose, but really, Jim inspired me to pursue it wholeheartedly.

We kept in touch over the years, from lunches to texts to sharing the stage at a nonprofit event to support young kids. I feel blessed that he is a friend and mentor. I'd hung onto his wisdom on energy all those years, and it allowed me to plug into a higher level of performance. Then a few years later, after I launched my training company, I invited him to join me on one of the first episodes of my podcast. Jim told me: "Energy is life. Energy brings life to time. If you have a lot of time and no energy, you're not going to do much with that time. The essence of what life is about is the energy you bring aligned with what matters most to you."

As the coauthor of the national bestseller *The Power of Full Engagement*, Jim brings together the value of energy combined with purpose. He advocates the power of "full engagement," in which you're aligning your soul and energy right here, right now.[3]

The importance of energy management is magnified in endurance sports, where athletes have to compete over extended time periods and long distances. It's what Olympic marathoner Steve Spence calls "managing your energy pie." He remembers the advice that physiologist David Martin gave him during training: "There are always going to be runners who are faster than you. There will always be runners more talented than you, and runners who seem to be training harder than you. The key to beating them is to train harder and to learn how to most efficiently manage your energy pie."

All the things that take time and energy make up your energy pie, and there's only so much room in the pie. What are the pieces that make up your energy pie? Do they all belong in the pie? Or do you need to make some changes?

For Spence, running was his priority. He made the tough decision to quit graduate school and run professionally. He went on to compete in the world championships and made the 1992 Olympic marathon team.

That's the major difference that refocusing our energy can have on our performance. You must have the guts to ditch the things that don't bring meaning to our priorities in life. Invest more time in the things that sustain and replenish your energy and eliminate or better manage those things that drain your energy.

It's time to get clarity around who and what matter most to us and put our energy toward those things. Engaging in "deep work" rather than remaining engaged in more superficial tasks will allow you to be more creative and productive.

A key component to managing our energy is focusing on what we can control and not investing our energy in things we have no control over. There are lots of things in life we can't control and plenty we can control. Knowing the distinction can make a huge difference in energy

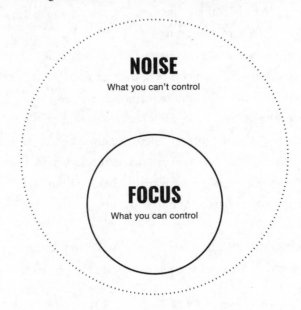

management. Until you get clear on what's most important, your decisions around your energy will not be optimal.

For an athlete, awareness might mean not letting a ref's bad call bother them during the heat of the game. For an executive, it might be recognizing moments that they shouldn't invest energy in—an employee's attitude in a meeting or a naysayer's opinion.

I think of this like an outer circle and an inner circle. The outer circle has the things I can't control. The inner circle contains things I can control. The things that need my energy. Where my energy makes the biggest difference.

In the inner circle, write down the things you can control in your life. This is where you should focus.

Here are some examples:

- Attitude
- Effort
- Mindset
- Choices
- Actions
- Beliefs
- Values
- Perspective
- Response
- Energy!

In the outer circle, write the things you can't control in your life. This is noise. Here are some ideas to consider:

- Other people's actions
- Circumstances
- Opinions
- Gender/race/age

- The past
- The future
- Results

When I was working with athletes, at the end of every season I'd quarterback a meeting with my client and other key players in their life. We'd go through the successes of their season, the challenges, what worked and what didn't, who is helping them, who is holding them back based on their high-level short- and long-term goals, and what support they might need to achieve them. My role was to hold my players accountable against their goals. Imagine the sheer volume of requests and demands on their energy—from friends' and family members' requests, to charity organizations, to endorsement obligations—it's endless. When you have a jersey on your back and make a lot of money, your phone rings all the time.

It was my role to bring them back to the question: What do you want most? What matters most? At that point in their life, it's maximizing the short window of time they had in their career to set themselves up for the future.

For a baseball player, it often is making sure they are strategic about their offseason and in-season obligations in order to perform on the field.

For a golfer, it might be passing up a paid private outing to ensure they are fully prepared for the next tournament.

For you, it might be saying no to the unnecessary business lunch or the conference call that you really don't need to be on (particularly if your approach is to be multitasking with email and other projects during the call). Instead, use the time for head-down work, and lock into the calls and meetings that do matter.

I've seen the best athletes in the world fiercely protect their energy. There are so many distractions and so many demands on them, and maintaining energy levels and focus in the face of so much noise can be a challenge. Everyone who has achieved anything over a sustained period of time has had to engage in periods of recovery. We usually hear about people who succeed but we don't hear about the training, and we certainly don't hear about the recovery.

Just like the athletes and coaches I represented, you too can take back control of your energy. How you protect it and invest it becomes a critical component of Dynamic Drive.

The Energy Audit

The Energy Audit is a process I implement with my clients both in business and sports, after first testing it on myself. It provides a framework to focus on what matters most and to understand the prioritization that must occur to show up ready for your most important moments and relationships. The best athletes and leaders proactively look at their life through the lens of energy.

Choose where your energy goes, before the world chooses for you.

An Energy Audit simply means looking holistically at all of your energy outputs and determining where you are gaining energy and where you are losing it. That awareness is the first step in creating change. This is where clarity and discipline around managing our energy comes into play.

When you manage your energy levels, your tank remains full, even after a long day. When you don't, it can feel like you are running on empty. Learning to manage your Energizers, Drainers, and Neutrals will help you build awareness as well as tap into a reservoir of energy and help you be focused and prioritized.

Identify What Affects Your Energy

Energizers: Energizers feed your soul and renew your energy. They might be things like a morning workout, an exciting new work project, meeting friends for dinner, strategizing with your team, volunteering in the community, or engaging in activities with family. *Find what energizes you and do more of it.*

Drainers: Drainers make you feel exhausted. They might be things like nonstop travel, back-to-back meetings, toxic relationships, too much scrolling on social media, overcommitting to social events, or balancing your financial accounts. *Find whatever it is that drains your energy and eliminate it, or better manage your energy around it.*

Neutrals: Neutrals simply exist. They might be things like running errands, your daily commute, household chores, or answering emails. These things may not be your favorite, but they are part of daily life. *Get more efficient at doing these things to minimize their impact.*

I recommend you start with the personal first. Enter your Energizers and then your Drainers first, followed by the Neutrals. Consider the physical, mental, emotional, relational, and spiritual realms within your life. Then go back and do the same with work.

To complete your own Energy Audit, visit www.getdynamicdrive .com/resources.

ENERGY AUDIT

What increases your energy and is meaningful to you?

What doesn't increase or decrease your energy, but you have to get it done?

What decreases your energy?

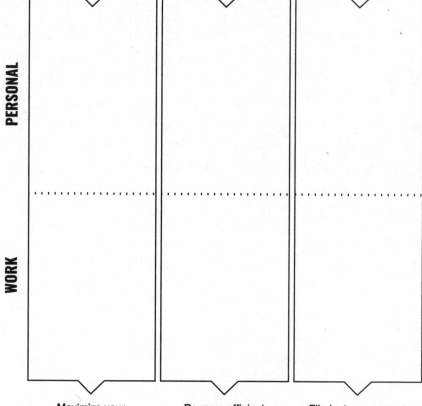

PERSONAL

WORK

Maximize your Energizers

Be more efficient with everything in between

Eliminate or manage your Drainers

ENERGY AUDIT

What increases your energy and is meaningful to you?	What doesn't increase or decrease your energy, but you have to get it done?	What decreases your energy?

PERSONAL

walking my dogs	Going to the grocery store	Negative people
Talking to my family and friends	Doing laundry	Bad nights of sleep
Going to church	Mowing the lawn	Difficult neighbors
		Skipping workouts

WORK

Closing a sale	Organizing my desk	Unrealistic clients
Shorter meetings	Cleaning out my inbox	Difficult contracts
Clear goals		Last-minute fire drills
Collaboration with colleagues		Technical issues

Maximize your Energizers	Be more efficient with everything in between	Eliminate or manage your Drainers

Let's review this completed Energy Audit from a friend of mine who asked for help. Stella is a busy working mom with two young kids. Like so many, she works hard and is spread thin across many different areas of life. Let's dig in!

As you can see from her audit, she's lacking Energizers in her personal life and needs to find ways to mitigate the effect of the Drainers. I sat with Stella and helped her brainstorm ways to work with the demands and responsibilities in her life and to prioritize the Energizers when possible. Here's what we came up with:

Drainers

1. Negative people can be so draining, but sometimes they can't be removed from your life completely. When I asked Stella for more details, I learned that her in-laws have strong opinions and a desire to visit regularly, creating a huge burden for her. I suggested she minimize her exposure by meeting them at neutral locations for the afternoon or sending her husband and children to visit for the day.

2. I worked with Stella to be honest about her phone habits before bed and the clutter in her bedroom that can be distracting. There are realities to having young kids, but do what you can to prioritize good sleep habits. Start by creating an ideal environment: cool, quiet, and low lit.

3. Schedule your workouts in your calendar and protect the time. Remember, it's better to do something rather than no workout out at all.

Energizers

1. I reminded Stella that she must prioritize these, and that they won't happen unless she is intentional. She set up a monthly dinner with her closest friends so they don't have to do the work of finding a date and picking a place each time.

2. Stella also told me she loves to read. So we're adding that to her Energizers list and finding ways to reincorporate it into her routine. I suggested she keep her book on her bedside table so she can read for a few minutes before bed instead of looking at her phone. And I suggested she join a book club so she is held accountable and has another opportunity to socialize with her friends.

Neutrals

1. Find ways to be more efficient with household tasks. I suggested that Stella have her groceries delivered. As your kids age, teach them how to do their own laundry, to make their own beds, and to independently manage simple chores.

2. I also suggested that she use mowing the lawn as a meditative or restorative time to herself. She can listen to an audiobook, a walking meditation, or a podcast.

The point of the Energy Audit is to become much more aware of how we're spending our energy: what's replenishing it and what's depleting it. There are some days that seem like it's one fire alarm after the next. You can get pulled into meetings or professional crises that require you to shift from other tasks and demand a high level of attention, draining your energy. The unexpected childcare needs, the last-minute favors, the demands of juggling so much between work and family all add up. There are positives that still drain energy. Just think of the holiday season with its many social events and family obligations. A festive time, no doubt, but one that takes a lot of energy. All of this is a part of life and cannot be avoided.

So what can you do? You find your nonnegotiables and hold tight to them, whether it's eight hours of sleep no matter what, or solid nutrition, or an hour walk at the end of the day while talking to a friend. Delegate and hire when you can. Be proactive in anticipating the drainers in your life so you can get out ahead of it. Plan carpools for the kids. Sign up early to bring paper plates to the class party instead of baking brownies until

2 a.m. Start projects at work early, and engage your team in anticipating time-sensitive items.

1. Maximize Your Energizers.

Become clear and intentional about what gives you energy, and find ways to support and protect that time. Scheduling, habits, and routine and systems are critical to feed your energy.

Protect time in your calendar for your yoga or workouts. Schedule lunch with friends so you always stay connected without letting it slip. Write in your journal, take time in the morning or evening for yourself. Whatever it is for you that gives you energy, protect that time in your schedule consistently.

2. Eliminate or Manage Your Drainers.

This is where most people struggle to make change. There's no way of sugarcoating the effects of the Drainers in your life. As we know, many are unavoidable parts of doing business and often out of our control. So, try to eliminate energy drains wherever you can and manage them better where you cannot. Ask yourself these two questions:

- Is this something I can eliminate or delegate?
- If not, how can I better manage my energy around it?

Once you identify the Drainers in your life, consider the ways to both offset them and prepare for them. Being proactive is key. Leave extra buffer room in your daily work schedule to address urgent messages and tasks between meetings and allow for some appointments running long. I always build in time to my travel schedule to allow for me to reset and prepare for a speaking engagement. If I'm landing late at night in Las Vegas, I won't schedule early morning meetings the following day, which ensures I have time to rest and get in a workout. Then I'm fully locked in on the event and ready to perform at my best. Try doing the same in your own life by blocking out the thirty minutes before a big presentation or sales pitch to ensure you have time to review your notes and take a few deep breaths before you begin.

3. Be More Efficient with Your Neutrals.

What you've identified as Neutrals is where you can simply be more efficient—not just physically, but mentally and emotionally as well. You don't have a problem here, but you aren't really reaping any rewards, either. The Neutral zone can easily be a trap if you aren't paying attention. Awareness is the key here.

Look for opportunities to make Neutrals into Energizers. For me, cooking has always been tolerable, but not enjoyable. It was a Neutral, and a necessity for our family. I considered ways to turn it into an Energizer, and I decided to try one of the meal-kit services that supplies recipes and prepped ingredients. With the tedious work of cooking done, I was able to focus on the more fun elements and began to bring my daughters into the kitchen to help. This allowed me to enjoy quality time with my children at the end of the day.

There isn't always a way to infuse meaning or pleasure into a Neutral activity and that's okay. Sometimes, driving to work or running errands just is what it is. Mindless activities can be meditative, an opportunity to slow our mental activity and daydream. Recognize what is peaceful and restorative and when it might slip into a Drainer. That's when you need to shift.

Put It into Practice

Now we need to take what we have learned from our audit and bring it to life in our calendar. Leaning into Dynamic Drive is about being intentional and disciplined—intentional about protecting what gives us energy so we can show up for ourselves and others and disciplined about saying "yes" and "no" based on our intentions.

Let's start by making sure you have a calendar. It may sound rudimentary, but if you're not working with a calendar system, it will be difficult to maintain the structure and intention required to engage your Dynamic Drive. Now, looking at your existing schedule, color-code everything in there based on your new audit system. Drainers are represented in red, Neutrals in orange, and Energizers in green to create a highly usable calendar. For example, that Monday morning meeting that happens every week, what color is it? The upcoming Wednesday client meeting, what color is that? Your daughter's basketball game on Thursday, what color is that? You get the idea.

Now you can clearly see your future days, and just by glancing at the colors, you can see where you are likely to feel your energy dip and where you might need to make some changes. You can see where you might have space for your greens or the need to add in more.

Assign a color to everything that is on your calendar now.

Next, consider your priorities. Remember the Alignment Audit you did? Let's start there. Look out in advance of your calendar, annually, quarterly, monthly, and weekly—for example, annual might include family trips, important dates for your family, like parents' weekend at college, company annual meetings, or employee and client birthdays. More frequently, you might add in date night with your significant other, exercise, and more frequent meetings with your team at work. Add these all in and color-code them based on your audit.

Of course, as the days and weeks happen, client meetings change, kids' schedules change, and adjustments will need to be made. The long view is important, but we also have to zoom in by anticipating monthly and weekly. That's why I suggest always revisiting at the top of each month and each week.

Once you drop in any new items on your calendar, assign them a color—green (energizer!), orange (blah), or red (ugh!).

All moments, meetings, and conversations are not created equally, and over time you'll learn to anticipate and protect your energy for the moments that matter most. You should consider building in time for preparation or quiet work before the big ones so you're entering those important moments prepared and fully present.

Many people I speak to complain that they don't have control of their calendars and where their energy goes. When you work in a corporate environment, you have more control than you think. You can choose how things affect you, the energy you give to it and give away. You may not have control over what drops in your lap from your boss, but you absolutely have control over your response to it.

Of course, there are plenty of events that can't be controlled or which might require a tough conversation and boundaries. Mandatory company meetings and requests from supervisors can make this challenging, but not impossible. Often, I encourage our training clients to advocate for their own individual priorities and needs while trying to serve the department or company's goals. For example, this may mean asking to attend only the portion of a long meeting that pertains to your job function so you can make progress an another project. Or, requesting to work remotely on a certain day so you have the hour of commuting time back and can use it to hit or exceed an upcoming deadline. It's asking yourself what matters most to them *and* to you. Then considering the next right step from there. For example, I speak almost one hundred times a year, and there is often an evening reception the night prior that I am invited to attend. But here is what I know without a doubt matters most to the client: that I deliver a keynote that impacts everyone in the room. So if attending a late-night event could impact that, I respectfully decline in the spirit of what I know matters most.

How did I get here, living by my crazy color-coded calendar? Through struggling with managing my energy just like you, and thinking there has to be a better way! When my daughters were in elementary school, my mom flew down from Michigan to help with them because I had a busy travel week with multiple speaking engagements. In addition, there was an "optional" board meeting on my calendar that I felt obligated to attend in Miami. That meeting added two nights to my already packed schedule, right in the middle of two keynotes.

As I landed for the not-required-but-feeling-obligated meeting, I felt so empty. Just awful. I missed my girls and husband and thought, *I don't really have to be here.* I called my mom in tears. She reassured me that the girls were fine, which was great—but I wasn't. I was still crying when I called my husband. I needed to reset my energy clock for the short term; I needed to reconnect with what fulfilled me. Luckily, there was still time to adjust.

I went to only part of the optional meeting, and I rearranged flights so that I could spend a day at home before heading to my next speaking engagement. I landed in Atlanta at 9:30 a.m., hustled home, and dropped off my bags. Then I headed to our girls' school and surprised my daughters. I checked in at the front office and walked into their lunchroom, where they were eating. They lit up.

"Mom, I thought you weren't going to be home today?"

"I wasn't, baby, but surprise! I am now. After lunch, do you want to scoot for ice cream and an afternoon at the park? It's beautiful outside."

"What?"

"I already talked to your teachers. They said it was fine."

We had a blast. Ice cream. Picnic. Conversation. The beautiful weather made it feel like it was meant to be. We spent that afternoon and evening together before I had to get back on the airplane—but this time I left with a full heart and clear head.

Two nights later, I returned home determined to come up with a new process to avoid this scenario in the future. I created a system with my internal team for managing the number of keynotes I committed to weekly. I created clarity as to what to say yes and no to, and I asked my husband to help me weed out the not-required-but-feeling-obligated requests. He's always been my sounding board, and it's so important to have this kind of support.

These moments happen to all of us at some point in our lives. We can't beat ourselves up every time, but the important thing is to make sure it's the exception and not the rule.

Bottom line: until you get clear on what's most important, your decisions around your energy will not be optimal.

As teams and as organizations, we need clarity, focus, and accountability as we seek the important. The more success you have, the easier it is to become scattered and to do the unimportant. It's easier to say we are busy than to admit that we might actually be unproductive and even chasing the wrong stuff. We must also ask ourselves: "What do I want most?"

Meet a friend of mine. Let's call him Frank. Frank is a sales executive at a large pharmaceutical company. Every time I talk to him (particularly lately), he is always exhausted. He's more stressed, he says, than he has ever been at work because of a recent promotion. He has more to do than time to do it. I can see it affecting his home life, too. He's talked about his wife of twenty years and their children he feels he is neglecting—especially a teenage daughter he snaps at more than he hugs.

"I'm exhausted," he told me. "It's this client. It won't last that long, maybe six more months tops, but I'd better get a raise and a nice bonus after this, that is for sure."

I knew that his promotion had come with no raise, only a promise of a bump later. Whenever later is.

"What are you chasing?" I asked him.

"What?" he said.

"What are you chasing?"

"What the hell do you mean?"

"Why are you putting all your energy into something that's clearly consuming you? Your health is slipping. You said that your family is being compromised. What is the end goal? The raise?"

He looked down, then back up at me. "I don't know."

Beyond being exhausted, my friend was clearly feeling confused and drained. His wheels were turning as he began to recognize the unintended consequences of his actions.

Following that conversation, Frank agreed to do an Energy Audit with me.

Frank needed the audit badly. I believed he could make adjustments that would get him back on track, but we had to start with three basic questions.

First question: "What increases your energy and is meaningful to you?" I asked. "Let's start with some personal examples."

He perked up. "Going for a run," he said. "I'm training for a 5K in March. Date nights with my wife, coaching my daughter Sarah's basketball team, and volunteering every Saturday morning through my church. Those are all the personal areas of my life when I feel energized and like I'm doing something that's meaningful."

I jotted his answers at the top of my page:

- Running
- Date nights
- Coaching daughter's team
- Volunteering

"What about at work?" I prompted him. "What are the things that bring you energy there?"

"Business-development opportunities," he said immediately. "I love prospecting new business, and I get excited every time I see a new opportunity evolve. My colleague Sam, he keeps me grounded and focused and knows how to shift my perspective when I'm having a bad day. I love working with him.

"Going out in the field . . . It might sound old-school, but I love the face-to-face contact with my customers and seeing firsthand what's going on in their practices, and I've been working on a new partnership with a well-respected hospital here locally that's going to really expand our market share, so that's got me excited."

I added those to his answers:

- Being out in the field
- Business development
- Working with Sam
- New hospital partnership

Next, I asked for the exact opposite. "What decreases your energy? Give me some personal examples first."

He paused. "Managing my kids' schedules—it's never ending," he said quickly. "And recently, my relationship with my best friend, Jason. He's going through a divorce, and as much as I love him, the constant negativity and complaining is starting to get to me."

"And what about at work?" I asked. "What's draining your energy there?"

"Travel," Frank said, shaking his head. "I've been on the road three of the last four weeks and it's starting to take its toll. My relationship with my boss. I hate to say it, but I just dread going into the office when I know he's there. He always focuses on what we are not doing and never points out the good work we are doing . . . and then probably just the typical office drama. We are going through a lot of change in our sales process, and it hasn't been an easy transition."

I wrote these down too:

- Kids' schedules
- Relationship with best friend
- Work travel
- Relationship with boss
- Office drama
- Change in sales process

"What's in the middle?" I asked Frank last. "What are the things that don't necessarily increase or decrease your energy, but they exist? You need to accomplish them and keep them on your radar each week."

"I've been on the board of my neighborhood association for a few years now, so that takes up time and energy," he responded. "At work, managing my direct reports. I have five now, and I'm part of the team that's working on our rebranding and website launch."

I captured these too:

- Board commitment
- Managing direct reports
- Rebranding and website launch

Now we could see what his choices were doing for him—and what they cost to his energy. So let's break it down further.

"Okay, now tell me this: How do you feel when you are here?" I pointed to the Energizers.

Frank lit up. "I feel ready to take on the world—optimistic, energized, focused. Like I'm doing things that matter."

"How often have you been feeling that way recently?" I asked.

"Rarely!" he said, staring at me. "Very rarely!"

"Okay, now tell me this: How do you feel here?" I pointed to the Drainers.

"Ugh . . ." he said. "I feel anxious and frustrated, and I know I'm short with people. Tired. I get more defensive with my wife and people at work."

"How often have you been feeling that way recently?"

"A lot. More than I want to, that's for sure."

Frank's story illustrates the critical importance of clarity in prioritizing our energy and efforts. Without a clear understanding of what truly matters most, we risk spreading ourselves too thin and chasing after the wrong goals, ultimately sacrificing our well-being and relationships in the process. By regularly asking ourselves what we want most and making deliberate choices to allocate our energy accordingly, we can avoid the pitfalls of burnout and inefficiency that Frank has experienced.

The Importance of Being Present

If you stay present, you can stay dialed in on what's important. As former Alabama football coach Nick Saban constantly reminded his players, "Be where your feet are." I love this way of putting it. Being present means that you're focused and fully engaged in the task at hand without distraction.

Being present is essential to managing your energy and can enhance productivity. Being deliberate in prioritizing tasks can help you focus on the important and eliminate the unnecessary, thereby increasing your productivity. Think about it. If you are present, you aren't thinking about the last meeting or phone call, you aren't anticipating the next one, you are locked in on exactly what you need to be doing in that moment. Plus, this heightened focus can help you complete tasks more efficiently and with fewer errors. Letting go of the anticipation of a tough meeting or high-stakes presentation and being there, where your feet are—in the boardroom, or at the sales meeting, or on the field. The freaking out is often worse than the thing itself. When you can see what's right there in front of you and take it in, you'll have the best possible chance at proceeding skillfully.

The author of *Essentialism: The Disciplined Pursuit of Less*, Greg McKeown,[4] talks about focusing on what is most important and removing the rest. When we do this, it is much easier to be present. We have less coming at us. Our society makes us think more is better. But we can't do it all; we can't have it all, and are we even sure *everything* is what we really want? We have to get clear on who and what deserve our energy and why. McKeown points out that most things aren't essential, so we have to shift our mindset and start the hard work of focusing our energy on what is.

Being present is anchored in discipline. It's hanging up the phone on our way into our house so we can be present when we circle up with the people in our lives who matter most. It's the ability to maintain eye contact—not screen contact—during meetings so we can be focused and connected to our teams. It's going on date nights and family outings without devices, or putting them on silent in our pockets or purses, so that we can give our full selves to the finite time we have for the people who are most important to us.

Distractions Drain Energy

Here's the truth: distractions add up. Over time, they can even destroy us if we aren't locked in on what matters most. Identify your distractions and you will be on your way to focusing your undiluted energy on your purpose.

One of my favorite examples of a top athlete avoiding distraction comes courtesy of right fielder Jason Heyward. He was a top draft pick in 2007, and our agency represented him throughout the draft and his MLB career.

Before the draft, we were sitting in my office discussing the deals that were coming in. On the table, he had opportunities to make a lot of money from card signings, car deals, appearances, and endorsements. He was an eighteen-year-old kid who could watch cartoons on his couch while signing his name on baseball cards and earn fifteen grand. Or, he could stop by the grand opening of a convenience store on his way to the ballpark for twenty grand. That's a lot of money, made pretty easily. But when I presented the opportunities to him, he responded swiftly: "I'll pass."

I was shocked. Most guys at this stage will take a couple of those deals right away and infuse some cash into their families.

But Jason said: "Molly, these are distractions to what matters most: crushing it in the next few years on the field and getting stronger, faster, better in order to get to the big leagues. The quicker I do this, and the better I do it . . . all these kinds of deals will be there and more when I get to the show."

He was right to focus on his craft, on getting in shape and training to operate at the highest level possible on the field. These distractions were small thinking, and he was focused on building his Dynamic Drive. As his agents, our job was to bring the opportunities forward to him, but it was also our job to support what mattered most to Jason—not line our pockets with commissions.

You may think of yourself as a successful multitasker. Maybe it's even a source of pride that you're able to juggle multiple projects simultaneously. But in reality, it's preventing you from engaging in more productive and creative output.

Author and professor Cal Newport researched the impact of distractions on what he calls "deep work," which is the most valuable, meaningful work done in solitude.[5] Deep work is brainstorming approaches to solve a problem, whereas shallow work is responding to emails. Newport says that the more we engage in shallow work, which does not require the same cognitive spark, we increasingly lose the capacity to perform that deep, intellectually stimulating work. It's a "use it or lose it" reality.

Newport cites a 2012 McKinsey study that found the average "knowledge worker" (someone who regularly engages in nonroutine problem-solving) spends more than 60 percent of the work week engaged in electronic communication and Internet searching, with close to 30 percent of a worker's time dedicated to reading and answering email alone.

So, how can you protect your energy? As Newport explained to me on my podcast, start with a digital declutter. Step away temporarily from technological distractions; remove the apps from your phone for social media, news apps, games, and streaming services. For thirty days. If you're already quivering at the thought, then this exercise is definitely for you. He suggests putting aside an amount of time each day in lieu of mindless scrolling to actively reflect. Ask yourself: "What do I really care about? What makes my life more satisfying?"

After thirty days, consider if that time would have been "notably better" if you had engaged with the apps you removed from your phone. You can begin adding back in those tools that are truly serving you, but I think you'll come to see that they're not adding as much to your life as the time they're consuming.

Listen, I know a thirty-day digital fast is a lot to ask for many people. If the idea of going cold turkey for thirty days isn't a fit for you at this time, there are ways to be more cognizant about where you're spending your digital energy. Start here. For the first week, pay close attention to how much time you spend on the apps (your phone keeps track), then try to reduce that by an hour or so each day. Or, consider trying the thirty-day declutter from one or two of your most-used apps, but allowing yourself to use the rest.

Once you fully live into Dynamic Drive, this digital reset won't feel as challenging. You'll be engaging a different mindset, focusing on long-term fulfillment through hard work, curiosity, and connection.

Distractions lead to multitasking. Multitasking is another word for a habit guaranteed to drain you. Your energy at the end of a day of multitasking is lower.

Psychologists have been studying the effects of multitasking for years, and the results are conclusive. Earl Miller, a professor of neuroscience at The Picower Institute for Learning and Memory at MIT, has been at the center of studying multitasking and productivity for years. In no uncertain terms he cautions: Don't try to multitask. It ruins productivity, causes mistakes, and impedes creative thought. As humans, we have a very limited capacity for simultaneous thought—we can only hold a little bit of information in the mind at any single moment.[6] In fact, research found that the brain lacks the architecture to perform two or more tasks simultaneously.[7]

As an example, think of how we naturally turn down the radio in the car when faced with a tricky turn in the directions or traffic up ahead. Attention is a limited resource, and in those instances, we innately know not to attempt to split ours.

McGill University psychology professor Daniel Levitin found that multitasking is, in fact, a myth. We think that we're doing a whole bunch of things at once. But we're not because the brain doesn't work that way. A number of studies now have shown that what we're really doing is we're paying attention to one thing for a little bit of time and then another and then another and then we come back around to the first. And all of these are separate projects that are occurring in separate parts of the brain, they require a separate start time, a separate monitoring process. And you end up fractionating your attention into little bits and pieces, not really engaging fully in any one thing. All that switching across tasks comes with a neurobiological cost. It depletes resources. So after an hour or two of attempting to multitask, if we find that we're tired and we can't focus, it's because those very neural chemicals we needed to focus are now gone.

Levitin points to how certain professions that are forced to multitask handle the cognitive load. There are some jobs that require rapid switching between tasks, such as an air traffic controller, a simultaneous translator at the UN, or journalists. They're monitoring all of these different things at once. We can take a tip from the air traffic controllers who, as part of their duty cycle, are required to take a fifteen-to-thirty-minute break after every hour and a half or two hours of work. It's a mandated unplugged, disconnected break where they go for a walk or listen to music, they exercise, or find something restorative to replenish all of the burned-up neurochemicals.[8]

As if the ineffectiveness of multitasking isn't bad enough, Russ Poldrack, a neuroscientist at Stanford, found that learning information while multitasking causes the new information to go to the wrong part of the brain. If students study and watch TV at the same time, for example, the information from their schoolwork goes into the striatum, a region specialized for storing new procedures and skills, not facts and ideas. Without the distraction of TV, the information goes into the hippocampus, where it is organized and categorized in a variety of ways, making it easier to retrieve.[9]

Recover and Reset

Rest and renewal are essential states within your Dynamic Drive. Yes, it's about pushing, challenging yourself, and holding yourself accountable to your highest purpose. But also remember that intentional, short-term periods of rest are essential to your sustained journey.

Rest is the short-term way to downshift several times throughout your day. It's a proven way to continue operating at a high level. And renewal is the longer-term period of scheduled down time.

Think about it this way: if you decided you wanted to get in amazing shape fast, you can't go into the gym for days on end without coming out to let your body and muscles recover. It's no different in our daily lives. "Gutting it out" works for a while, but it isn't sustainable without rest and recovery; it ends in burnout. Oscillation between hard work and recovery is important.

I spoke to *New York Times* bestselling author Daniel Pink for my podcast about the importance of taking breaks, and it was an inspiring conversation about the role they play in peak performance. Pink himself was someone who very rarely took breaks, preferring instead to power through. He told me that the research on taking breaks is powerful and led him to change his ways. Breaks aren't a deviation from our performance; they are part of our performance.

Pink now integrates breaks into his life daily, and it's made a big impact. His approach now includes scheduling his breaks in advance the way he would schedule a meeting. He sits down each morning to determine what time he's going to take a break and what he's going to do during his break.

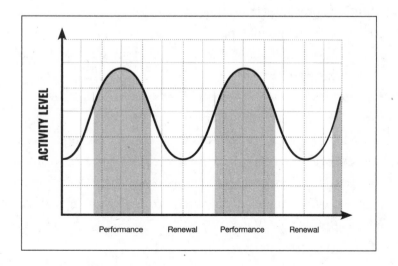

If you want to manage your energy better, build in microbreaks. Microbreaks are quick recovery periods to reset and show up for the next big moment. Based on his research, he prioritizes breaks intentionally to be the most restorative, according to the following guidelines:

1. Something beats nothing. Research says microbreaks under sixty seconds are effective. Looking up from your computer and stretching every twenty minutes can rest your eyes and improve your posture, both of which will prevent fatigue.

2. Social beats solo. Engaging in short conversations with colleagues, friends, or family members during a social microbreak can provide a sense of connection and belonging, reducing feelings of isolation and loneliness.

3. Moving beats sedentary. Take a short walk while on a call, or pace around your office. Walking, even for a short distance, involves movement and exercise, which can help improve blood circulation, reduce muscle tension, and prevent stiffness. It also encourages deeper breathing, which can provide a quick burst of oxygen to the brain, enhancing alertness.

4. Get outside. Being in nature has a calming and rejuvenating effect on the mind. The sights, sounds, and scents of the outdoors help reduce stress, anxiety, and mental fatigue.

5. Pull the plug. Disconnecting for a brief period gives your brain an opportunity to recharge, making you more alert and productive when you return to your work. Plus, allowing your mind to wander can lead to creativity and generating new ideas.

For most people, the day is split into three phases: the morning is the peak, the afternoon is the trough, and the early evening is the recovery. So, Pink schedules his longer, fifteen-minute breaks for the afternoon to get the most out of a slower time of day, and schedules shorter microbreaks in the morning during a period he can engage in sustained work. Time of day explains the 20 percent variance between who is performing well and who is not in workplace tasks.[10]

However you construct your workday, it's clear that regular breaks are key for sustained productivity. Insert them between calls and meetings. Have you ever spent the first ten minutes of a call thinking about what you need to do based on the last call? Create time to reflect on a meeting after it ends, and then space to prep for the next one. Back-to-back calls may seem efficient in your calendar, but it leaves you fried. Just five or ten minutes between calls can create a calm and present mind to fully engage in your work.

Whatever kind of microbreak you take, keep in mind that studies found relaxation, socialization, and cognitive microbreaks were related to increased positive affect at work, which, in turn, predicted greater performance.[11]

Recovery comes from the inside out, but support is critical. Whom do you reach out to to make decisions about where you are investing your energy? Connecting with people who can support you in that process and help you navigate what to prioritize and deprioritize can be helpful. Personally, I lean on my husband and my parents, and my COO, a lot for this.

Our energy is our renewable resource. It's the fuel we need to keep us moving on the road toward a better, more productive life. It also requires time to recover and reset. In fact, that is what gives you the strength, energy, focus, and perspective to not just recover, but come back stronger.

Consider the ways you bring on stress in your life physically and mentally and consider how you can recover. Ideally schedule those recovery tactics or at the very least keep your go-to recovery list somewhere consistently visible to you.

People give away energy very freely, without intention. Be proactive and intentional with your energy to build habits that support your Dynamic Drive.

Take a look at the chart that follows. Our goal here is to be consistently operating on the right side—in an ideal performance state or in renewal.

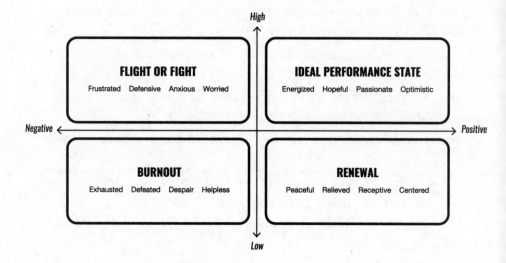

We can't be in an ideal performance state all of the time, because the ideal performance state is very energy "expensive," meaning we burn through energy quickly there. Plan to intentionally and proactively dip down into the renewal state in regular intervals in order to replenish your energy stores. This allows you to access the ideal performance state again and, therefore, your best self.

There will be things, people, situations, that will find you in fight or flight or even burnout at times, but if you create awareness and intentionality in this space, you can position yourself to bring the energized and engaged version of yourself more often and when it matters most.

Key Takeaways

- Energy can be systematically expanded and regularly renewed by establishing specific rituals—behaviors that are intentionally practiced and precisely scheduled, with the goal of making them unconscious and automatic as quickly as possible.

- Discover how to effectively handle your Energizers, Drainers, and Neutrals with our Energy Audit, enabling you to enhance your energy allocation. Holistically review all of your energy outputs and determine where you are gaining energy and where you are losing it. We need to recognize the costs of energy-depleting behaviors and then take initiative to change them.

- Distractions add up. Over time, they can even destroy us if we aren't locked in on what matters most. Identify your distractions and you will be on your way to focusing your undiluted energy on your purpose.

- Rest and renewal are crucial components of maintaining your Dynamic Drive. While it's important to push yourself, face challenges, and stay accountable to your highest purpose, it's equally vital to incorporate intentional moments of rest into your routine. These brief breaks serve as opportunities to recalibrate throughout your day, ensuring sustained high performance.

Stage 2

Sustaining Your Dynamic Drive

The second stage of Dynamic Drive empowers you not only to keep your momentum going but to increase your speed as you learn how to sustain your drive over time.

When you are starting out on anything new, it requires a lot of hard work without a lot of reward. It can be easy to give up. Discipline will keep you going back and it will become a habit. That is when you will begin to see the payoff from your efforts. Temporary discomfort creates long-term benefits.

Curiosity creates chances for you to learn, grow, and evolve. It unlocks new opportunities and strengthens connections. It shows up in every aspect of life: your work, your relationships, your self-development, and how you view the world and your role in it. You'll learn ways to connect to your innate curiosity through asking open-ended questions, setting learning goals, surrounding yourself with curious people, listening to learn, and valuing vulnerability.

As your Dynamic Drive begins to kick into high gear, you will undoubtedly face setbacks. High performers recover faster from adversity and view pressure as a privilege and obstacles as temporary. Resilience isn't a one-time thing where you either have it or you don't. Resilience is cyclical. It is a constant process where you build it over time. You fail, you recover, you show back up better, and you repeat. You'll learn the Fail, Recover, and Come Back Better model built to help in recognizing what pieces you can control and changing them as needed.

Chapter 6

Third Key: Discipline

dis•ci•pline \'di-sə-plən\: the process that takes you from where
you are to where you want to be

As an NFL quarterback, Alex Smith was used to being hit hard. But
in the fall of 2018, he suffered an infamous injury that almost cost
him his career—and his life. After being tackled by two linebackers at the
same time, his leg snapped; he had a compound spiral fracture of the tibia
and fibula, and the bone had broken through the skin. His leg was an open
wound, and the infection ravaged his skin and muscle. Smith developed
sepsis, a potentially life-threatening condition that occurs when the body
is fighting infection.

Smith's body fought for weeks while he was sedated, until finally he
was stable enough to make a harrowing decision: to amputate the leg or
try like hell to save it. He chose to save his leg. It was rebuilt with screws,
plates, and muscle taken from his other leg. All in all, he underwent

seventeen surgeries. But his journey to recovery was far from over. Once he was stable, and the infection was under control, it was time to rehab.[1]

Smith went to a military rehab facility because his injury was similar to those endured by wounded soldiers, akin to stepping on an IED. He couldn't walk for months. He struggled with the anxiety and the uncertainty of what the future would look like for him until he had a vision that he was going to get back to football. He held onto the image of standing behind the center, taking snaps, and competing at this level again. That's what drove him.

Smith missed the following season. Then, incredibly, he made it back to the active roster for the 2020 season. In October of that year, in a game against the Los Angeles Rams, Smith entered the game, almost two years after his life-changing injury.[2] He started for seven games as he led the team into the playoffs. He retired the next year, but what that single season of play meant to him will last a lifetime.

In his TED Talk, Smith said that the recovery from his catastrophic injury to playing in the NFL is the thing he's most proud of.[3] That battle, through the mental game and the discipline he embodied daily for almost two years, made him who he is today. He proved to himself that he was strong enough to return to the NFL, that he could overcome a life-threatening injury to play at the highest level. And, he says, it was the best thing that ever happened to him.

Athletes who are rehabbing from an injury are required to do the grueling work without the excitement, visibility, and tangible rewards of playing. They've got to rely on their mindset, they must hold tight to their purpose, and more than anything, they have to use discipline to go and do that every day, day after day, to get themselves back.

This part of the grind happens away from the game action, away from the cameras and fans, in the solitude of the training facility. Discipline often happens when no one is looking, in the moments of hard work, done day in and day out, in the personal commitment you make to yourself.

When you understand the value of discipline, it becomes a lifelong habit. But you have to get comfortable with being uncomfortable. Discipline sometimes means ignoring what you want right now to focus on what you want most in the long term, and that in itself is uncomfortable. But that discomfort creates freedom from regrets, from looking in that rearview mirror and wondering what you could have amounted to. Give yourself the gift of knowing your greatest potential.

Discipline is a key ingredient in peak performance. The research also supports the power of discipline, even demonstrating that it is a greater determiner of success than IQ.[4]

Most people overestimate talent and underestimate discipline. But here's the truth: hard work beats talent. Discipline drives your behavior when you don't feel like it. Which happens often, doesn't it? Discipline isn't complicated and it's available to anyone, but most people aren't willing to do what it takes. Discipline is your secret weapon to reaching your goals.

Discipline is less about lofty goals and more about stacking days on days of improvement. The 80/20 principle (aka the Pareto principle) states that 80 percent of the output results come from 20 percent of the input or action.[5] If you can't do your hour-long workout, do twenty minutes. Do something instead of nothing. All-or-nothing behavior is less effective than taking the small win or just doing something in the long run. Practicing your discipline day in and day out is more beneficial than waiting until you have the perfect set of circumstances. It's also about identity. Be a person who doesn't miss a workout, even if you can only do ten minutes.

There are a lot of buzz words out there to get you to buy products, programs, and books as a shortcut to success. But here's the real deal: discipline closes the gap when motivation vanishes. You won't always be motivated to do something, but your discipline—your system of rules for your conduct, your training—will become the unshakable and consistent behavior that enables you to set goals and reach them and, even more importantly, to engage with your Dynamic Drive. Discipline eats motivation for breakfast.

Discipline is easier when you've effectively managed your energy. It's easy to throw in the towel when you don't have energy to do the hard things. Managing your energy well moves you to your highest self and highest goals. It's difficult to be disciplined if you don't have the empowering, positive mindset to engage with difficult work.

Discipline isn't something you buy, borrow, or inherit. There's no hack or cheat to get it. There's no way to acquire discipline other than to build it within yourself through commitment, through actions like those I've outlined here.

The Freedom of Discipline

People with Dynamic Drive love discipline. It's not about the painful act of doing things you don't necessarily want to do. Discipline is freedom from regret, from disappointment, from wondering what you're capable of. Discipline requires that you hold yourself accountable to your highest aspirations, to be the person you truly want to be when you engage in the daily work to achieve your dreams. Investing in yourself will give you the opportunity to serve others in a greater way.

Discipline is the tool by which you bring closer the things you want in your life. But discipline doesn't work without purpose. Discipline requires you to know your purpose. When you can go to your purpose, it drives the behavior when you don't feel like it, when you don't want to at all. Through your purpose, you'll remain connected to your work even—or especially—when it's challenging. Know your talents and align with your goals. When you follow your natural abilities with hard work, you'll be less bothered by the friction you encounter along the way. We often talk about discipline as going against the grain of what feels good or natural to us. But if you harness your purpose, mindset, and energy—if you're engaging in actions that feed your dreams—it should feel like you hit a rhythm.

Showing up with discipline is often seen as a physical feat, but it's also a mental game. For me, I had to lock into my discipline last year when I tried meditation.

The benefits of meditation are widely acknowledged, and I believed I needed to incorporate it into my own life. Clear your mind? I'm in. I've heard over and over again from top athletes and business minds whom I've interviewed how much meditation helps with focus and performance. It seemed like an important tool that I was missing so I dug a little further and researched how meditation affects the brain. Those who meditate regularly have been shown to experience beneficial effects, including the ability to react faster to stimuli and being less prone to various forms of stress.[6]

The first time I tried to meditate, I struggled to sit quietly, to turn off the part of my brain that was running through my to-do list, to-dos for my family, upcoming travel, the text I hadn't replied to, the next call and meeting. I couldn't flip the switch to "off." I was antsy. Even though I knew that this was part of the process, it still felt so uncomfortable. Maybe I needed to create a space in the house. Nope, didn't work. Or maybe, I do it with my coffee in the morning for just ten minutes. Nope, the slew of texts and emails were prioritized. Okay, at night, then, right before bed. Nope, my husband and I enjoyed our evening catch-up conversation, and then I was tired so I flipped the light switch and set my alarm for the morning, meditation soon to be neglected.

Surely, the right tools would ease my transition. I bought myself a $500 headset someone recommended. Attached to the headset is a flip-down visor that covers my eyes and flashes blue or red LED light to promote further "healing and well-being" while I listen to a guided meditation. My family thought I had lost my mind when I would lie in bed tapping into my inner self. Still, I struggled. The fancy headset didn't help either. Neither did the paid app. I was still miserably sitting up in bed or in our study, trying to find my Zen.

What was I missing? I needed to more deeply connect meditation to my purpose and my faith. I run multiple companies, have a family, travel often to speaking engagements around the country, and find myself in high-pressure scenarios regularly. I wanted to perform at a consistently high level in everything I do, and I'm often pushing myself to new heights. Meditation has been shown to improve how you respond to stress[7] and reduces anxiety.[8] It's very aligned with my purpose of inspiring all those who attend my keynotes, listen to the podcast, or engage in our training programs. I was not, however, exhibiting the discipline to successfully meditate.

So, I reminded myself of it being an opportunity for me to connect with purpose and my faith in God and leaned into the discomfort of sitting still in silence. It wasn't always pleasant or seamless, but I consistently showed up and engaged my discipline to build five minutes at a time. Now, I'm up to twenty minutes every morning, and not only am I reaping the benefits of a consistent practice in the morning, but throughout the day I find myself embracing the silence and stillness that draws me closer to God. Overcoming the initial struggle required discipline, connection to my purpose, and faith, which has fueled me and the way I show up for others.

Discipline can help you unlock who you are. It shows you who you really are and what you are capable of when you take on the daily work and the focused habits.

Recently after a keynote, I was talking with guests during their break. As I shared and connected with people, I saw a woman patiently waiting in line, even as the next session was starting. Then it was just the two of us in the lobby outside of the ballroom. She spoke quietly, turned her back to the check-in desk. She was frustrated with her financial situation, feeling underpaid. In part, her world had changed—with kids and daycare expenses, there were more outflows so she felt squeezed in light of the added expenses. The more we talked about her sales pipeline, her systems, consistent touch points with clients (or lack thereof), what she was prioritizing from a sales perspective, the clients she was going after (or not), it was clear she needed a more disciplined approach to her sales process. Almost six months later I got a note from her:

> Molly, I know that you're busy, but I had to update you after our conversation at your keynote in Dallas. I realized the problem was my inconsistent work ethic and lack of systems to connect with

my most important clients. I was half assing it a bit, waiting for the phone to ring instead of being proactive. Not anymore. Here is what is so cool, I've doubled my monthly commissions, just through greater intention and discipline. Thank you so much! (My husband thanks you and my boss thanks you too btw.)

I was thrilled to hear this update. After struggling for so long, some consistent engagement and discipline helped this woman level up her sales. The proactive approach, the building of systems and streamlining of her practices, created freedom for her. During our conversation, I encouraged her to identify her top fifty business relationships—both those that she is already working with and those that she wants to work with—and then get in their head and heart to uncover gaps that she can close to support what matters most to them. By demonstrating your understanding of their business and offering insights and solutions, you're showing the ways in which you can add value. For example, make introductions that open new revenue streams or diversify supply chains, send a thoughtful article on new technology in their space, or write a heartfelt congratulatory note—all of which show you understand what's happening in their world. She did the work and landed several new accounts. She created financial freedom from the double in sales commissions, but also freedom around her identity. She now knows that she is a disciplined person. She's free from the constant worry and nagging feeling of not living up to her potential.

The Discipline Bridge

Dynamic Drive isn't about achievement but rather fulfillment. Focusing solely on the goals, the trophies, and the accolades minimizes the journey itself, and sets you up for the hollow pang of disappointment or disorienting lack of continued focus. True satisfaction in life is about a consistent and sustainable journey toward being better.

Having a clear goal can serve as a powerful motivator. Goals help you focus on what's important and prevent you from getting distracted. When you have something specific to work toward, you're more likely to stay committed and put in the effort to achieve it. Goals provide a measurable way to track your progress. They allow you to see how far you've come and how much closer you are to your desired outcome.

Goals help you think about the long term and create a vision for where you want to be in the future. This can provide a sense of purpose and direction in life. To fully embrace your Dynamic Drive, you must begin to get a sense of who you want to be.

While setting goals is a great starting point, achieving them requires consistent effort and discipline. It's important to break down your goals into actionable steps, establish a routine, and maintain focus even when faced with challenges.

Whenever there's a gap between your present state and future state, you build a bridge between the two. Those skills will serve you over and over again every time you reach a gap in the road. Discipline gives you the tools to build the bridge. You don't build a bridge in a day. There are small steps that must be taken to close the gap. The bridge is the daily grind, the behaviors and habits that get you to your goals. Skill acquisition is uncomfortable; we learn best when challenged. Struggling and occasionally failing are part of it.

Imagine that life is a cross-country road trip. Along the way, you'll face many obstacles that prevent a clear passage. There are many lakes and rivers along your journey, and you'll constantly find yourself with opportunities to level up. Discipline will give you the ability to build a bridge and cross into new frontiers, arming you with new skills and experiences. The more bridges you build, the more capacity you have for bigger, bolder bridges. You start by building a bridge over your local creek, and later, you can build a bridge over the Mississippi River.

How to Build a Discipline Bridge

1. **Identify.** Identify a desired future or goal.
2. **Seek success models.** Look at success stories. Identify people who are doing what you want to do. What are the differences and similarities between them? What have they all done? What sets someone apart? When you look at a blueprint for success in the category, you can begin to assess what makes sense for you personally. Ask for advice and listen deeply.
3. **Scrutinize the gap.** Scrutinize your current situation and the gap to your desired goal.
4. **Put in the work.** Work hard. You build a bridge brick by brick, day after day. Focus on the daily behaviors that will take you there without obsessing over the other side. Recognize that adjustments will need to occur along the way. Focus more on the process, then the goal. Appreciate who you are becoming as a result of the journey.
5. **Repeat.** Accept success. Celebrate the win. Show appreciation to those who built it with you, and help others build their bridge.

I developed the idea of a Discipline Bridge through building my first training experience as part of what would grow into my present-day, multi-faceted training company, Game Changer Performance Group. For years, I had been speaking to audiences around the world as a keynote speaker. As a former sports agent, I usually found room for a couple of negotiation stories from the stage. The stories were helping people, but more so the philosophy, tactics, and methodology I had deployed over almost two decades in one of the world's most competitive businesses. You can only say so much in an hour, so I wrote a book about it called *A Winner's Guide to Negotiation*, and I learned firsthand about the discipline it takes to write a book. Writing a book is all about putting in the work day after day, even when you're not feeling it. It took me about one year of writing to finish the manuscript, leaning into my purpose to help people and share my message more broadly.

Once it was published, I appeared on radio shows and podcasts, and wrote articles sharing my methodology, tools, and frameworks. I saw my discipline and purpose come to life. People were getting better results, they were building better relationships, they were seeing more opportunities to ask for what they want—and getting it, too. From there, I started with a vision for how I could make a bigger impact and got to work.

1. Identify. I pictured the future, helping people on a larger scale, creating valuable programming that would take each individual to the next level in their lives and careers. I knew this reality required me to create scalable materials and methodologies that would allow me to reach more people than I could physically touch. I needed to reverse engineer the path to achieve it. I knew what I wanted to do, and I was confident that I brought a unique perspective to the category as someone who lived in negotiation daily as a former sports agent.

2. Seek success models. I began by asking for advice. I needed help building out a framework from people who understood adult learning and corporate training experiences. I did a listening tour with friends and colleagues who were working and innovating in a similar space to learn what they wish they knew now, mistakes, market landscape, and competition. I hired an instructional design team to help develop the framework.

3. Scrutinize the gap. I piloted the negotiation training experience personally multiple times in different industries for feedback. We measured it. We measured everything from real-time feedback from the group that day, to longer-term key metrics like speed to close, margin percentage increase, and deal size.

4. Put in the work. How do you build something so big? Bit by bit, day by day, through hard work and curiosity. By seeing a gap in the market and closing it with something you are uniquely positioned to solve and scale. There are a lot of levers to building a company that is profitable, but one thing is for sure, it takes consistent, focused, collaborative work.

5. Repeat. We needed scale to make our greatest impact, more facilitators and technology. In less than one year after setting out to make my vision a reality, our coaches were training people in Russia, London, and Dubai—all over the world. We launched an application that lives in a CRM (Customer Relationship Manager) to enhance the experience and provide metrics. Today, our training experiences—offered in person, virtually, and on demand—are creating meaningful change in people and organizations' bottom lines.

The Discipline Bridge serves as a motivation multiplier, a life regulator, and focus guardian to make you indestructible in pursuit of your purpose. It shrinks the distance between who you are and who you want to be. Without discipline there's no way to get there.

I don't think I have to work hard to make the case that Tom Brady is one of the most accomplished and disciplined athletes in the world. Just check out his seven Super Bowl rings if you need a reminder. Tom Brady's career in the NFL spanned twenty-three seasons, and he attributes that longevity and success to discipline. He enjoyed the process of working out, of practicing and improving, and he knew that he couldn't cut corners.[9]

On my podcast I spoke to Alex Guerrero, Tom Brady's longtime trainer and business partner. Their partnership has been central in Tom's incredible approach to mindset, energy, and discipline—which all played a key role in the success and longevity he maintained.

It's clear that one of the characteristics that separates Brady from the rest is discipline. Brady does the tedious, monotonous training, getting in the reps. Brady's throwing coach, Tom House, has observed: "What separates these elite athletes, the Hall of Famers, is that they try to get better every day not by 20 percent but just 1 or 2 percent."[10] That's what sets Brady apart—the willingness to work hard when the daily reward is so small. It's about incremental improvements over time.

Brady himself famously said: "If I don't really work at it . . . and if I don't play to my strengths, I'm a very average quarterback."[11]

Guerrero and Brady talk about goal setting all the time, and the way they approach it is very much a Discipline Bridge mentality. Brady trains in the present to support long-term goals. They set goals three years out and work backward to determine what they need to do to reach them. Guerrero suggests asking yourself what you want to accomplish, not what you think you can accomplish. This distinction makes all the difference in achieving the lofty goals that will fulfill you at the highest level.

Brady's longtime teammate Julian Edelman recalls seeing this discipline and focus firsthand. A loss in the AFC title game at the end of the 2013 season only intensified Brady's offseason preparation. "We started training in February," Edelman recalled. "He had the location of the Super Bowl on his whiteboard in his gym ... I was like 'What's this?' and he's like 'That's where we're going to be the last game of the season, bro.'" That city was Glendale, Arizona, where (you guessed it) Brady led the Patriots to a Super Bowl victory the following season.[12]

It's easy to imagine Brady could slip into complacency with such a high level of sustained success. But Guerrero says they never look in the rearview mirror. They look forward to new goals and new opportunities.

The Genius of the Grind

Magic happens in the day-to-day, especially when fueled by a higher purpose. Rather than waiting for lightning to strike, or for the opportunity to achieve the "big goal," the person who embraces Dynamic Drive knows that the secret lies in the day-to-day process that powers incremental improvement—and the by-product is achievement.

Believe it or not, Steve Nash was a self-proclaimed late bloomer when he joined the NBA in 1996. Coming out of high school, Nash was totally under the radar. Although his high school coach sent letters of inquiry and highlight reels to over thirty universities, only one responded. Nash earned a scholarship offer to one school, Santa Clara University in California, where he joined his team in three NCAA tournament appearances and was twice named the West Coast Conference (WCC) Player of the Year. He came out of college in 1996 and was selected by the Phoenix Suns with the fifteenth pick in a star-studded draft. His selection was met with a chorus of boos from Suns fans, who didn't know this relatively unknown player from a small mid-major college. During his rookie season with the Suns, he averaged just 10.5 minutes a game.[13]

Nash calls himself a "late bloomer" because his career didn't really take off until he was in his thirties. So how, despite a slow start, did he end up playing eighteen incredible seasons, becoming an eight-time All Star, seven-time All-NBA selection, and member of the Naismith Memorial Basketball Hall of Fame? Steve is regarded as one of the greatest point guards of all time, and the daily grind was the secret to his success.

Steve explains, "I had miles to catch up. My thought was always to keep getting better every day. Where will I be in a year, three years, or five years, if I just keep stacking days on top of each other and don't give away days?"

Don't underestimate the compounding power of doing it consistently and being able to generate that passion and discipline every single day. Keeping his foot to the gas, Steve busted his butt every single day to get better. He learned from the more seasoned players around him, he pushed himself in workouts, and he did anything he could to earn a competitive edge.

During his second season, Steve worked so hard that he ended up doubling his minutes and tripling his scoring. Coach Danny Ainge believed in him enough to play three point guards at once on the floor, which is rare, especially in those days. That was validation for all the hard work, time, and effort he put in.

Steve admits: "I was never the biggest, strongest, fastest, most explosive so I always had to find ways to win in the margins. To be able to compete, I had to make sure that I was extremely efficient in a lot of ways."

He focused on learning more about diet, sleep, and recovery, all sorts of different levers to bring the totality of his impact up. He fell in love with the daily grind.

Nash's approach to a few bad days or a slump was to bury himself in the work. He would work hard every day, focus on the details, and approach his training with passion. He learned how to analyze his progress without being discouraged by the negative. He says being diligent in his preparation and what he could control allowed him to go into a game feeling prepared. He knew he'd put in the work and he could show up confident.

"I loved training. I loved going to bed thinking about doing it and waking up ready to go, and then seeing how I can pack more into a day, be more efficient with my workouts and be more thoughtful. I love to play when you go out there with a bigger arsenal because you put the time in; competing and playing is a lot more fun, with a lot more impact."

Nash clearly leaned into his discipline to play such a long and storied career in the NBA. His work ethic shows the importance of stacking one day on top of another.

Discipline inherently requires sacrifice, although sacrifice is a matter of perspective. It may seem like you're giving up the second cookie or the blissful hour of sleep in the morning—sacrificing these comforts and indulgences. But really, you're gaining the satisfaction and pride in working toward your goals. Remember that fulfillment is in the journey toward improvement. Do what you need to do for what you want most, not what feels good right now—delayed gratification. Discipline is what you rely on when you don't feel like it. And if you do it enough, it starts to feel more rewarding than it does painful.

Accountability

David Goggins is often considered one of the greatest examples of discipline. He's a former Navy SEAL, renowned ultra-endurance athlete, and motivational speaker, and he knows better than most the power of turning the effort into the reward. For those of you not familiar with his pursuits, take a look at this list of massive feats that tested him in every way: he is the only person to go through three Navy SEAL BUDS Hell Weeks; he trained as a soldier for the SEALs, Delta Force, and Air Force; he ran a one-hundred-mile race in nineteen hours, despite never having run a marathon; and he placed second in the Moab 240 ultramarathon, a 241-mile event that he completed in sixty-three hours and twenty-one minutes.

That's discipline embodied, and his ability to achieve some of the toughest physical and mental feats in the world and the work that he's done to inspire others wouldn't be possible without it.

One of the tools that Goggins has shared widely is his Accountability Mirror. It's the first step he took on his own personal reclamation of life. Before running ultramarathons and Navy SEAL training, Goggins weighed three hundred pounds and worked in pest control.[14] One day, he snapped. He'd had enough. He was tired of being overweight, tired of looking at the Navy SEAL poster in his room and doing nothing about it. He stood in front of his mirror and took inventory. He looked at his reflection and said, "You're fat, you're lazy, and you're a liar. What are you going to do about it?"

"I got real with myself. I looked in the mirror." Goggins says that he asked himself: "What am I going to do today to change what I see in the mirror?"[15] As Goggins says: If you're not real and raw about who you are, nothing is going to change.

Goggins admits that he lied a lot growing up, and it was a bad practice he wanted to change. He made small steps, going just one day at a time without lying. When he slipped up and lied to someone, he held himself accountable. He forced himself to go back to the person he lied to and own it, which is a deeply embarrassing act.

Total accountability—of owning who you are, your strengths and weaknesses—is the key to rising above a mediocre life and igniting your Dynamic Drive. Goggins says the only way he became successful was running toward the truth—as painful, as brutal as it is. It changed him and allowed him to become who he is today.[16]

Goggins advocates for taking complete ownership of one's life and actions. He encourages people to stop making excuses and instead acknowledge their role in their successes and failures. He challenges us to embrace discomfort and confront our fears head-on. In his book *Can't*

Hurt Me, he warns readers: "You are in danger of living a life so comfortable and soft, that you will die without ever realizing your true potential."[17]

Accountability inside of Dynamic Drive is about ownership. Owning up to your actions, both positive and negative, fosters self-awareness. This kind of accountability means no excuses and no blaming others. You must own the role you play in your life. It means being the victim isn't possible, ever.

Someone with this level of accountability monitors their progress regularly, enjoys the achievements, and owns any setbacks. Their rearview mirror is used to learn, never to blame. They leave nothing to chance, and luck isn't in their vocabulary. Progress isn't an accident and neither is success.

Accepting responsibility empowers you. When you acknowledge that your actions have a direct impact on your life, you gain a sense of control and agency. This mindset enables you to make intentional choices that shape your future.

Accountability builds trust with others. When people see that you own your actions, they're more likely to trust your words and judgments. This is crucial in personal relationships and professional settings.

One of my clients, a top college basketball coach, asks all of his players to write down their personal goals on a 3 x 5 index card at the start of every season. He holds onto these cards in a box in his office during the season. If he sees a player failing to live up to the standards required to meet their goals, he will bring out the card and remind them of their highest purpose.

As a leader, he knows that he plays a key role in supporting his players' discipline. He tells the players he's going to hold them accountable to their dreams, but he also believes strongly in the ability to self-motivate. There's only so much a coach can do and so many hours spent with the players, so he sees the necessity of players improving on their own. In order to self-motivate, you need to be able to self-evaluate. His players love him because he gets the best out of them, and it's all anchored in what they actually said they want most.

Through this exercise, he teaches his players how to hold themselves accountable, a lesson in true discipline that will serve them for a lifetime.

Play the Long Game

Playing the long game means setting yourself up for longtime success. Discipline is the tool by which you engage with temporary discomfort in an effort to reap long-term benefits. Lean into what you want most, not what you want right now. Discipline over time becomes your habit. Habits increase efficiency during goal striving.[18]

Ask yourself: "What would a snapshot of my life look like in ten years based on my choices right now?" Your actions and your choices today impact your outcome in the future.

Think about it physically. If you gain five pounds a year, guess where you'll be in ten years? That's right, fifty pounds heavier and probably not happy about it. If you neglect your relationships with your friends, they'll stop calling you. If you spend more money than you save, you might be bankrupt one day.

Most people overestimate talent and underestimate discipline.

On the flip side, if you increase your muscle to fat ratio by a few points every year, in ten years you'll be healthier. If you prioritize special moments with your friends and make the incremental effort to connect regularly, the relationship will be stronger over time. If you save more than you spend, over time you'll have emergency funds and financial peace of mind. Little moments create enormous impacts. Discipline on a single day won't get you there. It's got to be consistent.

Playing the long game requires discipline in ways you may not anticipate. For some, it's long periods of working the grind, sustained efforts, and slow progress. For others, it's stepping back, reevaluating, and sitting in the discomfort of uncertainty on the path toward a new future. Academy Award–winning actor Matthew McConaughey did just that. His incredible career has spanned forty feature films that have grossed over

$1 billion, but it was a two-year period of playing the long game that gave him the breadth of roles he so longed for.

After starring in box-office hit romantic comedies such as *How to Lose a Guy in 10 Days*, *The Wedding Planner*, and *Failure to Launch*, among others, McConaughey wanted to break out of the rom-com typecast and try his hand at more dramatic fare. But he couldn't get those parts.

So he took a step back. He said no to many roles in romantic comedies that would have earned him a lot of money and made him an even bigger celebrity. But that wasn't his priority. He held onto his goal of breaking into dramatic roles. For almost two years, he lived in Texas, out of the Hollywood spotlight. There were no paparazzi photos of him shirtless on the beach, and he wasn't appearing regularly in the latest rom-com in theaters. He calls it a period of "un-branding," and it took a lot of discipline to wait for the right role. It was a limbo, and it was deeply uncomfortable. But he persevered.

Throughout this time, he focused on rebuilding his identity through elimination. He finds it easy to know what you're not and what you don't want to do, and by sheer mathematics, you will end up discovering what is true to you. Through this process you eliminate a lot of chaff—the people, the places, the habits that are not serving you, and are no longer worth your energy.

Finally, it paid off. McConaughey received a call about a role in *The Lincoln Lawyer*, and soon he was cast in *Killer Joe*, *Dallas Buyers Club*, and *True Detective*. A few years later, he received his first Academy Award and Emmy Award for those roles.

When I spoke to him for my podcast, he told me: "The long view is understanding that every action we take right now is building the compound assets of our future—how we are seen, how we are respected or not respected, how we're trusted or not trusted, and also what we think of ourselves."

McConaughey poses the question: "What are the choices and actions we can take today that we are going to look forward to looking back at tomorrow?"

Key Takeaways

- Discipline requires that you hold yourself accountable to your highest aspirations. Total accountability—of owning who you are, your strengths and weaknesses—is the key to rising above a mediocre life and igniting your Dynamic Drive. This means no excuses and no blaming others. Someone with this level of accountability monitors their progress regularly, enjoys the achievements, and owns any setbacks.

- Playing the long game requires discipline in ways you may not anticipate. For some, it's long periods of working the grind, sustained efforts, and slow progress. For others, it's stepping back, reevaluating, and sitting in the discomfort of uncertainty on the path toward a new future.

- Discipline serves as the means to achieve your desired goals, but it hinges on having a clear purpose. Understanding your purpose is essential for maintaining disciplined behavior, especially during challenging times when motivation wanes. Your purpose serves as the driving force behind your actions, keeping you connected to your work even amidst difficulties.

- The Discipline Bridge acts as a tool to bridge the gap between your current self and your desired future, enabling you to consistently pursue your goals with purpose and direction. By cultivating discipline, breaking down goals into actionable steps, and maintaining focus despite challenges, you establish the necessary habits to progress steadily towards your goals.

Chapter 7

Fourth Key: Curiosity

cu·ri·os·i·ty \kyür-ē-'ä-s(ə-)tē\: the spark that ignites possibility

Curiosity is defined as a need, thirst, or desire for knowledge. The concept of curiosity is critical to your success because it embodies the strong desire to learn without constraint. It's the driving force behind new discoveries in all fields, not just technology and science. It pushes the limits of what we know is possible and opens up the world to what we imagine is possible.

Curious people have a mindset that helps them move forward to do the things that lead them on the path to new discoveries. The world's most successful entrepreneurs are curious about improving society, they are creative in developing innovative ideas, and they are committed to their task.[1]

Consider how much of our time we spend seeking and consuming information, whether listening to the news or music; browsing the Internet; reading books or magazines; watching television, movies, and sports; or otherwise engaging in activities not directly related to eating, reproduction, and basic survival. Our insatiable demand for information drives much of the global economy and, on a microscale, motivates learning, and it even drives patterns of foraging in animals.[2]

People with a higher curiosity are more inquisitive and open to new experiences. They tend to generate original ideas and are counter-conformist. Individuals with a higher curiosity are generally more tolerant of ambiguity. Curiosity also leads to higher levels of intellectual investment and knowledge acquisition over time, especially in formal domains of education like science and art.[3] People are better at learning information that they are naturally curious about.[4]

It's awfully hard to remain complacent when you are insatiably curious.

Curiosity on its own without action is a never-ending loop that leads you nowhere. You can read books, listen to podcasts, and gather new information, but you need to recognize that there's got to be an action component to it. Scientists or professors still have to produce something with all of that knowledge. Curiosity is the interest to learn more about a subject; motivation is the desire to do something with that information.

In his classic 1890 publication *The Principles of Psychology*, William James described two types of curiosity. The first is an instinctual arousal to an unfamiliar object. Imagine our fascination being introduced to our first computer. That fascination was instinctual. The second type of curiosity is what James described as a scientific curiosity and metaphysical wonder in which the brain "responds to an inconsistency or a gap in its knowledge, just as the musical brain responds to a discord in what it hears." The underlying belief was that either form of curiosity was sufficient to compel us to some form of motivation. Hence, curiosity—of any kind—yielded motivation.[5]

When we seek certainty, we are looking for finality. This is in constant conflict with Dynamic Drive—hence the reason we need curiosity to keep our journeys going.

Spencer Harrison, an associate professor of organizational behavior at INSEAD (the Institut Européen d'Administration des Affaires, a multinational business school), and Jon Cohen, chief research officer at SurveyMonkey, surveyed more than twenty-three thousand people, including sixteen thousand employees and over fifteen hundred C-suite leaders, to understand how they view the role of curiosity at their organizations, across industries and at various levels of leadership. They found that curiosity helps employees engage more deeply in their work, generate new ideas, and share those ideas with others. When feeling curious at work, 73 percent of individual contributors report "sharing ideas more" and "generating new ideas for their organizations."

Curiosity creates chances.

Successful organizations are rooted in curiosity. To generate new ideas and add value to their organizations, employees at all levels need an environment where they can be curious, seek and absorb new information, and make new connections. A disconnect between leaders' and employees' assumptions about the value of curiosity within an organization prevents new information from flowing into the organization. Unless leaders can see the barriers to curiosity throughout their organizations and create systems for it to flourish, they will remain in a prison of their own construction: believing themselves free to be curious and therefore believing everyone else is equally curious and unimpeded.[6]

Curiosity is a core building block for professional growth. Curious people have hard conversations when things aren't going well. They ask direct questions of themselves and those around them. They continuously learn from experiences so they can improve relationships and careers.[7]

If you want to unlock Dynamic Drive and even more opportunity, you have to adopt curiosity as your default mindset in every situation. Curiosity is an engine for growth, and requires that we embrace uncertainty. Make curiosity who you are, not something you do.

The Curiosity Edge

Those who sustain success make it a point to listen. They take it on themselves to call people in and outside of their industries whom they can learn from. They always want to evolve for the better. As you gain trust in your ability to ask great questions and then listen, really listen, you'll begin to find ways to connect, not just communicate.

The best stay curious about how to employ their energy for the greatest results. Because here's the deal: you can't wait until the bottom falls out to change. This is a major thing I have seen with the best athletes and coaches, successful leaders and business owners: they lean into it before they have to.

Winning coaches don't start asking for advice from others when they are a few losses away from getting fired, and the best leaders don't ask for advice after they or their teams have missed quota month over month. They are always curious. They recognize that change is constant, and that to stay relevant, it's better to lead change than to fight change. As we ask, as we listen, we might just pivot a smidge with something that we can try. Or maybe that information gives you a sharper eye.

Researchers have determined that dopamine, the brain's reward chemical, is intricately linked to the brain's curiosity state. When you explore and satisfy your curiosity, your brain floods your body with dopamine, which makes you feel happier. This reward mechanism increases the likelihood that you'll try to satisfy your curiosity again in the future.[8]

The researchers found that "curiosity recruits the reward system, and interactions between the reward system and the hippocampus seem to put the brain in a state in which you are more likely to learn and retain information, even if that information is not of particular interest or importance."[9]

Studies also show that people are more likely to be curious about a topic if they perceive it to be useful personally and socially.[10]

Beyond learning, two pioneers in the field of positive psychology, Martin Seligman, PhD, and Chris Peterson, PhD, devised a scientific classification of the basic human strengths. This system was the end result of reading the works of ancient philosophers, religious texts, and contemporary literature, then identifying patterns, and finally subjecting these ideas to rigorous scientific tests. Their research eventually recognized twenty-four basic strengths. Of those, curiosity was one of the five most highly associated with overall life fulfillment and happiness.[11]

Research suggests that people who make growth a habit have what I call The Curiosity Edge, which is a desire to seek opportunities to learn, regardless of the discomfort it might create. The Curiosity Edge serves as a vaccine of sorts against complacency. Curiosity creates chances and unlocks opportunity.

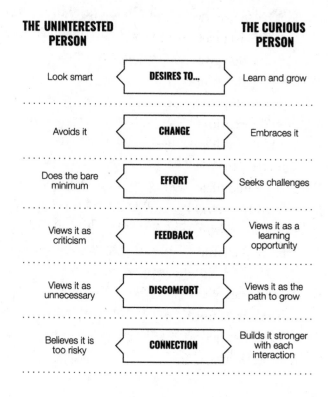

THE CURIOSITY EDGE

THE UNINTERESTED PERSON		THE CURIOUS PERSON
Look smart	DESIRES TO...	Learn and grow
Avoids it	CHANGE	Embraces it
Does the bare minimum	EFFORT	Seeks challenges
Views it as criticism	FEEDBACK	Views it as a learning opportunity
Views it as unnecessary	DISCOMFORT	Views it as the path to grow
Believes it is too risky	CONNECTION	Builds it stronger with each interaction

Kat Cole, president and COO of Athletic Greens, told me that curiosity is one of the main traits "that drive people who seem to cut through the clutter and wind up with more opportunities and more trajectory." Early in her career, Kat seized a chance from management at Hooters to help open a franchise in Australia. She had barely traveled and was only nineteen years old at the time, working as a waitress.

"I was curious to know if I could do it," she says. "I was curious to see how they did things in other places. No matter what I might run into that would be unfamiliar, I had confidence in my ability to build relationships and be curious."

Two months later, Kat was helping to open the first Hooters restaurant in Central America. Soon, she was not just a member of the training team, she was overseeing the openings herself. A year later, she took a corporate job running the employee training department and by the time she was twenty-six, she had been promoted as one of the company's vice presidents. She was led by her curiosity to understand her business and to explore each of the roles at the restaurant and within the corporation, which ultimately led to her success.[12]

Kat could have focused on her job as a local waitress, on the tasks in front of her. But instead she reached beyond, helping out in the kitchen when needed, asking questions and learning the business from every angle. By staying curious about changes in industries, technologies, and social dynamics, curious people can identify emerging needs and gaps that can be turned into new opportunities. Curious people question the status quo and explore unconventional ideas. This mindset can lead to innovative solutions and creations that fill a void in the market, creating new business ventures or artistic endeavors.

Learn and grow: The curious person cares more about learning and growing than appearing smart. The curious person knows that life is more fun when asking questions because when we do, we expand our knowledge and perspective. They'd much rather challenge their assumptions and learn something new than avoid information that doesn't reinforce their current view.

Embrace change: The curious person understands that growth happens through change. They believe that change is something to embrace, not resist. Instead of fearing what might be lost, they seek to understand what might be gained.

Seek challenges: The curious person knows that anything worth having requires effort. Instead of coasting through life and looking for shortcuts, the curious person seeks out new challenges.

View feedback as a learning opportunity: The curious person views feedback as a learning opportunity instead of criticism. Instead of getting defensive, they view feedback as an essential tool to get better and correct course. They don't assume that feedback is wrong; they assume it has value.

Trust discomfort: The curious person views discomfort as a necessary path to growth. Instead of viewing discomfort as a signal to change course, they view discomfort as a sign that they are on the right path.

Build connection: The curious person recognizes that putting yourself out there with an open mind helps form meaningful connections. Curiosity shifts our perspective outward, increasing our capacity for empathy and authentic connection.

When curiosity becomes a habit of the Dynamic Drive lifestyle, new opportunities unlock and connections strengthen as it shows up in every area of life. Even the brain begins to function differently as the potential for learning increases. In short, curiosity powers innovation and unlocks opportunity.

How to Build Curiosity

Allbirds cofounder and chief innovation officer Tim Brown famously refers to the origins of his company as a "curiosity project." As a professional soccer player who went on to represent New Zealand in the World Cup, Tim received so much free athletic gear, including more sneakers than one man could wear in a lifetime. He had studied design at the University of Cincinnati and he preferred a minimalist style, but at the time, the footwear landscape was all bright colors and overrun with prominent logos. Tim was not able to find a simple shoe—basic colors, no logos—on the market. So he decided to create his own. He admits that he knew little about shoes, but he began asking questions about both the style and the materials used, and he started to imagine making shoes from natural materials.

In 2007, Tim began to make shoes himself on the side, while still playing professional soccer. "I literally went on Google, found a shoe factory, and visited it in the middle of one of my off-seasons, just because I was curious," he explains. "This whole thing really started as a curiosity project—to solve a problem that was only my own."[13]

After creating prototypes, he began to share and eventually sell them to his teammates. He moved to London and earned his master's in management at the London School of Economics. He felt like he was starting all over again. He told me, "It was hard but you have to go backwards if you want to go forwards." The transition was difficult, but he knew he had to learn, ask the questions, and engage his curiosity if he wanted to pursue his new dream.

For Tim, he defines purpose as "devoting your time, career and your energy to solving urgent problems that are far greater than you in society."[14] Brown brought on a business partner, Joey Zwillinger, an engineer and renewables expert. Together, they created the Allbirds we know today—a company that's imbued with Brown's purpose, combining the minimalist style and natural materials that embodied Brown's vision from the beginning, along with an ethos of sustainability. In 2021, Allbirds raised more than $300 million in its initial public offering to give the company a valuation of $4.1 billion.[15]

Brown says: "Curiosity is the foundation of creativity and innovation but the assumption is that 'curiosity' is a nice or carefree state of mind. It is actually the opposite. Impactful curiosity is a lot about discipline, constraints, rigor and the courage to ask (and answer) the simple question. At our best I would like to think we bring that incisive form of curiosity to our daily work with the understanding that the answers in innovative organizations come from everywhere, not just the top."[16]

Curiosity is something that can be nurtured and developed. It's easily accessible and readily available to all of us, if we just take the time to cultivate it. With practice, we can utilize curiosity to transform everyday tasks into opportunities for growth or connection.

Eight Ways to Build Curiosity

1. Ask open-ended questions. When you are considering a statement you want to make, reframe it as a question instead.

2. Set learning goals. We set performance goals, but when was the last time you set a learning goal? Learning goals are critical to help you focus on developing skills and knowledge that support your long-term growth.

3. Surround yourself with curious people. The quickest way to kill your curiosity is to surround yourself with apathetic people. Think about the people you spend the most time with. Do they inspire you to explore, innovate, and expand your interests?

4. Listen to learn. Consider ways that you can become a better, more intentional listener. List habits you may have to work on to make this happen. Examples: Listening to respond, not interrupting conversations, putting your phone away, closing your laptop.

5. Make "cold calls." Make a list of people you want to learn from and ask for advice. Connecting with someone from a totally different industry or background is a great way to practice curiosity and expand your perspective. The goal is to get them to like and respect you enough to share what has and hasn't worked for them. Listen deeply and always have a little nugget up your sleeve that demonstrates you know something about them that they might not expect you to know—it helps drive connection.

6. Value vulnerability. Ensure you have at least three people in your life who will tell you what you need to hear, not what you want to hear. These will be your trusted sources to help you see your blind spots.

7. Rewind the tape. Get honest with yourself about ways you can get better. Athletes and coaches watch film to improve. We can take the same approach. After a sales pitch or a tough conversation with a colleague, take time to reflect on the way you showed up. What worked, what didn't work, and what can you improve next time?

8. Seek new perspectives. One of the common habits I've observed in peak performers is that they are avid readers and consumers of new information. Those at the top of their game are curious about different perspectives and possibilities, and they immerse themselves in all points of view on a topic. Find at least one book and one podcast to get you started. Hint: my podcast *Game Changers with Molly Fletcher* is a great place to start!

As a speaker when I get booked for a keynote, I understand that it's a big decision for an organization to put an external speaker in front of their people. Whether it's their employees or their clients, an organization's most valuable resource is people. I take the responsibility and the trust that they're extending very seriously.

Before each keynote, I ask to schedule a thirty-minute pre-call to discuss the goals for the event, key takeaways we are driving toward, opportunities and challenges in front of them, and more. It's an important opportunity for me to be curious in the spirit of connecting deeply with every head and heart in that room.

The organizations that I speak to value the opportunity to connect as much as I do. For the more than one thousand speaking engagements I've done to date, no one has ever canceled a pre-call and many of these calls include multiple high-level leaders as part of the conversation. I ask questions like:

- What are the best of the best doing consistently?
- What are three behavior changes you want to see from the people in the room? In other words, if we connect again in six months, what will people be doing differently?
- What are they worried about? Excited about?
- Is there common language you use?
- Any new products or initiatives, if so what?
- How is their energy overall?
- What is happening before and after I speak? (This helps me understand what types of information they are consuming.)

The answers to these questions unlock more questions, and ultimately enable me to create a tailored and impactful message to an audience.

Recently I spoke at a Champions Club event with top salespeople from a Fortune 100 organization. I learned on the pre-call that one of the areas they are all working to solve for is scaling relationships. In other words, these top performers needed to find a way to pull in other team members to support existing client relationships so that they can cultivate new business. Everyone was aligned on the expectations, but they were struggling to execute the plan. They had recently implemented a new technology platform to help the flow of information at scale in order to free up top performers' time and energy.

When I spoke, I specifically mentioned their proprietary language and programs, including the tech platform, which created connection and buy-in with the audience. People in the audience literally leaned forward. Using their language, specifically referencing an area of focus for them, created connection and validated my interest in their challenges and opportunities.

After the event, I had a line of people asking me to expand on that point. One after another sharing specific situations, what they were doing or could do given my knowledge of their gap. That keynote expanded into eight more small-group sessions where I have supported them even more tactically on this very specific issue of scaling relationships and focusing on new client acquisition. Everybody wins when you are curious.

Curiosity Creates Chances

Curiosity creates chances for you to learn, grow, and evolve. It unlocks new opportunities and strengthens connections. A mixture of confidence and vulnerability is necessary to be curious. It takes both to acknowledge that you don't have all of the answers.

When you can identify a gap, it's a chance to create value, to connect with people, and to lean into your pursuits. I utilized curiosity in a big way whenever I recruited players. Early in my career as a sports agent, there were five young rookies who all came up within the Braves organization at the same time. I knew it would be a big coup to sign as many of them as I could. I said to my boss, "I'm going to get all five of those guys into the office at once so I can build rapport and connect with them." I remember the look on his face. It was clear he thought it would be tough.

My client John Smoltz, the longtime Braves pitcher, was a veteran guy whom the rookies all looked up to as the clubhouse leader. Here is what I know about rookies: They're living out of a suitcase in a new city. They want to take advantage of this big stage, to make their mark. And, yes, they are a little bored. I called Smoltz, who wanted to break into television when he retired from baseball. In order to pitch him for broadcasting opportunities, I knew we needed to put together film showcasing his interview skills and on-air abilities.

"John, let's get you some reps with a mic, tap into the rookies, and shine a light on them to the city of Atlanta," I proposed. He was interested, so I continued. "Friday you have a night game. What if you and the guys come up to the office for an interview? You act as the host and ask them questions. We'll capture it all, share their story, and get some video for your reel." Smoltz agreed.

I had a lot to do, starting with cold-calling these five rookies and sourcing a media outlet that wanted the interview.

Luckily, everything lined up. The interview was scheduled for Friday at 1 p.m., in our office. The guys needed to be at the ballpark by 3 p.m.

The day of the big interview we set up an empty room in the office like the inside of a network studio. When the guys arrived, I greeted them at the elevator, one after another, as they rolled out. My colleagues were shocked. The interview was set up as far from the elevators as possible, giving me ample time to walk through the autographed memorabilia of our other clients—the Wheaties boxes, the endorsement deals, and, yes, that cheesy first record-setting contract plastered to the wall. All of which, in a perfect world, helps unlock their curiosity when they learn the caliber of clients we represent and the kinds of deals we've gotten for our clients.

As we're rounding the corners, I'd start up a conversation in hopes of getting to know them better. I'd ask them questions like: Where are you living? Is your family here with you? What does your wife like to do in the area? How's the clubhouse? Have you begun working with any nonprofits yet? Where are you planning to train in the offseason? I'd also add in some observations about their position in the lineup or the previous night's game and ask about their plans for the forthcoming off day in San Diego. Through these questions, two things happened: I discovered opportunities to add value and demonstrated my knowledge of their world. This was not only a way to gather information, but also understand them better.

Smoltz delivered and the guys responded. It was in the can.

Now the real work began. My philosophy was always this: act like you have the business before you have the business. Certainly there were things I couldn't do yet, as I wasn't officially their agent. But thanks to curiosity, I discovered a lot that I could do. A nonprofit connection for one. A hard-to-get dinner reservation for another. Tickets to a concert. And golf in San Diego for four of them on their upcoming off day. I had insights into their passions, their hobbies, and their pain points, and I could do something for each of them and build from there. Out of the five guys, I signed two.

Active listening, probing for more information, and remaining open-minded to possibility—all crucial elements of curiosity—can reveal untapped opportunities. Curiosity can lead to conversations with new business partners or mentors, and it can drive new initiatives. If you ask great questions, you are much more likely to find greater success.

As a sports agent, I regularly had people coming into the office to pitch our clients. Whether it was financial advisors, insurance agents, or endorsement opportunities, it happened constantly. So much so that it became rather predictable for me.

I remember once I had a coach come into the office sourcing a new financial advisor. The first financial advisor walks in and he has a forty-five-minute meeting with our coach. He greets the coach, and then he sits down and pulls this brochure out of his briefcase and opens it up. It's a beautiful brochure and he's dressed to the nines, the whole thing. However, as he started going through this brochure, I watched the coach completely check out.

And then a woman from another firm came in next. She sat down and she popped open her laptop. Again, it's a great presentation and she shares her incredible credentials, but the coach remains uninterested.

Finally, the third guy walks in and I'll never forget it. He looks at the coach and he says, "Before we dig in, tell me this: What's your philosophy on money?" The coach became quickly engaged and shared his thoughts with the financial advisor for the next twenty minutes.

In this Goldilocks tale, the third financial advisor got it "just right"! He came in curious. He asked questions that engaged the coach in his personal philosophy on money. Once he learned the coach's perspective and how he thinks about his money, he leaned into that approach and offered a tailored solution. And he got the business.

Sometimes curiosity means pushing back on the way things have been done or the commonly accepted knowledge to really ask, "Why?" Unlearning or rethinking information is a key ingredient to the successfully curious.

In Adam Grant's book *Think Again*, he explores the idea that the most important cognitive skill is the ability to rethink and unlearn. He advocates for seeing disagreements as an opportunity to learn and for opening our minds to hear things with which we might disagree. He argues that "embracing the joy of being wrong" can turn us into lifelong learners. As lifelong learners, we have a greater opportunity to build our relationships, become experts in what we do, and generate more innovative ideas and solutions.

The next time you feel certain about something, use that feeling as a gut check. Ask yourself: "Is your certainty causing you to ignore certain clues that exist?"

Finding opportunities to be more curious and seek out information can help you succeed in a number of ways. Approach feedback and conflict from a position of curiosity, and you'll turn those moments into opportunities to learn and grow.

Innovation

Curiosity drives innovation. It is pure impulse to pursue a thought, find a solution, seek new possibilities, or keep on a path to see what might be around the next corner.

The Zen Buddhist concept of Shoshin, also known as "beginner's mind," refers to having a lack of preconceptions about a subject.[17] When you're a true beginner, your mind is empty and open. You're willing to learn and consider all pieces of information, like a child discovering something for the first time. As you develop knowledge and expertise, however, your mind naturally becomes more closed. You tend to think, "I already know how to do this," and you become less open to new information.[18]

Children are born with this same type of innate, open-minded curiosity. They have no preconceived ideas about the world around them as they explore for the first time. According to Harvard-based child psychologist Paul Harris, a child asks around forty thousand questions between the ages of two and five. If you're a parent, you may feel like it's forty thousand questions every day.

When you leave your assumptions at the door—even when you know something about the topic—you'll be poised to learn new things and gain a new perspective. When in doubt, ask "Why?" The question of why is always a focus, whether it's why a business decision makes sense, why there isn't a regulation in place, or why there is a need for a certain tool.

The best athletes, businesspeople, and entrepreneurs have tough days, tough weeks, hear no, but step into—not away from—these moments of possibility. They cultivate and engage a mindset of what is possible, rather than what is impossible.

Joe Gebbia, one of the founders of Airbnb, engaged this curiosity mindset at a high level when launching his company. Not only was the idea for Airbnb completely innovative in the space, he also employed curiosity and innovation when struggling to keep his young company afloat. I talked to him for my podcast and heard firsthand how curiosity was a core value.

If you've ever looked at Airbnb's core values, one probably stands out: be a cereal entrepreneur.[19] And if you have an ounce of curiosity, you might have wondered why!

In 2008, Airbnb hit a low point, making a mere $200 a week in fees. Gebbia told me that there was only one way out of it: sheer creativity. One late night, or rather early morning, Gebbia and his cofounder Brian Chesky came up with an idea to generate quick cash for the business. It was a play on their offerings at Airbnb—leaning into the "breakfast" of their company name, they decided to make a breakfast that all of the hosts could offer to their guests. It had to be accessible to Airbnb locations all over the country, so they decided to create a breakfast cereal. In 2008, anything that had to do with then presidential candidate Barack Obama was selling well, so they decided on "Obama O's," and to ensure bipartisan representation, "Cap'n McCain's."

Gebbia and Chesky called General Mills and Kellogg and were promptly hung up on. So they knew they'd have to bootstrap the project themselves. They asked themselves, "How do you make breakfast cereal?" Turns out, they realized, you just need to buy it at the store. They brought in a fellow Rhode Island School of Design (RISD) alum to design the packaging. They did a run of five hundred boxes of each cereal, creating a limited edition collector's cereal that they sold for $40 each. They took product shots, set up a website, and began sending boxes out to every media outlet they could think of. They got some coverage, including a live interview on CNN talking about breakfast cereal. Orders came flying in. Gebbia would run to the grocery store to buy boxes of cereal, and they turned their kitchen into an assembly line to put the boxes together and ship them to customers.

In the end, they sold out of Obama O's and had a quick $20,000 infusion that saved the company. Gebbia attributes a lot of his innovative vision to his background studying industrial design and graphic design at RISD. "You have to learn how to imagine something that doesn't yet exist. And then you learn how to make it real."

A key component of entrepreneurship is imagining something that doesn't exist. Gebbia says he encourages others to not edit themselves too early in the creative brainstorming phase. To me, this is a unique and powerful example of creativity, curiosity, and flat-out finding a way especially when it seems unlikely. And this philosophy of bold curiosity, of following an idea or discovering a solution in an unlikely place, remains intact at Airbnb.

Curiosity often drives individuals and organizations to explore new territories and ask questions about the world around them. Google's Eric Schmidt is well known for leading the company through a period of rapid expansion from 2001 through 2015, first as CEO and then as chairman of Google's parent company. Schmidt played a significant role in developing Google's advertising business, particularly the AdWords and AdSense platforms. These advertising platforms revolutionized online advertising and became a major source of revenue. He oversaw the purchase of Android and restructured its corporate organization, creating Alphabet Inc. as its parent company. He's famously said: "We run this company on questions, not answers." Schmidt encouraged Google to pursue ambitious, forward-thinking projects, often referred to as "moonshots." These were projects that aimed to solve big, complex problems, even if they seemed unlikely to succeed initially. The idea was to foster curiosity and a willingness to take risks in pursuit of groundbreaking innovations.[20]

There Are Stupid Questions

You have to prepare deeply before you ask busy people questions. When it comes to connecting with someone, especially those you care to make a good impression on, asking obvious or already published answers to questions is a surefire way to get shut down.

When you can show that you've done your homework on anyone that you care to connect with or make a good impression on, you can earn respect. So many people make the mistake of asking questions they could have found out on their own. You can lose people really fast when you're lazy and unprepared. Demonstrate a level of knowledge, of preparation, then ask questions.

Questions can show how you have prepared and sometimes bring to light a gap you want to expose, all while gathering information.

Bad Questions	Good Questions
Who is your ideal client?	I saw you just started working with Target and CVS—congrats; what is it about those clients that makes them ideal for you?
When is your fiscal year?	Since your fiscal year starts in November, when do you lock in your budgets prior to November?
How many salespeople do you have?	With over forty-four thousand salespeople, how do you break up your sales teams—geographically, by product or industry?

Early in my career, I was working for Leeman Bennett, the former head coach of the Atlanta Falcons, as part of the Super Bowl XXVIII host committee. Toward the end of my six-month stint with the committee, Leeman and I were playing catch with a football in the office while we were waiting for someone to come up for a meeting. I felt comfortable, too comfortable. After a couple of back and forths, I said, "Coach, where did you play college ball?"

He caught my spiral, tucked it in like a running back, and said, "Molly, I like you, so I am going to tell you something I hope you never forget," in a kind, almost fatherly tone. "Don't ask someone a question you could have found out on your own!" He cocked his arm back, stared at me like I had a number on my chest, and threw me a bullet. Just as I caught it, he said, "University of Kentucky, I played there, quarterback and defensive back." He smiled and nodded toward the reception area, where his visitors had just arrived.

I never forgot what he said; it filters my questions to this day, and I hope yours now, too.

Key Takeaways

- Curiosity is critical to your success. It's the driving force behind new discoveries in all fields, not just technology and science. It pushes the limits of what we know is possible and opens up the world to what we imagine is possible.

- Curiosity on its own without action is a never-ending loop that leads you nowhere.

- A mixture of confidence and vulnerability is necessary to be curious. When you leave your assumptions at the door, you'll be poised to learn new things and gain a new perspective.

- Curiosity drives innovation. It is pure impulse to pursue a thought, find a solution, seek new possibilities, or keep on a path to see what might be around the next corner.

- Individuals who consistently prioritize growth possess what I call The Curiosity Edge, demonstrating a keen inclination to pursue learning opportunities, even amidst discomfort. This mindset acts as a countermeasure against complacency, unlocking potential opportunities.

Chapter 8

Fifth Key: Resilience

re•sil•ience \ri-'zil-yən(t)s\: the mental toughness to repeatedly
get back up BETTER when you're knocked down

I'm standing on the range at the Masters Tournament behind my client, former professional golfer Franklin Langham, while he warms up.
It was early in the morning in Georgia, and only a few guys were on the
range. I looked down the range and I saw legendary golf instructor Butch
Harmon standing behind Tiger Woods, who was also warming up. Both
players were just starting their routines and getting loose. I had met Butch
a few nights before and I was eager to continue our conversation.

Every April, during Masters week, about a dozen of us in and out of
the golf business get together for dinner near Augusta National. I found
myself in conversation with Butch, one of the foremost swing coaches
in the game and among the top-ranked teachers in the country. He had
worked with some of the best golfers on the PGA and LPGA Tours—Tiger
Woods, Phil Mickelson, and Annika Sörenstam, to name a few. He's one

of the most sought-after, revered, brilliant minds in the sport, and he has witnessed his players hoist trophies time and time again. I had a lot I wanted to ask him about, so I edged my way over and reintroduced myself.

"Butch, I've got to ask you," I said as Tiger continued to drop wedges right on top of the pin, "you've worked with some of the best golfers in the world. What would you say is the one thing, the biggest difference between the ones out on tour that are winning tournaments, making cuts, holding trophies over their heads on Sundays? What's the difference between them and everybody else?"

"That's easy," he said. "Molly, the best are resilient. The best recover from adversity fast. They're disciplined and intentional about their recovery. The difference between good and great is the ability to recover from adversity fast." He paused. "Faster than everybody else."

It isn't about the mistake, the missed putt, the sprayed drive, the shanked bunker shot. It's about resilience. Resilience is the difference between just hitting a bad shot and letting that bad shot ruin the hole or the round. You're going to hit bad shots. Resilience is about how you choose to respond.

Because here's the thing: we're all going to make mistakes and have a bad day. That's fine. We're going to get no, right? I always used to love to say to my young sports agents, "No, it's really just feedback. That's what no is. Feedback." The difference isn't what happens. It's how we choose to respond to it. That we don't let it unravel us, that we recover.

Resilience is the "capacity of a system, enterprise or person to maintain its core purpose and integrity in the face of dramatically changed circumstances."[1]

What does a lack of resilience cost you? Progress, at best. Resilience is trying, failing, building on those misses, and trying again, and again and again. Failure and success go hand in hand.

It's not the first miss, or the messy second try. It's about the fourth, the fifth, the hundredth time that you go for it and prove to yourself that you can do it. It doesn't matter if it hurts, or it looks ugly, it matters that you get up and go back at it. Resilience is built through action. You can't think your way into it; you have to do it. A resilient person views pressure as privilege, setbacks as temporary, and obstacles as opportunity.

Most people think about resilience as just coming back. Yes, that's important, but it's about coming back better, stronger; not just showing back up.

It's inevitable that your Dynamic Drive will be interrupted—that's what makes it dynamic; it may not be consistent and perfection is not the goal, nor is it sustainable. Life is full of the unexpected. Resilience is the key to embracing the unexpected hiccup as just that, and not the decline of your Dynamic Drive.

Come Back Better

Diana Nyad is one of the most incredible examples of resilience on the planet. In her record-breaking feat in 2013, she swam 110 miles from Cuba to Key West, Florida. At sixty-four years old. It was a dream thirty-five years in the making and accomplished only after four crushing failed attempts. The swim itself took just under fifty-three hours to complete. Diana knows better than most what it means to pursue a dream with unwavering resilience.

Diana grew up in Fort Lauderdale, Florida, and she was nine years old when the Cuban Revolution broke out. She remembers that overnight thousands of Cubans emigrated to Fort Lauderdale with nothing. She remembers standing on a beach in Fort Lauderdale, looking out at the water, asking her mother where Cuba is. Her mother told her it was just across the horizon, and that she could actually swim there. That phrase stuck with her for years and years, until, at the age of twenty-eight, she decided to see if her mother was right.

The first time she attempted it, in 1978, she swam inside a 20-by-40-foot steel shark cage for nearly forty-two hours, before team doctors removed her due to strong westerly winds and 8-foot swells that were slamming her against the cage and pushing her off-course toward Texas.

For decades after that, Diana put her dream on the shelf. She worked as a sports broadcaster covering others chasing their dreams before she finally decided to pursue hers again. Thirty-three years after her first attempt, Nyad entered the water again in August 2011, this time without a shark cage. She stopped after twenty-nine hours in the water, after encountering strong currents and winds that pushed her miles off course to the east and suffering an extended asthma attack.

A month later, in September 2011, Nyad began a third attempt, again without a shark cage, but stopped after forty-one hours, because of jellyfish and Portuguese man-of-war stings that caused respiratory distress.

On August 18, 2012, Nyad began her fourth attempt, without a protective shark cage. Nyad and her team ended the swim two days later, reportedly because of two storms and nine jellyfish stings.

Until finally, she completed her fifth attempt.

Diana's level of discipline is staggering. Resilience is getting stung by one of the world's most venomous creatures, the box jellyfish, and almost dying of respiratory failure, and jumping into those same waters again, undeterred.

After the fourth failed attempt, most people told her that it was impossible. Sanjay Gupta and CNN, who had followed all of her attempts, didn't send anyone to cover her fifth attempt. The message was clear: we think this isn't ever going to be accomplished, by anyone. Even her own team, and her trusted partner, Bonnie, told her that maybe it was impossible. But Diana says she never considered quitting. She told me, "I never stopped . . . and put up my hands and said I can't, I'm done." She always saw learning opportunities. She valued the intel in the failure and used it to get smarter and better each time.

The definition of resilience is to come back stronger after a setback, instead of getting back to where you were. Dynamic Drive isn't just about recovery, it's about standing back up taller, stronger, smarter, better.

When you consider what Nyad put herself through in training and in each of those attempts, you can see her level of Dynamic Drive—the mindset, the discipline, and the resilience—that she utilized to persevere. Consider that Diana swam alone, in the open water, throughout the night. It's a sensory deprivation experience, with hours upon hours spent with her own thoughts.

When I spoke to her for my podcast, she told me a story of a sixteen-mile training swim where she realized that she was 0.01 mile short of the 16-mile mark upon returning to the boat. Many people would have called it good enough. Not Diana. She went back out to finish the swim, going one minute out and one minute back. Dynamic Drive—discipline—is what you're doing when no one is watching.

Just like Nyad, the best in any field view setbacks as temporary, as fuel or something to learn from. More of a challenge than an obstacle. Nyad cultivated this "find a way" mindset, and she never, ever gave up.

Diana Nyad is the perfect example of coming back better. Who would imagine that she could accomplish something at age sixty-four that she failed at in her twenties? If she was going to come back, she wasn't just going to come back. She was going to come back better.

When you're faced with adversity, you must reconnect to your purpose. Why does recovery matter to you? Why do you need to be disciplined? If you're going to be resilient, you first have to know why it's worth persevering in the face of the obstacle at hand.

The reality is things don't always go perfectly as we plan. We are going to have tough moments, that's life. It's not about what happens to us, it's about how we choose to respond. Resilience is a choice.

As you engage your drive, you will stumble and fall. Reframe it as progress. You will encounter setbacks and detours. That's okay, that means you are going for more—which is good. But what you do when those challenges happen can either fuel your drive or let complacency in the back door. Children are innately wired to push past resistance, to naturally seek to surmount setbacks, to get back up when they fall. But as we get older, we become conditioned to avoid failure entirely. We risk complacency becoming our default setting.

Have you ever heard about the pain associated with Achilles tendon injuries? It's known as a career-ending injury as many athletes just don't come back from them. The pain is excruciating and the movement is immediately limited. On April 12, 2013, Kobe Bryant, legendary NBA star, tore his Achilles in the middle of a game. In true Kobe fashion, he walked the length of the court and nailed two free throws before leaving the game. Yes, that's an act of heroism, or discipline and strength. But what really speaks to me about resilience is his mental state after the injury, which he shared with the world on Facebook.

He wrote, in part:

There are far greater issues/challenges in the world than a torn Achilles. Stop feeling sorry for yourself, find the silver lining and get to work with the same belief, same drive and same conviction as ever.[2]

Even in his late-night, post-injury state, he embodies the "mamba mentality" he was known for, which he defines as: "to be able to constantly try to be the best version of yourself."[3] Kobe's response to his injury underscores a "setbacks are temporary" mindset. He endures and conquers.

He returned the following season, in 2014, after a year of battling back to playing shape. He spent the rest of his playing career as a top contributor and a living demonstration of the will and discipline required to play at the highest level.

Top performers in any pursuit view setbacks as temporary. This mindset fosters resilience, allowing you to better cope with challenges, stress, and disappointments. Resilience helps you maintain a limitless mindset and keep moving forward, allowing you to maintain a long-term perspective on your goals and aspirations. You understand that obstacles are a natural part of the journey and that the path to success is rarely linear.

Next Play Mentality

The concept of next play mentality is simple: don't let one mistake affect how you play for the remainder of the game. Don't let one stumble in the race make you quit. Don't let one "no" during a sales call cause you to walk out of the room. Don't let one mistake make you give up.

A next play mentality demands that you don't dwell on what happened but focus on what happens next.

Life is a face-paced and continuous game. If one play doesn't go your way, you try again. Recover and step back. Control what you can, and let go of the rest.

Life isn't fair, so it's helpful to stop expecting it to be. When the umpire calls a ball on what clearly was a strike, the pitcher has to let it go. If the conditions on the golf course are subpar, focus on what you can control, not what you can't.

Now of course that's easier said than done. There are immediate physical responses after a mistake—quickening heartbeat, flushed face—and emotional ramifications, too—anger, embarrassment, fear. The next-play mentality requires emotional regulation. Don't get too high; don't get too low. Move forward.

My tennis coach used to tell me, "When I look at you, I don't want to be able to tell if you are winning or losing, regardless of what happened on the last point."

Controlling the controllables is key to recovery but stems from discipline. It requires discipline to remain steadfast on your path and not be deterred by a setback. When faced with life's obstacles, resilient people explore them as opportunities for a new way, a different way, and very likely a better way.

Consider your life and the value of resetting in various moments—be it a meeting and someone shutting down your idea, a sales pitch and you get an objection, or a temper tantrum from your toddler. Some moments allow more time than others; a surgeon or an airline pilot's next play mentality might be different from a salesperson's. That's okay; it's about moving on and showing up in a way that allows you to execute.

The next play mentality applies to more positive moments too. Someone loves your idea in a meeting, you close a big sale, or someone pays you a compliment. Acknowledge it with a concise "thank you" or high-five with a colleague and then refocus on the present. Just like you can get stuck in your mistakes, adopt that next play mentality and climb the next mountain.

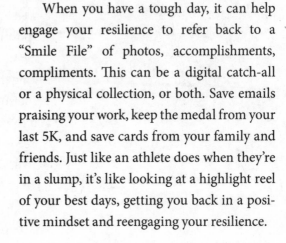

The difference between good and great is the ability to recover from adversity faster.

When you have a tough day, it can help engage your resilience to refer back to a "Smile File" of photos, accomplishments, compliments. This can be a digital catch-all or a physical collection, or both. Save emails praising your work, keep the medal from your last 5K, and save cards from your family and friends. Just like an athlete does when they're in a slump, it's like looking at a highlight reel of your best days, getting you back in a positive mindset and reengaging your resilience.

Expected to Be Tested

Golfer Billy Horschel has a strong mental game that has helped him capture, to date, seven wins out on the PGA Tour. Billy told me one of the keys to his success out on tour is knowing how to handle pressure and to recover quickly from a bad hole. Resilience is at the heart of what golfers need to move through eighteen holes, four days in a row, with players battling week in and week out for over thirty weeks a year. The next play mentality is an absolute necessity. For professional golfers, you must be fully invested in the next shot and let go of the last one—fast. You cannot hold onto the baggage of a bad hole as you step onto the next tee box. When Tiger Woods was consistently out on tour, guys often lobbied to get in a practice round with him. Billy was one of the guys. A piece of advice Billy received from Tiger Woods changed his mental approach. Heck, wouldn't it change yours? The man has won 110 professional golf tournaments and

15 majors. I'd beg him to play practice rounds if I was out on tour and pepper him with questions the whole time—that's what Billy did.

Billy explained Tiger's approach: "He sees himself miss hit a shot and be in a spot of bother, and really grind through it in his mind. He's prepping his mind in case he doesn't hit that perfect shot, and he's got to work hard to save something. He's already prepared himself for that."

Every athlete is taught to visualize the positive, to see themselves succeeding. But the greats like Tiger take it a step further.

Tiger told Billy don't just visualize sinking the birdie putt, holding the trophy over your head, or holing out on eighteen. Visualize yourself in the rough, in a trap having to get up and down to save par. Visualize yourself in tough moments. But visualize yourself recovering. That way when you are out on the course, you are prepared for whatever adversity comes your way. Billy embraced this advice and it helped prepare him to be tested.

You will be tested. You will be in the rough sometimes. Visualize and prepare for those moments, and then visualize yourself recovering.

The key to visualization is to close your eyes and imagine the scenario in detail. The more detail the better. It works because the brain cannot distinguish between something that's very vividly imagined and what's real.[4]

Billy offers great insight into how the best move super quickly from setback to comeback. He spends time visualizing executing his best shots, hearing the gallery applause, and holding the trophy. He also programs his mindset for great recoveries.

By rehearsing your reaction to adversity, you will develop the mindset to recover quickly from defeat in real time, and be better poised to handle change. Start practicing his visualization techniques now to help you bounce back quicker when you need to.

1. Visualize overcoming obstacles. Give yourself a clear picture of your ability to pick yourself up. Billy imagines himself grinding out a good score after a poor start, knowing that the capacity to do that is critical to his long-term success in professional golf.

2. Make the obstacles specific. Billy mentally rehearses saving par from a green side bunker, for instance.

3. Limit self-criticism. It's easy to beat yourself up for a mistake; top performers spend very little time in this space. "They are fully invested in the next shot and they let the past be bygone," Billy says. After a miss, they quickly shift into preparing for the next best step.

4. Practice patience. Billy echoed my long-standing belief that success rarely if ever happens all at once, and building this mindset is key to picking yourself back up. "You're not going to have everything be easy and successful right away," Billy says.

5. Collect memories of success. When you practice mentally, you have already reminded your brain of its capacity for success. This powerful practice is transferable to other challenges. "Whether you are meeting quarterly sales numbers or playing golf, you have got to envision yourself as being successful, then you can be successful in reality," he says.

6. Relax. When you've prepared as well as you can physically and mentally, you deserve to perform well and bounce back quickly. Relaxing helps Billy let all of the preparation and self-belief flow into his golf game so he can focus on being present.

7. Manage expectations. To control his emotions, Billy tries to play without expectations. He follows the process of preparing as well as possible and staying present. The more he claims this as his mindset, the more likely the results will follow. "If you believe in yourself, you can conquer anything," he says.

8. Give yourself positive feedback. When you battle through adversity, remind yourself that you can do it. "I can say I have handled the good and the bad," Billy says. Failure is simply feedback.

9. Find what works for you. After picking the brains of Tiger Woods and many others known for their strong mental games, Billy takes one or two points "and molds it into what works for me." Makes sense, because none of us are carbon copies.

What I have observed working alongside the top performers for many years is that they view pressure as a privilege and failures as opportunities to learn. Success and failure have a much closer relationship than most people think. The research supports this as well, indicating that the one quality high performers have, across a wide variety of fields, is the refusal to quit.[5] It suggests that healthy curiosity drives resilience[6] and that, once again, a limitless mindset is the key to functioning with grit.[7,8] The truth is that trying and failing may have benefits and implications beyond what we might initially think.[9]

Kelly McGonigal, a psychologist and author known for her work on stress and its effects, examines the concept of viewing pressure as a privilege. I had the chance to sit down with her for my podcast, and we discussed her work on stress, as detailed in her book *The Upside of Stress*. She explains that changing our perspective on stress and pressure can lead to positive outcomes. Instead of viewing stress and pressure as purely negative and harmful, we can choose to see them as opportunities for growth, learning, and even as signs that we are engaged in meaningful and challenging activities.

McGonigal's work highlights the concept of "stress mindset," which suggests that our beliefs about stress can influence how stress affects us. When we view stress as harmful, it's more likely to have negative effects on our health and performance. On the other hand, viewing stress as manageable and even beneficial can mitigate its negative impacts and help us thrive under pressure.[10]

When we're under pressure, our bodies release stress hormones like adrenaline, which can enhance our focus, energy, and performance. We can capitalize on the heightened alertness and motivation instead of fighting it.

Facing pressure-filled situations allows us to develop resilience, adaptability, and problem-solving skills. Overcoming challenges strengthens us and helps us become better equipped to handle future difficulties.

Pressure often arises in situations that we care deeply about, such as important projects or responsibilities. By reframing stress as a sign that we're engaged in activities that matter to us, we can find a sense of purpose and meaning in these situations.

Billie Jean King, the former world number-one tennis player with thirty-nine Grand Slam titles and a tennis legend, has spoken about the concept of pressure being a privilege in the context of competition and high-stakes situations. She believes that feeling pressure is a sign that you're in a position where your performance matters and that you have the opportunity to excel. Her famous saying—"Pressure is a privilege—it only comes to those who earn it"—is one I think we all live by as we engage our Dynamic Drive.

Being in situations of pressure and high expectations is something to embrace rather than shy away from. As King suggests, pressure is a marker of success and achievement, as it often arises when you're striving to reach your goals and make a significant impact. Rather than being overwhelmed by pressure, King encourages individuals to view it as a positive challenge and an opportunity to showcase their skills and capabilities.

Flexibility

Mental flexibility is the ability to dynamically change one's course of thought or action, based on the requirements of a situation. It involves being able to abandon a previous pattern of responses in favor of an alternative response that better suits the current circumstances.[11]

Flexibility is a crucial component of resilience. You will be much more prepared to respond to difficulties or any crisis in life if you learn to be more flexible. When we accept that it doesn't exist forever, and that everything changes, we start to develop flexibility, and we won't crack under the pressure.

Resilience is the process and outcome of successfully adapting to difficult or challenging life experiences, especially through mental, emotional, and behavioral flexibility and adjustment to external and internal demands. Cognitive flexibility is frequently linked to resilience because of its important contribution to stress regulation.[12]

Flexibility is a trait that can come in handy in several situations. For instance, being flexible and open-minded at work can help you be more efficient and deal with unexpected stressors.[13]

Just consider the power of this in our daily lives, as we face stressors and unexpected setbacks. Being able to adjust is essential to resilience. For me, with regular travel, speaking in various settings all over the country, and working with a wide range of individuals and companies, flexibility and resilience is key. I've had birds flying around in large ballrooms, backstage noise, and technical issues while delivering keynotes. With mental flexibility, I am able to react favorably to what could otherwise be challenging situations. When you're adaptable, you're better equipped to recover from setbacks and find new ways to overcome obstacles.

Key Takeaways

- Resilience is built through action. You can't think your way into it; you have to do it. A resilient person views pressure as privilege, setbacks as temporary, and obstacles as opportunity.

- Most people think about resilience as just coming back, but it's about coming back better and stronger.

- A next play mentality demands that you don't dwell on what happened but focus on what happens next. Control what you can, and let go of the rest.

- Visualize yourself in tough moments and recovering. That way when you are in the moment, you are prepared for whatever adversity comes your way.

- Resilience is the process and outcome of successfully adapting to difficult or challenging life experiences, especially through mental, emotional, and behavioral flexibility.

Stage 3

Maximizing Your Dynamic Drive

The third stage is where the magic happens as your momentum is building. You've begun the process of creating the mindset and protecting your energy, and you've also engaged your curiosity to consider the possibilities for your future. It's not that the danger of complacency no longer seeks to get in. You will always have to guard against settling once you experience some success. But maximizing your Dynamic Drive becomes more frictionless as the Seven Keys become force multipliers in your life. Now, you take everything to another level.

Connection is a tool for self-motivation, a way to maximize our impact, and a pathway to fulfillment. Life isn't all about goals and success, however you define it. Connection adds meaning, and it's an essential component to finding true fulfillment. Connection takes time. It takes touches. It takes preparation and courage. Embrace the vulnerability it requires. The people you love, those who inspire you, and those who you inspire become your legacy. Confidence is often discussed and rarely understood in a deeper and more meaningful way. At its core, we can begin to embrace it as a tool to continue to push ourselves out of complacency, or our comfort zones, to face new and exciting opportunities. We grow because of our confidence, and we will continue to thrive within Dynamic Drive as we continue cycling through the Seven Keys.

Chapter 9

Sixth Key: Connection

con·nec·tion \kə'nekSH(ə)n\: the link or positive energy between people

Connection is the link to a meaningful life. It's an essential component of Dynamic Drive, a key to unlock an even higher level of performance and a must-have for a well-rounded, full life. Human beings are creatures of connection. Without it, we wilt.

Connection is a tool for self-motivation, a way to maximize our impact, and a pathway to fulfillment.

Connection has been recognized as a critical part of communication and persuasion since the days of Aristotle, back in 350 BC. He identified *pathos* as a critical element in communication and persuasion. *Pathos*, in philosophy and rhetoric, is a purposeful appeal to emotion to evoke specific feelings in one's audience. Aristotle understood way back then that the human connection makes a huge difference in provoking a desired action.[1]

Aristotle knew that people's sense of their connections and relationships to others and the social groups with which they identify themselves is also intrinsic to their motivation.[2] The role of social identity has been studied by Gregory Walton, psychology professor at Stanford, who found that it serves as a powerful source of motivation—especially as it influences achievement.

He also suggests that people's interests, engagement, and motivation all derive from their social identity. For example, people are often motivated to go to work when they may not be feeling well, primarily because of their affiliation with their work community. Membership in a social group appears to greatly influence persistence in pursuing tasks and goals that are seen as important to the group.[3]

In one study, college students were shown a newspaper article highlighting a former math major at their school. The only variable manipulated in this study was that of the math major's birthdate published in the article; in the experimental group, the date matched the participants', in the control group, it did not. Those who were told that they shared a common birthday persisted 60 percent longer when presented with an unsolvable math puzzle. In addition, these students also reported greater interest in the math department and their sense of potential "fit" for themselves in that department.[4] Connection—even in this seemingly superficial and arbitrary way—created a positive increase in motivation.

Connection is built through our behaviors and conversations. Yet we often avoid interacting with those around us because of fear. Social psychologists coined the term "the spotlight effect" to refer to the tendency to overestimate how much other people notice about us. We think there is a spotlight on us at all times, magnifying our mistakes or flaws for the world to see. We fear what people will think of us, how we come off, or that we'll say something wrong. We're so wrapped up in our own self-consciousness that we miss out—not just on the conversation, but on the connection that comes with it. But the truth is people aren't focused on us like we are focused on ourselves.

Connection takes time. It takes preparation and courage. We need to embrace the vulnerability it requires to deepen our connections and strengthen our relationships.

Use Connection to Get What You Want

Building strong connections is a powerful tool to find and sustain success. When you have big goals and sharp focus, it can get easy to slip into a transactional mentality, overly focused on the task, less on the relationship. But the real power happens when we stay relational because that is what unlocks opportunities for everyone. A rising tide lifts all boats. The more you create a culture of support within your network, the more everyone will find greater success.

When reaching out to connections, focus on how you can offer value to them as well. It could be through sharing information, introducing them to other valuable contacts, or providing assistance with their projects. We can't reach our goals or maximize our potential on our own—no one does.

When it comes to getting what you want in life, there is a counterintuitive truth: you get more by giving without any expectations. The legendary Zig Ziglar said it well: "You can have everything in life you want, if you just help enough other people get what they want."

Connection creates an opportunity to learn what truly matters most to other people and then find a way to add value. When you walk into the room with the goal of connecting—whether it's to pitch an idea to a colleague or navigate a tough conversation with your boss—you have to put in effort and energy to prepare. Anticipate what the gaps might be for someone else. Research opportunities for each of you to add value to a shared goal, or in the individual paths forward. This was my approach as a sports agent building relationships in a competitive environment where there are more agents than athletes to represent.

THE PATH TO BUILD CONNECTION

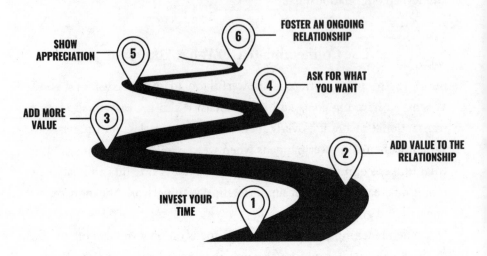

STEP 1: Invest Your Time
Find out what is important to them.

STEP 2: Add Value to the Relationship
Ask open-ended questions to determine what you have to offer.

STEP 3: Add More Value
Continue learning so you can continue to add more value to the relationship.

STEP 4: Ask for What You Want
Now that you have established that relationship and added value, ask for what you want.

STEP 5: Show Appreciation
Express gratitude for their generosity and share the impact it made.

STEP 6: Foster an Ongoing Relationship
Continue to show up consistently and provide value, touching base regularly to show you value the relationship.

Throughout my career, I've engaged this path to build connections with my clients and my team of agents and to strengthen the relationships within my speaking and training businesses.

Invest your time: Listen and get curious to understand what others value.

I signed a pitcher with the Detroit Tigers, Mike Maroth. As part of this process, I spent a lot of time getting to know him and his wife, Brooke. I wanted to know what mattered most to both of them, on and off the field. What would success look like for him in the short term and in the long term? His Christian faith is deeply important to him, as is his family. He believed that his platform as a professional athlete was an opportunity to serve other people. That focus on the value of his platform, the impact it could make on others, is what I love about him. This would inform the kinds of deals and opportunities that I would bring to him and how to approach negotiations for him. It wasn't just about money and landing a record-setting contract. It wasn't about being the highest-paid left-handed pitcher. It wasn't about the car or the bling. He was making more money than he had ever imagined doing something that he loved. I needed to spend time knowing him so I could represent him in a way that aligned with his values and goals.

Add value to the relationship: Work with values and connection in mind.

I signed Mike when he was inside of the arbitration window, meaning this was the time for him to come to terms with the team or we would go to arbitration. Arbitration wasn't in Mike's nature, which was, in part, the reason I was working to secure a multiyear deal, allowing him to avoid arbitration in future years. I remember calling Mike with the initial offer of $1,000,000 for a one-year deal. Mike was ready to sign. Heck, this was more than he ever thought he would make. But it would be a bad deal. I needed Mike to understand that and be patient. In light of the connection we had, and my knowledge of what drives him, I was able to point out to Mike that jumping on this offer would result in setting the market low for other left-handed pitchers. His "servant first" heart listened. He didn't want to jam up other guys; he wanted to help his fellow big-league guys. So, we pushed back, and weeks later we agreed to a two-year $5.25 million deal.

Ten percent of an agent's job is negotiating players' contracts; the other 90 percent is maximizing their unique window of time as a professional athlete. That's why a focus on securing appearances and endorsements mattered. A camp for kids. Alignment with nonprofits that were heartfelt to Mike and Brooke in his home and playing communities. None of this is anything for an agent to celebrate, it's expected.

Add more value: This is where the magic happens. It's doing things for clients that add value outside of the bottom line in the spirit of truly serving.

Maroth cares deeply about his community, and when he began to see the homeless people in Detroit on his way home from the ballpark, he couldn't stand by and do nothing. "After the games, the player's clubhouse is full of food for the guys and it's a big spread," Mike shared with me one day on his drive to the ballpark. He noticed how much of it was being thrown out and he couldn't live with that. He personally began packaging up a few plates of food at the end of the night and handing it to homeless people on his way home from the park. But there was still an enormous amount of food going to waste. So, I reached out to the Tigers' head of community relations as well as identified a nearby homeless shelter in the spirit of seeing if we could arrange for all the leftover food to get to the people in need. Within days, a shelter representative started to come to the ballpark, package up food, and take the leftovers back to the shelter.

Ask for what you want: Connection can also create a space for you to ask for what you want. And a space where people are happy to support you in that.

I did the work to build connections with all of my clients, seeking ways to add value that aligned with their priorities. As a result, my baseball clients, like Mike Maroth, would often recommend me to their teammates or make an introduction, which I took as the highest compliment.

I always appreciated their support connecting the dots to meet and sign new players. Other times, I would see an opportunity to work with someone, knowing that I could add value to an already stellar career, and I had to ask for help. I had the opportunity to represent Erin Andrews during her time covering college sports for ESPN. She was covering the Michigan State men's basketball game for ESPN, so she knew Tom Izzo better than me. I'd been in contact with Coach Izzo at that time recruiting him, in hopes of representing him one day. I needed existing clients to share their positive experience with me. I asked Erin to share with Coach Izzo how I have helped her in her career, in the spirit of helping me sign him. I asked Paul Hewitt, Georgia Tech's basketball coach at the time, to put in a good word when they played each other that season. I signed Coach Izzo shortly thereafter and I have been blessed to call him a dear friend, not just a client.

Show appreciation: Appreciation can look like unexpected and deep anticipation in the spirit of making someone's day or week better.

There are many ways to show appreciation, so be sure to tap into the best ways for the person. One of my baseball players was flying to San Diego in a few weeks for a series against the San Diego Padres. As a starting pitcher, he's on rotation to pitch every four games to keep his arm rested and ready for the next start. Knowing he loves to play golf on his off days and Torrey Pines is one of his favorite courses, I projected out the pitching rotation and I discovered that he was scheduled to land in San Diego at midnight, followed by an off day, and he wasn't scheduled to pitch during that series.

I called Torrey Pines, the beautiful golf course on cliffs overlooking the Pacific Ocean, where it's notoriously tough to get a tee time. I secured a spot for a foursome and called my client. He was so appreciative of the forethought and thought I put into anticipating something that mattered to him.

Foster an ongoing relationship: You can't fast-forward connection. There's no shortcut. Trust is built over time, so is connection. Laying the foundation of connection will lead to a steady, mutually beneficial relationship.

When one of my teenage daughters was interested in broadcasting, Jeff Francoeur and Chip Caray invited her to join them in the broadcast booth. Seeing her sitting between them overlooking the Braves game, with a headset on and all, was incredibly special. More than twenty years after signing them as clients, their support of my daughter was humbling.

And I do the same when I can. Recently, I received a call from George Lombard, aspiring baseball manager and former first-round pick, wanting some advice about speaking. I had attended George and Judy's wedding, watched their kids grow up, and now, almost thirty years later, we are still supporting each other.

People assume that Dynamic Drive might limit your connection to the world around you—that relationships are part of what you sacrifice to achieve your goals—but really, you bring Dynamic Drive to your relationships, making them stronger and more fulfilling for all.

Too often, people communicate without connecting, focusing on what they need to say—their script—without considering others. You have to build trust and connection, so when you're in a sales position—and we're all selling something on occasion—I encourage you to step back from your hard pitch and have an honest conversation. When you can get into the head and heart of other people, you can see their needs and how you can work together to fulfill them.

Have the courage to get off script because that's when we connect and that's when we can better understand how to serve. I want to emphasize the importance of authenticity, spontaneity, and genuine connection in our interactions with others. It means responding genuinely to the situation at hand rather than relying on preconceived answers.

When you walk into a room—whether it's a job interview, a client meeting, an office conversation, or a social event—people are asking themselves three key questions about you:

- Do I like you?
- Can you help me?
- Can I trust you?

If your goal is a path to connection, guess what, they need to say YES! to all three of those questions.

Relationships are nuanced. They require time, energy, and intention. A lot of times when we deal with tough people and difficult situations, our natural tendency is to shut down. We get defensive. We lose focus on what really matters most.

Be relational, not transactional.

Instead of shutting down, open up. Make the effort to walk into tough situations and get curious about how to make a connection. Curiosity creates connection.

Relationships That Amplify

When you lean into Dynamic Drive, you may find yourself attracting people who have a similar focus and pursuit of better. They understand the kind of commitment it takes to live with intention and they will encourage and support you along the way (as you will to them, too). They will challenge you when you get complacent, listen without judgment when you feel frustrated, and celebrate your wins. These kinds of relationships are important as you continue to have more and more success and increasingly prioritize your goals and purpose in life. These relationships amplify your Dynamic Drive, fueling you with optimism, furthering your curiosity, and deepening your sense of purpose.

You attract what you are putting out into the world. If you maintain an abundance mindset, believing that there are ample opportunities and resources available, you'll likely approach situations with a positive outlook. This optimism can attract opportunities and like-minded individuals who share your outlook.

Positive and ambitious friends and colleagues can inspire us to grow, learn, and push ourselves outside of our comfort zones. They may introduce us to new opportunities or experiences we might not have considered on our own. Close friends often provide emotional support and encouragement. They can help us through tough times and motivate us to pursue our goals and aspirations. The flip side of this is true as well: friends who care about our well-being may offer constructive criticism and encourage us to work on personal development areas, helping us become better versions of ourselves.

Building relationships that amplify success involves a combination of mutual support, effective communication, and shared goals.

How to build relationships that amplify:

- Relationships that push you to be your best begin with purpose. Identify individuals who share your values, whether it's in your personal or professional life. Having a common direction provides a strong basis for collaboration.
- Focus on how you can add value to the relationship. This could involve sharing knowledge, offering assistance, introducing connections, or providing resources. When you contribute positively, others are more likely to value your relationship.
- Instead of seeing others as competitors, view them as potential collaborators. Collaborative efforts often lead to innovative solutions and enhanced outcomes.

Remember that building relationships is a continuous process. It's about nurturing and maintaining connections over time. By fostering real and supportive connections, you increase your overall chances of achieving your goals.

In the agent business, collaboration with other established agents doesn't exist much, if at all. The Major League Baseball Players Association would coordinate conference calls with agents to discuss various topics. Their intent was information sharing in the best interest of our players. But that's not what happened. The calls were pathetic and a waste of everyone's time. It would be analogous to having two head coaches talk game strategy before a Super Bowl. It doesn't happen. And it didn't on these calls either, in part due to a scarcity mindset by the agents.

The speaking circuit, on the other hand, is full of collaboration and people who help amplify each other. For example, if I am booked for a particular date or if I don't think I'm the right fit for a client, I am happy to recommend another speaker in my place. It's an industry that could easily be seen as competitive, but is remarkably collaborative, which makes it that much more fulfilling! There's a common understanding that each of us has a message worth sharing with the world, and we each have a unique platform that we can leverage. I have mentored dozens of up-and-coming motivational speakers who are working to build their platform and build relationships with speaker bureaus, and I've networked with veterans in the space who reach out to compare speaking fees, travel budgets, and other best practices.

Some of this is a direct result of market share (or perceived market share), but being overly guarded can hurt our clients. What's at risk for noncompeting sports agents to collaborate on best practices? When I led our agency's initiative to expand from baseball to golf, I found the knowledge from baseball was helping me better serve our golf clients and vice versa. When I help a client source a speaker for an upcoming event, it strengthens our relationship, too.

Relationships are the most important decision we make in our lives. So, why aren't we remarkably intentional about whom we spend our time with and how we engage with them? And why don't we put more intention and effort around investing in and maintaining them? Complacency can creep into relationships too—when we stop putting in effort, take others for granted, and don't prioritize investing in those we care about.

Our happiness is a direct reflection of the small group of people we consistently surround ourselves with. They influence our beliefs, behaviors, and attitude. Your inner circle influences your perspective. The people you spend the most time with shape who you are.

Studies show that people's happiness depends on the happiness of others in their lives. This provides further justification for seeing happiness, like health, as a collective phenomenon. Clusters of happy and unhappy people are visible in the network, and the relationship between people's happiness extends up to three degrees of separation (for example, to the friends of one's friends' friends). People who are surrounded by many happy people and those who are central in the network are more likely to become happy in the future.[5] This couldn't be truer in motherhood (or parenting in general); it's often said "you are only as happy as your most unhappy child," and as the mother of three girls, I can promise you this certainly rings true for me.

People are influenced by the behavior of those around them. If your friends engage in certain habits or behaviors, you may be more likely to adopt or be influenced by those behaviors as well.[6] So choose wisely!

I've found that when I spend time with friends who are excited about growing their businesses or pushing themselves professionally, I'm eager to tap into that energy in my own work. On the other hand, when I spend time with friends who are feeling stuck, who lack the spark of passion and excitement that I have for my work, and who complain about their lack of momentum, I leave feeling drained and with some lingering feelings of malaise.

Surrounding yourself with motivated and ambitious friends can inspire you to set and pursue higher goals. Seeing their accomplishments can motivate you to strive for your own success.

Why You Should Build Trust

Trust is a key ingredient to relationships that amplify your Dynamic Drive. In any relationship—whether it's between friends, family members, romantic partners, or colleagues—trust creates a sense of emotional safety and security. When you trust someone, you feel more comfortable being vulnerable, expressing your thoughts and feelings openly without fearing judgment or betrayal.

Building a solid foundation of trust encourages collaboration and teamwork. In professional relationships, for example, when team members trust each other, they are more likely to share ideas, support one another, and work together cohesively to achieve common goals. Research shows that employees in high-trust organizations are more productive, have more energy at work, collaborate better with their colleagues, and stay with their employers longer than people working at low-trust companies. They also suffer less chronic stress and are happier with their lives, and these factors fuel stronger performance.[7]

One important way to build trust is through consistent anticipation. Trustworthy individuals are more likely to be dependable and consistent. They follow through on their commitments, and their actions align with their words. This predictability creates a stable environment, which is crucial for the growth and stability of any relationship.

Anticipating others' needs (sometimes before they have even recognized them themselves) is a powerful way to build trust and show that you're attentive to their well-being. It demonstrates consideration, builds rapport, and helps unlock a closer relationship.

For me, building trust was a top priority when working with my clients. I'd spend a lot of energy anticipating their needs so I could best serve them. I had a baseball player get traded, and he was slated to pitch for the new team the very next day. After learning of the trade, he was on a plane to his new team within hours. I knew that his wife and kids would want to be there to support him for his start, but would be overwhelmed with the logistics and unclear on how to pull it off so quickly. I arranged for a private plane to take her and the kids out and back to watch his debut with the new team.

Anticipation in a relationship involves being observant, empathetic, and proactive. Here are some practical ways to show anticipation in a relationship:

- **Use active listening:** Pay close attention when someone speaks and try to understand their thoughts and feelings. Listen for cues about their needs and desires in both verbal and nonverbal communication.
- **Ask thoughtful questions:** Ask questions that go beyond small talk. Inquire about their goals, their struggles, and their fears to gain a deeper understanding of what matters to them.
- **Remember important dates and events:** Take note of special occasions and important milestones in their life. Sometimes being there for someone and building trust is as simple as an acknowledgment of a key moment in their lives.
- **Offer help without being asked:** Take initiative to offer assistance with tasks or responsibilities that may be causing them stress or overwhelm. This proactive approach shows that you are attuned to their needs.
- **Support their passions and goals:** Encourage their interests and support their personal and professional goals.

Anticipating someone's needs might not always be perfect, but *your effort* is what demonstrates the consistency to create a deeper bond.

Boundaries and Tough Conversations

Boundaries provide a framework for maintaining focus, establishing priorities, and ensuring that your energy is allocated effectively. Establishing boundaries empowers you to say no to commitments or requests that don't align with your goals or values.

Boundaries communicate your expectations to others. When people know your limits and what you are willing and unwilling to do, they can respect your decisions and work with you more effectively.

Boundaries also communicate a level of self-respect and self-regulation. You're telling others how you're allowing yourself to be treated in a relationship, which communicates how you feel about yourself. Acknowledging and prioritizing your needs and limitations show that you respect your own well-being and are willing to take care of yourself.

For many of us, saying no in an important relationship—or any relationship—is hard. Learning to say no and remain open (and supportive) to the person or people you value in your life is key. There's an art to saying no and staying open. It's a mindset that will truly empower the way you communicate. It's a core habit for the most effective leaders. And it is essential for balancing important connections with your commitment to Dynamic Drive.

A clearly defined purpose will help you to say no and mean it. When you are clear on what you want and how it aligns with your personal mission, saying no ultimately means saying yes to other possibilities. Performing against a purpose encourages you to decide the best use of your time, talent, and resources. It forms a boundary that shows you clearly that you can't do it all and shouldn't. When you are clear on purpose, you can say no without guilt and mean it.

Boundaries are part of healthy relationships. When we are afraid to ever say no in a relationship with someone we care about, that's a red flag. Dr. Henry Cloud, author of *Boundaries: When to Say Yes, How to Say No to Take Control of Your Life*, defines a boundary as a personal property line that marks those things for which we are responsible. Relationships falter, he told me in a recent conversation, when we reach over the fence and begin taking responsibility for other people's behaviors, moods, etc. Boundaries aren't destructive to relationships; they are essential to maintaining healthy relationships.

Boundaries don't have to mean a door slammed. Tap into your creativity to suggest alternatives. It's being able to say, "No, I can't do this, but here's another person you might ask who is even better at that than I am" or "No, but here's a resource that will help you get that done." When you add a comma after a no, instead of a period, it keeps the conversation open. When the solution you provide is even better, your "no" may even end up serving them better in the end.

Saying yes to everything is a myth of being perfect that many of us—consciously or not—buy into. We say yes on autopilot out of a misguided sense of responsibility (we have to do it all) or fear (if we don't do it, who will?). When we say no, we show others how to reject the myth of doing it all.

By reserving yes for the requests that are most aligned with your purpose, you can counteroffer with respect and openness to the needs of others. The more that you practice the art of saying no and staying open, the more you will move away from toxic perfectionism and model saying yes to what's most important.

So remember:

- Say no to the meeting so you can say yes to deep work.
- Say no to attending a client dinner to say yes to attending your kid's game that night.
- Say no to a promotion requiring a move for the family to say yes to your spouse's career.
- Say no to the overdramatized fire drills at work so you can say yes to showing up ready for your meeting.
- Say no to picking up your phone in a meeting so you can say yes to being fully present.

Saying no is a choice; it's your choice. Step into your power in these moments. In the end, those on the other end of no will likely respect you for it, learn from you, and deploy it in their own life for good.

I learned this firsthand with one of my clients, none other than coach Tom Izzo. Tom and I are good friends today, but at that moment you would not have known it. In fact, our relationship was on the line.

What unfolded that week of the NCAA Final Four, the pinnacle of Tom's sport, was a chess match. It was April 2007, and my family was already in town for Easter. In the middle of the Final Four, Kentucky expressed interest in Tom. If you know anything about college basketball, you know that this is one of the most high-profile positions in all of coaching, one that almost every college coach would entertain. But like most negotiations, this one was a delicate dance between Tom's passion for Michigan State, where he'd been coaching for more than a decade at that point, and what the folks in the Bluegrass State were looking for in their next head coach.

Kentucky, though, had many choices, and we began to hear of other conversations they were having. News travels like lightning in the small world of college basketball's elite coaches. While Tom wasn't rushing to say yes to an offer, he would have appreciated if an overture was made from Kentucky.

I was in bed asleep at 2 a.m. when Izzo called. I had barely answered when he launched into me just moments after the media announced Kentucky's new head coach. Tom was furious that we hadn't heard from Kentucky directly. I had seen him countless times on the sidelines of the court, down to the last seconds of close games, and knew he had a temper, but it had never been unleashed on me. After all, I was the person he counted on to help him and the reason he hired our firm five years earlier. He knew that we delivered.

After an hour of unloading his frustration on me, he abruptly hung up. All I had was a dazed "oh my" feeling. What just happened? Trust is everything in my business, and it wasn't just Izzo I might be losing. But my oldest daughter, then age five, needed me. When she woke up, I hustled to her room to rub her back so that she could go back to sleep. In five minutes, she was sound asleep. But when she woke up again at 6 a.m., I was still staring at the ceiling.

The trust I had carefully nurtured with Izzo was the foundation of our relationship. Was it all crashing down now?

I knew I needed Izzo, but I didn't need anyone to speak to me like that. There were serious consequences for tolerating it. Backing down to him could make me a doormat, which wouldn't serve me well or our relationship going forward. From my standpoint, we had worked hard for Izzo, too. I paced for two days trying to figure out my next move.

I knew what I had to do. I knew that I had to reestablish common ground with Izzo. In our world, the verbal tirade he had just unleashed was a challenge. Was I going to take it? And if I did, would I be able to stand up for him the next time we entered negotiations? The stakes were high for me as Izzo was an important client and one I cared deeply about.

My house was full of people visiting for Easter, so I found the quietest spot I could think of: my daughter's closet. Crouched among her tiny soccer cleats and Lego collection, I dialed his number.

As soon as Izzo picked up, I started in, only to be interrupted. "Why haven't you called me?" he said. "I have the media calling me asking me what happened!"

"I don't help people who light me up like you did the other night," I replied, practically snarling. "I don't get calls like that. I get thank-you notes and flowers. Up and down my client list, there isn't anyone I care more about than you."

I kept going. "No one has ever talked to me like that. I'm not an eighteen-year-old in the huddle, Tom. We were clear on what you wanted. But we both know in no way were you ready to take a pay cut to go to Kentucky. We had more to discuss with them, and other guys didn't. Kentucky has an ego, and they couldn't have it hit the media again that another coach wasn't diving in. We might have tap-danced around the job for days. Kentucky wasn't about to let that happen."

There came another pause. *Embrace it; don't kill it*, I told myself.

Even in the silence, I felt he knew how much I cared.

"You're right," he finally said in a quiet voice. "I wasn't going to position myself like he [Gillispie] did. I didn't want to be in the middle of this. I'm a Spartan."

This was about as much of an apology as I was going to get, and that was okay. The call wasn't long, but it was powerful. We recovered our working relationship. Izzo's breaking point for our relationship became the turning point. We'll always be friends with a great respect for and trust in each other in part because of that experience.

Having tough conversations demonstrates honesty and transparency in your relationships. It shows that you are willing to be open and authentic, which fosters trust and strengthens emotional bonds. Relationships can become complacent without tough conversations. Issues within a relationship don't get better on their own. And it's also worth thinking about how setting our boundaries positively impacts other people, too. If I'd have let Tom yell at me without saying something, do you think he'd be confident that I was standing up for him whenever I was negotiating on his behalf?

Let's be honest, we all have those conversations in our lives we've been avoiding. We leave that meeting and think, *Wow, they didn't bring it up . . . I'm off the hook!* But while it might feel good in the moment, it's still there. That problem didn't go away.

Real conversations are the building blocks of deep, rewarding connection. Every conversation is an opportunity to connect. Think about your closest relationships. I bet you can think of a tough conversation that you've had to have. We assume tough conversations are what will cause relationships to unravel, but it's actually what most important relationships are built upon.

Don't be afraid to ask yourself the tough questions when it comes to decisions and relationships.

Best Practices for Having Tough Conversations

1. **Listen.** Above all else, tough conversation are about listening. Focus on the other person and process what they say. Don't get caught up in preparing your own response. Don't interrupt. Affirm what they've told you.
2. **Gather the facts.** Facts and information are crucial to a fair and productive conversation.
3. **Shift your mindset.** Drop your judgments and start the conversation with an open mind. Your default going into a tough conversation is likely to think "worst-case scenario." Instead, ask yourself: "What could go right? What is the best-case scenario?"

4. **Make it a live conversation.** You can't solve difficult situations with a text or an email.

5. **Timing is everything.** Be cognizant of what's happening in the other person's world and with your own mindset.

6. **Be aware of your nonverbal communication.** Your physical cues communicate a lot. Sitting down, not standing, uncrossing arms. Creating a safe environment is key.

7. **Use curiosity to overcome disconnects.** Ask questions to drive clarity around what matters most to the other person. Ask, "What role did I play in the situation?"

8. **Embrace the pause.** Be thoughtful around what you say and be willing to slow down and think.

9. **Know when to walk away.** Have the courage to step away to gain intentionality around how you're showing up. Tough conversations don't have to happen all at once.

10. **Reflect and learn.** Engaging in tough conversations is a skill, and it takes time to develop.

You will solidify your relationships through the willingness to engage in difficult conversations. So often we brush the tough stuff under the rug, but for our relationships to be authentic, for longer-term connection, the tough stuff needs to be discussed. The best way to make a problem big is to set it aside and watch it grow. Most of us don't like tough conversations, but we need to embrace them.

Meaningful Impact

As an agent, it's easy to get transactional if you aren't truly connected to your clients. That's why it's crucial to understand their values and their goals. The why behind what I do.

One of my favorite broadcasters, Ernie Johnson, Jr., mans an anchor booth on *Inside the NBA*, along with three former NBA superstars:

Kenny Smith, Charles Barkley, and Shaquille O'Neal. During the league's super-long season, he is the bland but likeable filling in a celebrity sandwich with his lively analysts and a rotating roster of fill-ins.

Barkley and Shaq are both extraordinary personalities, creative and hilarious, and worth tuning in for even when the games are lackluster. EJ, in contrast, is dialed way back. But Barkley and Shaq are only able to have that kind of free reign because EJ and Smith excel at playing supporting roles. Ernie has won two Emmys, competes in a pool of stellar broadcasters, and he's still making a great salary.

I know what a good salary does for EJ. His late son Michael was disabled and used a wheelchair. A good salary for EJ meant Michael used a great wheelchair. EJ is terrific at what he does, and what's at stake for him is taking care of his family. Each week EJ goes to the grocery store and always stops to buy a bouquet for his wife, Cheryl. He always buys an extra bouquet, and as he leaves the store, he looks for a stranger to give those flowers to. Who knows how many regular folks have been blessed by EJ's flowers? There's no telling, but these bouquets bring him so much joy.

As his agent, I look for these details. These are part of his inner baseline. Take away his ability to get the wheelchair or buy the flowers—which, granted, may not be a lot in terms of dollars—and his life has a lot less joy.

Because EJ's values align so closely with my own, I love being a part of his negotiations. Ensuring a fair salary and compensation for him is fun for me. Sure, I can help a client whom I know is going to spend his paycheck on vacations and fancy cars, but I have more compassion for EJ and the clients whose drive is to do good in the world. When he won the John Wooden Keys to Life Award given to individuals who live out faith, integrity, and character, I was beyond thrilled. His professional platform is all about him being a great role model in life. I know that EJ's work, and his heart, is all about the impact.

My most memorable deals to negotiate were the ones that changed lives, not ones that lined my pockets. For instance, we repped an MLB player who needed ten more days in the big leagues to qualify for his pension. He was done physically; his career was over. But we were able to get him on a major league team roster for eleven days and he received the pension for the rest of his life. He's an incredible guy, and this was important for him and his family. It wasn't about making money for me; it was about making a lasting impact

Without connection, you'll minimize the opportunity to multiply your impact, which comes down to other people. Connection is about transcending our own success to empower or otherwise benefit others. Without it you might find achievement, but you'll never find real meaning or fulfillment.

Dynamic Drive isn't about status or accolades. It's about your contribution to others. That's what creates legacy. One of the easiest fears to succumb to is the fear of losing status. It can be your income, job position, social rank, or anything you perceive as an important measuring stick to others. Threats to status are often immediate and urgent. It's hard to step back and see the big picture. And it's so important to create space to consider your legacy—what you want people to ultimately remember you for. Your legacy is built on all the small moments that you string together.

When you trade status for legacy, you anchor your values in the big picture of your life. You can make decisions that may be hard in the short term, in a way that makes you proud of what you stand for, even if those decisions risk failure. In fact, you should expect that taking a stance for legacy will have high stakes.

By trading status for legacy, you cement your values. You can make difficult decisions in the moments that create big outcomes, even for generations to come.

When you move through life's moments with humility instead of entitlement, you don't fear your truth. You claim it by fearing less. You begin to think that your own approval is more important than that of others. Sharing the credit can be scary. What if outsiders miss your importance?

That is the fear that keeps people focused on themselves. When you stop hanging on so tight to what other people think, you can stand up for what is important to you.

Retired Hall of Fame baseball manager Bobby Cox still holds the record for the most ejections ever as a manager. Bobby was ejected a record 162 games. On the surface, most would think this is not a record to set, let alone still hold well after retirement. In fact, the next closest manager has over thirty fewer ejections. So, he is well positioned as the leader in this category. A hothead, Hall of Fame manager, leading in ejections, is there more to this story? You bet. Bobby was a selfless leader, just ask any of the veterans who stayed for less money to play for him. When a player was disputing a call with the ump, Bobby wobbled out there, put himself between the player and the ump—he protected his guys—and took the ejection. I picked Bobby up at his house one day to take him to an appearance. The night before he had been ejected from the game. The Braves won. Bobby told me in the car on the way to the event, "It was 1–1 game, bottom of the sixth inning, my number-three hitter slides into second base, thinks he is safe, but the ump calls him out. He pops up and starts arguing the call with the ump. I am watching this escalate from the dugout, thinking, I need him, I need him in the seventh, eighth, and ninth in the field and at the plate." Bobby put his players before himself, always, well more than 162 times in fact. Just ask any of them.

It's not about you; it's about the people you lead and serve.

Key Takeaways

- A rising tide lifts all boats. The more you create a culture of support within your network, the more everyone will find greater success.

- When we deal with tough people and difficult situations, our natural tendency is to shut down. Make the effort to walk into tough situations and get curious about how to make a connection.

- Boundaries communicate your expectations to others. When people know your limits and what you are willing and unwilling to do, they can respect your decisions and work with you more effectively.

- You attract what you put out into the world. If you maintain an abundance mindset, believing that there are ample opportunities and resources available, you'll likely approach situations with a positive outlook. This optimism can attract opportunities and like-minded individuals who share your outlook.

Chapter 10

Seventh Key: Confidence

con•fi•dence \'kän-fə-dən(t)s\: your secret weapon that makes you unstoppable

The road of Dynamic Drive is ongoing, it's for the long term, and you need confidence to keep going as the conditions change, you face the unexpected, and things flat out get hard. Confidence is the final level to accomplish. You're close enough to taste the end zone, but you still need to lock into your skills and execute. You can't achieve authentic confidence until you've worked on the previous keys. Confidence ebbs and flows. Sometimes you need more of it. You'll need tools to get it back when you lose it, because you will. You're not always operating on a full tank of confidence. If you are, you're probably not challenging yourself!

Confidence is the belief in oneself and in one's abilities. People with healthy self-confidence have an assertiveness we admire. They have a strong sense of both their strengths and areas for improvement. But instead of letting these perceived weaknesses foment insecurity, they reach out for support.

Confident people inspire trust in those around them and can receive constructive feedback without getting defensive. Confident people welcome feedback.

Confidence comes from understanding that self-worth isn't measured by achievements, failures, or the opinions of others.

I learned about the importance of confidence when I was a young mother. I had taken my three girls, who were two and three at the time, to the beach in northern Michigan. The girls were walking in front of my mom and me in the soft sand. I turned to my mom and asked her, "Mom, what is the most important character trait for me to instill in these girls as they grow up?"

"Confidence," she replied without missing a beat. "Molly, if they're confident, they'll make the right decisions when it's hard. They will go after what they want in life. They will be less afraid of failure because their confidence will lift them back up. They will stay true to their values. Their confidence will make saying no to things easier for them. Confidence, Molly."

She was right. She saw how confidence was a throughline for everything I wanted for them as they grew up. I wanted them to know themselves and stand up for their sense of self in tough situations. I wanted them to put themselves out there, take risks, and face new challenges head on. To have the courage to make the right decisions in tough moments, and the courage to ask for what they want and what they need.

Self-confidence is considered one of the most influential motivators and regulators of behavior in people's everyday lives.[1] Stanford psychologist Albert Bandura found that our levels of self-confidence significantly shape our everyday lives. Your confidence reflects how you judge your capabilities and how much you believe in yourself.[2]

Because confident people aren't staking their sense of self on outcomes, they're more likely to collaborate, celebrate the achievements of others, ask for help, take calculated risks, and pursue opportunities for growth. Research shows that a strong sense of self-esteem is linked to greater happiness and mental strength.[3]

Without confidence, receiving a simple "no" can send you spiraling. Confident people know that "no" is just feedback. No is just data. It's an opportunity to dig deeper inside of yourself. To embrace the feedback, learn from it, and keep going. A no from a boss, a client, a colleague—it's just feedback. The best of the best have heard no and the reason you know their name is because they didn't view the simple two-letter word as a brick wall but rather a speed bump. Or, for some, it's motivation.

Psychologist Carol Dweck says that true self-confidence is "the courage to be open—to welcome change and new ideas regardless of their source."[4] Real self-confidence is not reflected in a title, an expensive suit, a fancy car, or a series of acquisitions. It is reflected in your mindset: your readiness to grow.

However, overconfidence is something to be cautious of. When confidence overwhelms your desire to learn and improve, you lose your curiosity and stop challenging yourself, leading you toward the path to complacency. Overconfident individuals may believe that they don't need to prepare adequately for a task or challenge because, in part, they may underestimate the task or their opponents. And most importantly, without acknowledging areas for improvement, they may become stagnant in their development.

Confidence Comes Through Action

There were so many things that made Michael Jordan great. Mike Greenberg has been well positioned to observe peak performance as one of the most recognized pundits on ESPN for more than a quarter century. Mike was twenty-four years old when he was assigned to cover the Chicago Bulls and Jordan in 1991, during their first championship "three-peat." He had a front-row seat to one of the greatest athletes of all time.

Greenberg told me that he was fascinated by Jordan's process and the thing that, more than anything else, made him stand out: his never-ending self-belief. It seemed innate and deep-seated. Jordan never seemed to question himself, and in the toughest, most high-stakes scenarios, he never questioned the fact that the answer to anything was always him. He'd say, "Give me the ball" or "Get the hell out of the way," knowing that everything will be well.

Greenberg has tried to distill this message and pass it on to his kids. He tells them that the best path toward success and achieving any goal is if you can get to a place where you genuinely believe in yourself. Greenberg saw confidence as coming largely through action, but Jordan taught him that there needs to be some element of that confidence prior to having proof of its reality. Doing it over and over again and genuinely believing you're doing it well is the best way to develop that confidence. But you have to walk in the door with some actual belief. Jordan exemplified this.

Taking action can build confidence, even through setting and achieving small goals. Each accomplishment reinforces the belief in your abilities and creates a positive cycle of building confidence. Confidence comes from the little moments of discomfort. If you want more confidence in your life or in maybe just different areas of your life, keep getting uncomfortable.

Confidence is not a fixed attribute; it's the outcome of the thoughts we think and the actions we take. No more; no less. It is not based on your *actual* ability to succeed at a task but your *belief* in your ability to succeed.

The good news is that new research into neural plasticity reveals that we can literally rewire our brains in ways that affect our thoughts and behavior at any age. Which means that no matter how timid or doubt-laden you've been up to now, building self-confidence is absolutely possible.[5]

As you first start to engage drive, confidence can feel elusive. We all experience self-doubt, but that doesn't mean we have to let it stop us. It's easy to think of confidence as a fixed trait—either something you have or don't have. In fact, confidence is a muscle that can be built to power your drive.

I suggest starting small. I didn't start negotiating for the first time as an agent with a $30 million deal. I started with an expired coupon at Target and built my confidence from there. Start with low-risk moments and build up to your goals.

Thoughts without action are pretty useless. You can be planning to learn Spanish or run a marathon or start a business, but if you don't do it, it's meaningless. Confidence helps you take action, and the more action you take, the more confident you become.

Taking action, even in the face of uncertainty or fear, can lead to increased confidence. By stepping outside of your comfort zone, trying new experiences, and achieving small successes, you can gradually build self-assurance and belief in your abilities.

Confidence comes through action. But in order to take those actions, you do need some level of self-belief or confidence. The confidence loop is the cycle of developing a little confidence, taking action, and building more confidence through the success as you develop your Dynamic Drive.

Lisa Bilyeu is the cofounder of Quest Nutrition, the president of Impact Theory, and the host of the *Women of Impact* podcast. For eight years, she worked behind the scenes alongside her husband, Tom Bilyeu, building their companies and launching Impact Theory, which Tom hosted. It wasn't her dream. She says she was happy to support her husband but knew there was more for her to do.

When Lisa began to step in front of the camera representing her companies and launched her own podcast, she began to get messages from her community asking about her confidence. Lisa was floored. She felt terrified of the spotlight, and questioned her abilities to take on such a public role. But she did it anyway. She didn't let the fears and insecurities stop her.

This is what Lisa now calls "Radical Confidence," which she defines as being scared or uncertain and doing it anyway. So many people focus on feeling confident as a precursor to taking that first step, but Lisa is living proof that sometimes, you have to take action first, and the confidence will follow. If you wait to feel secure and confident, you may miss out on important opportunities.

Confidence is not just a state of mind; it's built through experience and action. Taking action, even when faced with uncertainty or challenges, can lead to a sense of accomplishment and growth, which in turn boosts confidence. Sometimes you have to take a risk and jump into your next move.

It's easy to get stuck in what Lisa calls the "purgatory of the mundane," which means that life is just fine—not engaging or fulfilling, but not awful. Another word for it? Complacency. You hear stories of people with these amazing accomplishments that all come from the fact that they've hit rock bottom and it jolts them into action. But more often, it's years and years of a diminished life that doesn't quite feel right, habits that you don't even necessarily realize you have, and a series of seemingly small choices that are not moving you toward the thing you really want in life.

> **Confidence doesn't come from your comfort zone.**
>
>

When Tom asked Lisa to help out with Quest, Lisa started by shipping nutrition bars from her living room floor. Two years later, she was running a ten-thousand-square-foot warehouse with forty employees working for her.[6]

Lisa's experience underscores the confidence loop. Take action, and over time you'll become more competent. And as you become more competent, you'll build confidence. But you have to get started.

The Confidence Zones

"Everything you want is just outside your comfort zone."

—ROBERT G. ALLEN, *THE ONE MINUTE MILLIONAIRE: THE ENLIGHTENED WAY TO WEALTH*

The idea of the comfort zone originated in a classic psychological experiment in 1908, in which psychologists explained that a state of relative comfort created a steady level of performance. In order to maximize

COMFORT ZONE	STRETCH ZONE	PANIC OR STRESS ZONE
Where we spend too much time. Not ideal for growth.	Where we need to spend more time. The ideal place for growth.	Where we need to spend minimal time. Potential confidence killer.

performance though, we need a state of relative anxiety—a space where our stress levels are slightly higher than normal.[7] There are three zones, which researchers refer to as the Comfort Zone, the Stretch Zone, and the Panic Zone. The Comfort Zone is where we all tend to spend way too much time on autopilot. The Panic Zone is where we feel overwhelmed and spread too thin. The Stretch Zone is that ideal place where we get stretched but don't break. It is within the Stretch Zone that our confidence grows as we experience success in new areas of life. The research supports the fact that when we optimize our challenges, we grow exponentially and enjoy the journey! In short, confidence doesn't come from your comfort zone. You have to be willing to embrace the uncomfortable as part of the Dynamic Drive lifestyle in order to build your confidence.

The Comfort Zone is where you feel most at ease. It's familiar, safe, and—well, comfortable. This is typically where your day-to-day routine happens as if on autopilot. It's easy. There are no surprises. You feel confident and competent. But there's very little reflection or learning in the comfort zone, so you remain unchallenged. As a result, you can become unmotivated, complacent, and disengaged. Confidence doesn't come from your comfort zone.

The Stretch Zone is in between the other two zones—outside of the secure environment of your comfort zone, but far enough away from your panic zone. Things feel a little awkward and unfamiliar, but not enough to prohibit learning. It's here where you can expand your knowledge, explore your boundaries, and achieve growth. The stretch zone is where we build our confidence!

The Panic Zone is at the completely opposite end of the spectrum. Spending time quickly becomes overwhelming. It's like jumping off the deep end when you don't really know how to swim. It's terrifying! You experience stress, fear, and challenge in a way that makes learning impossible. All your energy is spent trying to control your fear and anxiety. When you stay in this zone too long, you never feel like you have a grip on things, and it can be a confidence killer.

Show Up As You Are

Authenticity is the key to genuine confidence. Show up as who you are and own your skills and accomplishments fully. When you try to "fake it until you make it," what you're really doing is telling yourself that you're not good enough right now and you have to act as if you're better. If you get there by faking it, it creates misalignment because you've created this persona. That display of confidence isn't real and it's not sustainable.

Embracing your individuality promotes self-acceptance. When you're comfortable with who you are, you're more likely to have a positive self-image and be less affected by external judgments or the need for validation from others. This inner strength enables you to navigate through challenges more effectively.

If I hadn't been comfortable being myself as a sports agent, there is no way I would have had as much success or impact. I leaned into my identity and what I uniquely brought to the table as a female sports agent, and it was a positive differentiator that set me apart.

In fact, when CNN called me "the female Jerry Maguire," my natural inclination was to shy away from it. But it resonated with people. So finally I decided to lean into it. I had to own the confidence to not take it too seriously or overthink it when it came up. The best part is that at a recent keynote the woman introducing me said, "Molly is going to come up here not as the female Jerry Maguire, but as Molly Fletcher. Now, ladies and gentlemen, Jerry Maguire will be known as 'the male Molly Fletcher.'"

The idea of "fake it until you make it" is about pretending to be something you're not. Pretending to be confident when you are not can lead to overestimating your abilities. Misrepresenting yourself as more skilled or knowledgeable than you are can be misleading to others. It can create false expectations and may erode trust once your true abilities are revealed.

Katty Kay is the author of *The Confidence Code* and *The Confidence Code for Girls* and has spent years researching and studying the science of confidence. Kay says that confidence is something that comes from inside you that is real and tangible and you don't have to fake it. Kay explains that you should learn to acknowledge "I've worked hard and I'm good at what I do, and I'm talented, and that's why I've been successful. Therefore, I can take on this new challenge. There's nothing to stop me from trying."

When you're authentic about your skills and experience—and not hiding behind a facade of false success—you can learn new skills and develop at your own pace, building genuine confidence when it's earned.

Emmy Award–nominated sports journalist Taylor Rooks is the host and executive producer of *Taylor Rooks X*, her interview show for Bleacher Report, and a feature reporter for Amazon's *Thursday Night Football*. She's got great confidence and authenticity on and off camera, and yet she faces negative comments and criticisms.

Rooks knows how to handle herself at this point. She sat down with me for my podcast and it's clear that she knows who she is and what she's accomplished. This helps her be able to disregard the doubters, critics, and online trolls that come with the territory.

"There are always people who want to criticize and cut you down," Rooks says. "It's important to tell people: it doesn't get better, but you get better."

Rooks credits her parents with instilling such a strong sense of confidence. Every day they told her she could do and be whatever she wanted. Even so, she says that confidence is something that only you own. Rooks says, "I just always want to feel confident and emboldened. I want to step into places with people knowing how I feel about myself. Because I think that that bleeds into how people treat you."

How to Rebuild Your Confidence

Confidence is believing in yourself and your own abilities without needing validation from others. It's having faith in your judgment and being secure in who you are. At the same time, that doesn't mean that you completely disregard the opinions of others. You can learn from their feedback, even if you don't agree with it.

We all have an innate need to be validated by others, so it can sometimes feel triggering when people point out the areas we need to work on. But being able to take feedback like a pro is a key marker of a confident person. Remember: if you want to build true confidence, learn how to identify where you need improvement—then do the work necessary to become more competent at those things.

Rebuilding confidence will be a gradual process. Establish achievable short-term goals that gradually challenge you to step out of your comfort zone: these serve as baby steps toward boosting your confidence. As you achieve these goals, you'll experience a sense of accomplishment. Remind yourself of your accomplishments and strengths when in doubt, even if that means referring back to your "smile file" on occasion.

Confidence killers can significantly undermine your self-assurance and belief in your abilities. Once you start to recognize these confidence killers, you can begin work on overcoming them to foster confidence.

Here are some common confidence killers:

- **Negative influences:** Surrounding oneself with negative or unsupportive individuals can contribute to a decline in confidence.
- **Comparison to others:** Constantly comparing oneself to others, especially on social media where you have no context, can lead to feelings of inadequacy or inferiority.
- **Negative self-talk:** Constantly engaging in self-criticism, doubting one's abilities, and focusing on perceived shortcomings can erode self-confidence over time.
- **Fear of failure:** A deep-seated fear of failure can prevent individuals from taking risks and pursuing their goals, leading to a lack of confidence in their abilities.
- **Past failures or rejections:** Lingering feelings of disappointment or rejection from past failures or setbacks can impact

one's confidence in tackling future challenges. Embrace your next play mentality and move on!

- **Lack of support:** A weak support network or feeling disconnected from others can lead to a lack of validation and support, affecting confidence.
- **Perfectionism:** Setting unrealistically high standards and striving for perfection can create constant feelings of inadequacy and undermine confidence.

If you recognize these confidence killers, you're not alone. We all have doubts. We all have moments when our confidence wanes. But those who experience the greatest success are the ones who step into the fear and self-doubt, push past it, and overcome it. We all encounter the unexpected, the wrinkles and bumps in the road that ding us a little or a lot. Everyone experiences self-doubt. And we all need tools to help us recover inside of those tough moments!

I remember lots of moments when I lacked confidence. And stayed there for far too long.

One March day, I was sitting in the lobby of a hotel in Florida during spring training, in a meeting with a baseball general manager about a client's contract. I respected the general manager; he was a veteran in the business. He'd been in baseball management since before I was born. My stomach was in knots. I couldn't nibble on the appetizers we were pretending to share. My confidence seemed to have vanished when I needed it most. The fear, the negative self-talk; I was feeling totally alone in the moment. He was confident, direct, and a man of few and pointed words. He didn't mind the silence or pressure of the situation at hand. I, on the other hand, had a loop of negativity in my mind. I remember thinking, *What if I fumble this deal for my client? I am not ready for this.*

When he got up to go take a call and stepped away from the table, I signaled to him "one minute," holding up my index finger. I stepped outside. I needed a TMR. I needed my confidence to navigate this important conversation. This was a negotiation that could land my client a multiyear, multimillion-dollar deal, which would set him and his family up forever. A deal that my client had worked for since his days in the backyard playing catch with himself. Here is the kicker with athletes: the clock is ticking; their body is only capable of this for so long, which means that every year, every deal matters. It was my responsibility to capitalize on it for him. I needed to belly back up to the table with confidence, and fast. I needed to acknowledge to myself my intense preparation for that moment and remind myself of the many successful deals I had struck.

Less than five minutes later, I walked back up to that high-top table, and he was off the phone. I didn't sit down. I wanted him to know I might not stay.

"We haven't made much progress," I said. "Do you want to get a deal done?" I paused, giving him time to answer. I grabbed a piece of pita bread and dipped it in the hummus, resisting the urge to fill the silence.

"I do," he said, after what felt like an eternity.

I sat down. This time the conversation was different and the result for my client was a deal that set him and his family up for the rest of their lives.

People often ask me where my confidence comes from. And while I consider myself a confident person, I don't always feel that way. My confidence has wavered in countless moments, literally, from the hallways of high school, the tennis court, to a tough conversation with an employee, to an annual review, to starting a company; it rears its head. Guess what? It does for everyone.

Confidence is fluid, but what isn't is the consistent opportunity we have as humans to reload our mind and body with an essential ingredient to a life of Dynamic Drive.

Confidence is not the goal. People say "I want to be confident," but that's not the end goal. You have to ask yourself what you want to be confident in. Lisa Bilyeu suggests identifying your purpose and connecting it to your confidence. Just like my mom advised me on the beach all those years ago: confidence will open the doors and give you the strength to walk into rooms knowing your worth and your goals and how to stand up for yourself when needed.

Key Takeaways

• Confidence comes from understanding that self-worth isn't measured by achievements, failures, or the opinions of others.

• Beware of overconfidence. When confidence overwhelms your desire to learn, to improve, you lose your curiosity and stop challenging yourself, leading you toward the path to complacency.

• Taking action, even in the face of uncertainty or fear, can lead to increased confidence. By stepping outside of your comfort zone, trying new experiences, and achieving small successes, you can gradually build self-assurance and belief in your abilities.

• Researchers have identified three zones: the Comfort Zone, where we often stay on autopilot; the Panic Zone, where we feel overwhelmed; and the Stretch Zone, where we grow and gain confidence through manageable challenges. Confidence doesn't stem from staying within the Comfort Zone; instead, embracing discomfort in the Stretch Zone is vital for building confidence and experiencing growth.

• Confidence is cultivated through action, yet some initial self-belief is necessary to embark on those actions. The confidence loop involves incrementally building confidence through taking action and experiencing success. Initiating action is pivotal; as you gradually gain competence, confidence naturally follows, reinforcing the cycle of growth.

Part 3

All In

Chapter 11

Deep Purpose

Purpose is your sense of direction, your meaning in life. To discover your purpose involves identifying your passions, values, and aspirations and using that self-awareness to set meaningful goals and pursue a fulfilling life. These foundational elements determine where you invest your time, what your energy levels will be, and what actions you'll take. Research shows that people who find meaning in their efforts report higher life satisfaction.[1] I'm sure that doesn't come as a surprise.

A personal sense of purpose is less of a specific end goal and more of an ongoing impact that you have on the world. It's about having a clear intention or reason that guides your actions and decisions consistently over time. It's the fuel and the motivation to continue working toward your goals, even when faced with challenges or setbacks.

Purpose is a sustained goal, not a singular achievement. Athletes too often think that their purpose is to win the World Series or the golf tournament, and when the moment passes without purpose they become lost. Achievement is a necessary part of success, yes, but purpose is what gets you back in the training room and on the golf course fast. Think of Tom Izzo the day after winning the NCAA tournament: It's not what you do, it's who you become. Purpose is an identity. Achievements are a way to live out their purpose—be it on the field or off, in or out of the office or home.

Purpose is like a compass that guides you past discomfort, over speed bumps, and through inevitable uncertainty. Like the corner pieces of a puzzle, it guides you to fill in the spaces. Your life, your goal, the "glass half full" mindset, will all create the picture you have dreamt about.

So many people are no longer content with just having a job for the sake of earning money. They want their work to have meaning, to contribute to something larger than themselves. It's a privileged position, for sure. But weaving purpose into just about any professional pursuit is possible with Dynamic Drive. McKinsey researched individual purpose and discovered that about 85 percent of people feel they have a purpose, and about 70 percent of those people say they define their purpose through work. Millennials are even more likely than other generations to see their work as their life calling. So what that means is that people are looking for opportunities in the work they do day-to-day to be actually contributing to what they believe their purpose is.[2] That's a great thing. When people are working toward something they believe in, they tend to be more motivated and engaged.

A clear purpose drives you to live your best life. Purpose is the why that gives your life meaning, and it is distinctly personal to you. I think passion is great, as something that will *start* your engine. Purpose will provide the drive that sustains it.

Purpose is the pathway to deeper life fulfillment. It is not what other people think it is, it's what you know it is for you. Purpose is your ultimate motivator and gives you clarity to see and expand possibilities for your life.

Getting clear on your purpose will direct your drive, as the research on purpose and results demonstrates.[3] "Purposeful people are more likely to know the pathways to accomplish a goal, feel the motivation to do so, and have the passion and perseverance to overcome what it takes to succeed."[4]

Purpose is a dynamic and evolving concept, and it can change as you grow, learn, and experience new things in life, just as it did with me as I stepped away from one career into another. It's not uncommon for people to redefine or refine their sense of purpose as they encounter different life stages and circumstances.

Purpose can serve as a powerful antidote to complacency. When you have a clear mission in your life, you're inspired and determined to stay focused and engaged in your pursuits, even (and especially) when faced with challenges or obstacles. Having a strong sense of purpose creates intrinsic motivation, which means that you're motivated by internal factors rather than external rewards. This internal motivation is more enduring and resilient, keeping you consistently engaged in your endeavors.

The Role of Deep Purpose

I spent years helping high-performing athletes maximize their careers on and off the field, unleashing their full potential. I loved guiding my clients through a remarkably unique window of time as a professional athlete. After my first book (a book about how to secure tough jobs), I began receiving requests to speak to college students and athletes about sports business and my career as an agent. After my second book (a book more fitting for businesspeople), I began to receive requests from companies to speak on peak performance. Every time, it was evident that my stories, experiences, and application of such to their world was equipping leaders and teams with fresh and transferable skills, both at home and at work.

My heart was shifting. And my purpose was shifting.

What I was doing as an agent had always been fulfilling and impactful. I guided the seasoned pros through challenges, advocated for them, and helped them transition off the field into whatever was next. It felt important and I loved it. My clients were my friends, their families were like my families. Funerals, weddings, new babies, and big contracts, our relationships ran the gamut. But I couldn't shake the sense that there was more for me to do. I couldn't shake the middle-school girl who couldn't stop grabbing Zig Ziglar's books and cassette tapes. Every time I delivered a talk, I experienced the gap in the market I was closing in a way that was fulfilling, exciting, and, most importantly, making an impact on others.

In 2010, I left my secure, comfortable job as a sports agent to step into a new career as a full-time motivational speaker, a leap of faith, which I did with the support and encouragement of my family and my clients. I had to reengage my Dynamic Drive. I didn't necessarily have the specific discipline or curiosity practices, the right connections, or the confidence in this particular arena. But I did have Dynamic Drive memory muscle in spades from my years of leveling up as an agent, and I took myself through my paces to achieve the same level in my new pursuit. I had to build confidence speaking in front of increasingly large audiences, delivering important and often personal messages in a new way.

I had officially flipped the switch as a solopreneur bringing my insights on performance to corporations as a keynote speaker. My clients began asking for more tools and tactics to get what they want. I needed to unlock my curiosity and my Dynamic Drive to serve them.

In 2016, I launched what is now known as Game Changer Performance Group, a consultancy experiential training company, and since then we've consulted and trained individuals and teams globally on energy, negotiation, and leadership development for women.

When I launched my podcast, *Game Changers with Molly Fletcher*, in 2017, I tapped back into that curiosity to have conversations with thought leaders, athletes and coaches, and entrepreneurs to bring their messages of living into Dynamic Drive to the world. I wanted to connect, and to share these powerful conversations with others.

I know now that this was absolutely the right transition. My businesses have allowed me to spread my message and live into my purpose: to lead, inspire, and connect with courage and optimism.

I've had moments of awe and gratitude along the way, like when I shared a stage with the legendary Billie Jean King, Magic Johnson, or big-brand CEOs, or when my Game Changer Performance Group changes outcomes for organizations and their people globally.

The more you engage with Dynamic Drive, the more you unlock deeper, more meaningful moments. The work you've been doing with the Seven Keys anchors you back to your purpose, and in the process of building your mindset, energy, discipline, curiosity, resilience, connection, and confidence, you will also deepen your understanding of your purpose.

Choosing to take ownership of your life—identifying what matters to you and what you're chasing—is at the heart of Dynamic Drive. Don't wait on the baseline for life to come at you. Step forward and make it happen. Trade complacency for ownership and tap into your fearlessness.

Purpose can unlock your drive, and drive can unlock your purpose.

When you know your why, it will change what you do. There's fascinating research in which individuals are confronted with big challenges in their life and then their brains were studied using fMRI technology. The control group was just told about these big changes with little context. The experimental group was told to reflect on their core values for a few minutes before they were presented with the same big changes. Researchers found that the group that reflected on their core values showed activity in the brain associated with taking on challenges and taking action, and decreased activity in the part of the brain associated with fear and overwhelm. The control group that did not reflect on their core values showed much more activity in the part of their brain associated with fear and overwhelm. When researchers asked the people how they felt, people who had reflected on their core values felt confident that they could do the right thing. Unsurprisingly, the people in the control group felt completely overwhelmed.[5] When you have a clear understanding of your values and purpose, your actions take on a deeper meaning and obstacles don't seem as daunting.

Your purpose also helps you filter out distractions and focus on what truly matters. It becomes easier to say no to activities or tasks that don't align, allowing you to allocate your time and resources more effectively.

Consider the role purpose plays in this story: There's a plank between two New York City high-rise buildings, with no net underneath it. There's an 80 percent chance you'd make it if you walked across, and there's a 20 percent chance you would die. Would you walk across it for $1 million? When I share this story from the stage, about 5 percent of the room raises their hand.

Then I ask, "How about three million bucks?" A couple more hands go up.

"How about five million?" And then a few more hands.

And then I ask, "What if the most important people in your life were on the other side of that plank, and you could only save them if you walked across to get them, would you walk across the plank?" Before I can finish the sentence, every hand goes up.

When you know why you do what you do, it changes what you do.

When there's a real why, you do things that are unimaginable.

Your Purpose Will Evolve

Different life stages bring various responsibilities and priorities. For example, what was once a primary focus on career success might later shift toward building meaningful relationships or contributing to a cause. Life experiences, both positive and challenging, can lead to personal growth and self-discovery. These experiences can shape an individual's values and passions, influencing their sense of purpose.

It's never too late to change your life. Ten years into a successful career as a nightclub promoter, Scott Harrison felt empty and unhappy. By many standards he had achieved success, but in his own words he was emotionally, spiritually, and morally bankrupt. His lifestyle wasn't sustainable: he was eating dinner at 10 p.m., arriving at the club by midnight, and then going to the after-hours party until 5 a.m. He was doing drugs all night and taking an Ambien to come down the following day. At twenty-eight years old, he realized it wasn't working for him anymore. The outside world would have thought he was crushing it, but the truth was he felt empty. What was he chasing? The superficial look of success? The exciting but destructive and soulless pursuit of what feels good in the moment?

Scott had a wake-up call and asked himself the very question I suggest you start asking yourself: "What do you want your tombstone to say?" His answer? Pretty alarming.

Scott told me, "I had enough of the things that I was chasing and none of them made me happy. I contributed nothing to the planet. My tombstone was going to read: 'Here lies a man who got a million people drunk.'"

Desperate for change, he signed up to volunteer on a humanitarian mission. He figured he'd spent ten years living selfishly, and this would be an opportunity to give back. He sold everything he owned. In 2004, he joined a mission as a volunteer photojournalist on a hospital ship in Liberia, where he first learned about the impact of the global water crisis.

That experience inspired him to start the nonprofit charity: water to bring clean water to developing countries around the world. Today, the organization charity: water has helped more than 14.7 million people get access to clean water. Scott is walking proof of the power of finding your purpose and why it's never too late to make a change.

Connecting with deep purpose like Scott did can lead to a new and unexpected path. Life is a dynamic journey, and as people experience new things, learn, grow, and face different challenges, their priorities and perspectives can change. I see this all the time in our training courses.

A few years ago, a prominent litigation attorney participated in our Energy: Optimize Your Performance training. He was fifty-five years old and had worked his entire adult life toward making partner at his firm. He came to our energy training when he was feeling stifled, burned out, and disconnected at work. He knew he needed a jumpstart to get him out of the drift of complacency. The experience with us helped him to unlock a deeper understanding of his mission in life. A year later, he wrote to me to share that he retired from law and became a high school English teacher. He loves kids and he loves teaching. He didn't wait it out, suffering and passing time until retirement, as I hear so many people do. And he didn't care about the external opinions of the career shift. He opted into his Dynamic Drive.

Purpose is something that you can uncover through doing, through action, and through showing up. Get clear on the direction, do the work of reflection, and then take it out to the streets. You'll continue to refine it. You're molding it constantly. Putting yourself out there, even in less-than-ideal circumstances, allows you to learn about your purpose and to dig deeper into how it feels as you're engaging it. You'll see the gifts and benefits of a clear purpose when you start to live into it.

Achievement does not bring fulfillment, purpose does.

While waiting for perfection, opportunities may pass you by. Go for progress, not perfection. Taking action can create its own momentum. Once you start making progress, you may find yourself inspired and motivated to continue pushing forward.

Purpose takes time. Don't rush it.

Allyson Felix is a five-time Olympian who recently retired as the most decorated American track-and-field star of all time with thirty medals. Felix was at the top of her game, when through a difficult experience, she found her purpose shifting and strengthening. In November 2018, Felix's daughter was born, and she says it was a terrifying time because she was negotiating a renewal of her Nike contract, which had ended in December 2017.

It's fair to say that negotiations did not go well. Despite all of her victories, Nike wanted to pay her 70 percent less than before.[6] Felix asked Nike to contractually guarantee that she wouldn't be punished if she didn't perform at her best in the months following childbirth. While Nike agreed to her terms, it declined to extend these terms to all female athletes, and Felix moved on. She says she wanted to set a new standard for female athletes.

Without a footwear sponsor and fueled by her experience, Felix started her own shoe and lifestyle brand called Saysh. She became the most decorated track-and-field athlete at the Tokyo Olympics in 2021, all while wearing her own shoe. It was a true full-circle moment.

Ultimately, because of Felix's outspoken stance along with that of several other top female athletes, Nike announced a new maternity policy for all sponsored athletes guaranteeing an athlete's pay and bonuses for the eighteen months surrounding pregnancy. Three other athletic apparel companies followed suit and added maternity protections for their own sponsored athletes.

Felix was able to work for incredible change and continues to serve as an advocate for women's rights, maternal health, and gender equality in sports.

Clarifying Your Purpose Statement

Just as companies develop core values and mission statements, you must do the same. Crafting a purpose statement forces you to explore a deeper understanding of your values, passions, and what truly matters to you. When faced with multiple options, you can assess which choice aligns best with your purpose and values. This clarity can help you set meaningful and achievable purpose-aligned goals. Your purpose becomes the filter through which you make decisions, define priorities, and clarify your goals.

A personal purpose statement is a compass that can guide our way through the inevitable moments of discomfort and uncertainty en route to our goals. It reflects who you are, and want to be. Taking the time to drill down to your essential beliefs and personal story will help you understand your true self—on your way to your best self. In only a few words, you have a motto that's easily accessible when you need it most.

Many years ago, I was away from home at a personal development retreat, working on crafting my personal purpose statement. I was feeling great about my progress when I called my husband, who, aside from handling his professional career, was also handling all the normal daily issues at home with our three young girls.

While I was feeling inspired and focused from my time at the retreat, I could tell my husband had experienced an exhausting day. Sometimes those long-distance parenting calls can be challenging when you aren't in the same physical location to support each other.

This call was a bit different when my husband told me that one of the girls had lice, and he was stuck combing through three little heads alone. His frustration and exhaustion were palpable through the phone. He was being pulled between the heavy responsibilities of our family and urgent work matters. It was a tough spot to be in, made all the worse by my absence.

In that phone call, I didn't default to trying to micromanage the situation, even if that was my first thought. I paused to reflect on my ten-word purpose statement, which is "to inspire, lead, and connect with courage and optimism." At that moment, I asked myself: "How could I connect? What could I say or do to inspire him through this frustration, to lead him to a new and better place mentally?" Instead of frustration or caving in, I reflected on my purpose statement, which allowed me to shift and show up in a way that was going to serve us better.

I asked him what I could do from afar to support him at this moment. I reached out to a local salon near our home that specializes in lice treatment and I made appointments for the girls. I couldn't do much else, but I made sure to reassure him that he was an amazing dad and he would be able to shepherd our family through this with grace. And I tried to bring some levity to the situation, even managing to elicit a few laughs with my lice jokes. I didn't actually comb through anyone's hair that day, but in approaching the conversation through the lens of my purpose statement, I was able to offer my best self when my husband and girls needed it.

My entire response changed in light of the lens I was now looking through. So did the conversation, and the next one with my mom, and the next one with my client, and the others after that. I was focused on my purpose, not on fixing and getting frustrated, but rather offering my best thinking and support to others. When I can keep my purpose as my lens, it changes the entire dynamic of the conversation in a healthy way. For me, these ten words are my why.

My personal purpose statement has become so much more than words for me. In a conversation with my employees, I think about my purpose statement and dig deeper. In parenting our now young adult daughters, I think about my purpose statement. This phrase grounds me and helps me bring my best self to most (because it's a work in progress) moments every day.

A meaningful personal purpose statement contains a few basic elements.

- Who do you want to be?—What values you want to live into consistently, how you want to show up in the world, who you are when you are your best self.
- What impact do you want to make?—What you want to accomplish, what contributions you want to make. Consider your natural gifts.

One way to start this somewhat overwhelming process is to think about your deepest values. Consider your top five values. Write them down.

Then ask yourself who you are when you are your best, your truest self. With that in mind, ask yourself the questions below:

- What are you deepest-held values?
- What do you want your legacy to be?
- What contributions do you want to make?
- How do you want people to describe you?
- What does success look like in your life?
- What matters most?
- What are your gifts and passions that you want to live into?

Write your answers down. Sleep on it. It's important to remember that there are no right answers. Purpose statements take work, time, and thoughtfulness. Be gentle and patient with yourself as you unwrap this important collection of words that become your North Star.

The next day, review what you captured and highlight your top values, the phrases and words that pop off the page as the truest for you. Now begin to combine it into a sentence. I recommend one strong, powerful, memorable sentence.

We regularly help people home in on their purpose statements during our training experiences. These are examples from people who have gone through the process:

- To enthusiastically connect, energetically engage, and purposefully challenge others to be their best selves.
- To inspire others to act with curiosity and confidence.
- To educate young minds and create compassionate, empathetic, and hard-working members of society.
- To bring beauty to the world through my unique perspective and artistic talents.
- To act as an instrument of positive change in my family, my work, and my community and to use my voice to inspire change in others.
- To contribute to a sustainable future through conscious choices and meaningful actions.
- To bring new technology to the forefront of our culture and to develop groundbreaking solutions.

Remember to keep it precise and simple. A purpose statement should be easy to remember and share. Once you have your purpose statement, review it periodically. It can serve as a constant reminder of your core values and aspirations.

Keep your purpose statement visible. I keep my purpose statement written on the whiteboard in my office. Some people keep it as their screen saver on their computer or phone. One woman who experienced our training framed prints of her purpose statement and put it around her house to look at and read consistently. And another commissioned a piece of art with her purpose statement featured.

For more guidance on crafting your own purpose statement, visit www.getdynamicdrive.com/resources.

Chapter 12

Alignment

Alignment refers to the state of harmony or congruence between different aspects of one's life, values, goals, and actions. Living your life in a way that aligns with your deepest values enables you to show up in the world better, happier, and kinder, and you are unlocking your best self every single day. Alignment means consciously integrating and organizing various elements of life to work cohesively and purposefully together. When someone is living in alignment, they experience a sense of fulfillment, authenticity, and balance.

Like all of Dynamic Drive, alignment is an evolving and ongoing process. As life circumstances change, priorities may shift, and new challenges may arise, requiring reassessment. Living in alignment doesn't mean everything will always be perfect, but it does help you navigate life's ups and downs with a stronger sense of purpose and contentment.

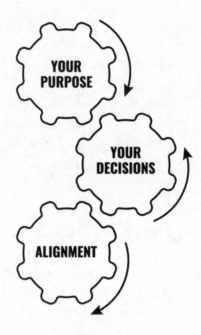

The Myth of Balance

The myth of balance is that not only can you achieve balance, but that it's an ideal state you want to attain. Balance implies that there's an equation to solve, that each side must equal out to operate optimally. If you add something in one area of your life, you must subtract from another.

It's such a catchphrase being thrown around to working moms, especially as some form of closeted judgment. It's a constant and exhausting cycle of trade-offs, with the unattainable goal of creating a life that is perfectly balanced. But is a "balanced" life even what we really want? Not if you are living with Dynamic Drive. I advise that you strive for alignment instead.

The key to engaging your Dynamic Drive and reaching your most meaningful goals is knowing when to focus on the different areas of your life and acknowledging that the pendulum may constantly swing back and forth. There are times to lean into a big presentation, a client pitch, or a season of travel, just as there are times when your personal life or family requires more of your attention.

This is alignment. Where balance is a fixed state, alignment is a dynamic process of adjustment and prioritization. This intentional shift of energy and focus is essential for high-impact and peak performance. Think about the way choosing a life of alignment instead of balance would impact your decisions. Let's say you got a huge opportunity at work that aligns with your values and fuels your purpose. If your end goal is balance, your default mindset is to think about what you must subtract from your life in order to say yes to this opportunity. Ultimately, you might even say no, staying exactly where you are even if that wasn't your optimal state. Whereas if you strive for alignment, you recognize the value of the opportunity and understand that it's natural to allow it to take up more space in your life. You go for the opportunity and move forward. Alignment gives you permission to put more into one place to reach a broad goal when balance demands that you compromise. The goal is all of the pieces coming together to move forward in the right direction. It's about not compromising what matters most to you.

Think of your car. When you balance your tires, you ensure the weight is evenly distributed to provide a smooth, comfortable ride. When you align your tires, you make adjustments so that all of the wheels are going in the right direction for optimal performance. The goal of a balanced life is ease and comfort. The goal of an aligned life is moving your potential in the right direction.

As vice president of fitness programming and head instructor at Peloton, Robin Arzón knows how to push people to connect to their limitless mindsets and dig into their resilience on the bike. According to Robin, balance is not necessarily something that you want to strive for. She says that it's been misrepresented and misinterpreted in society. She explains, "We have this illusion that balance means 'I am the best executive. I'm the best partner. I'm the best mom,' and all the titles and nouns that we have in the world. I think it's really disruptive, especially for caregivers, especially for women, and especially for folks who consider themselves multi-hyphenates who wear many hats, which I think in this day and age most of us do."

Instead of striving for balance, we should strive for defining our purpose as the filter for decision-making to support our life of alignment. Robin says she seeks alignment over balance. There are some days where she is 70 percent executive and entrepreneur and 30 percent partner and mom, and there are some days when she's 90 percent with her family to the exclusion of most everything else. She delegates and she prioritizes. She's taken the time and energy to get clear on her priorities, and that creates the opportunity to say "no."

The myth of balance hit me for the first time as a new mother. My husband and I had our first child, a healthy baby girl, and just twelve and a half months later, I delivered our twins. That's three babies in thirteen months. I had a team of agents, hundreds of clients, and now, three miracles (as I still call my grown daughters). I had a lot of demands on my energy, and I found myself immediately locked into the pursuit of balance. Perfect symmetry day in and day out. Just the right amount of focus and attention on my clients, my employees, my husband, my kids, my parents, my brothers, my friends. I forgot that I needed to create a little space for me in this balancing act, but that was okay, because I was going to handle everything else so well.

Guess what? I failed and I felt like a failure. In reality, it's an exhausting misguided attempt for that nebulous, unattainable, overused word: balance. In all of this searching for balance and consideration of the demands on my energy, one thing always seemed to me missing: me.

When we work to achieve balance, we often put ourselves last in order to do it. Then we find ourselves exhausted, burned out, and resentful. I usually was able to give the girls their first bottle, or nurse both twins football style (that really is a thing), or later feed all three in a high chair at once before racing out the door with a cup of coffee on an empty stomach. I gave it all away all day, mustered up enough gas coming back in the door to relieve the nanny only to suck down a glass of wine while my husband and I tag-teamed dinner, bath, and bedtime. Sometimes I remembered to scarf down a bowl of ice cream for dinner and went to bed praying no one would wake up in the night. I was a size zero (I'd never been a size zero in my life) just a couple months after delivering two full-term six-plus pound babies. I was evaporating, literally, in my valiant attempt at the impossible state of balance. My scorecard was wrong. Heck, I was playing the wrong game.

Imbalance is an inherent piece of pursuing a goal wholeheartedly. It's a reality of living a life of Dynamic Drive. As long as your decision-making is in alignment with your purpose, you'll be good. Make your choices with intention and clarity to ensure that you are aligning with your goals, your purpose, and your desired outcomes. Life is dynamic, and your alignment will be, too. Some days you'll over deliver as a wife or mother. Some days, on purpose, you'll be in full focus with your work. Your drive will narrow your focus, but it won't blind you to your intentions.

The drive that narrows focus for specific goals also widens opportunities because it conditions people to always seek ways to get better. It teaches you to concentrate and go "All In!" across all of life and tap into parts of your genius that may otherwise be ignored.

Alignment is an internal calibration. Balance is outward, but if you're aligned with your values and your goals it's okay. Alignment is an internal process where you ensure that your actions, decisions, and behaviors are in harmony with your core values, beliefs, and life purpose. It involves being true to yourself, staying authentic, and living in accordance with what you hold dear, not what others expect of you. When you're aligned with your values and goals, you have a clear sense of direction and purpose in life.

On the other hand, balance is an external consideration that involves the distribution of time, energy, and attention among different aspects of your life, such as work, family, hobbies, and relationships. Striving for balance relies on the external circumstances that you can't control, and may create more pressure.

Alignment is anchored in deeply rooted clarity of values, purpose, and legacy. Alignment in our choices and actions helps us to get clear on what matters more and gives us the courage to say "no." It becomes an essential filter for decision-making.

Like when you step out of a meeting when your child's school calls you instead of sending them to voicemail. Or when you say yes to a walk with your daughter instead of staying strapped to your computer. Or when you turn your phone on "Do not disturb" to have an important conversation with a colleague. When you say yes to contributing to your church community, when it means saying no to sleeping in on Sunday.

All day, every day, we're presented with choices. It's up to us to choose who and what we give our energy to. It's up to us to lean into the clarity of our life's purpose.

Dynamic Drive Offsets Burnout

People assume that drive depletes energy. They believe that level of intensity, focus, and daily effort leads to burnout.

What is burnout, really? Burnout is a state of chronic physical and emotional exhaustion caused by prolonged stress and demanding or draining activities. Your flame has been burning too hot for too long. Burnout is typically accompanied by feelings of cynicism, detachment, and a reduced sense of accomplishment. Sounds like a fast track to complacency to me.

Burnout has recently been defined as "a work-related state of exhaustion that occurs among employees, which is characterized by extreme tiredness, reduced ability to regulate cognitive and emotional processes, and mental distancing."[1]

Dr. Christina Maslach, a professor of psychology at the University of California, Berkeley, and one of the world's foremost experts on occupational burnout, defines the three components of burnout: the stress response of exhaustion; the negative response to the job of cynicism, which leads to suboptimal performance; and the negative response to self, of inefficacy.[2]

Maslach suggests that one of the ways to mitigate burnout is to ask yourself: "Is this really what I want to be doing? Does it align with my values?"

People feel burned out when they aren't aligning their work with their highest purpose. Dynamic Drive is infused with purpose at its core. This purpose, which is threaded through your daily efforts, infuses your work, your energy, and your output with a higher calling. It's not about a singular achievement, as we know, but rather about an identity that you're proud to own. So, when we hear people complain about burnout, it's often compounded by a misalignment toward purpose. The lens they are looking through isn't aligning with something bigger than the tasks at hand, causing it all to feel like something they have to do versus something they get to do. They drift through life, in and out of the stages of complacency, because they misunderstand how to go for more and don't have clarity on the path to a healthier journey.

Burnout is, in part, a result of a lack of alignment with your greater purpose. The solution to mitigate burnout is realignment with your purpose and values. When you do things that fulfill you, it's much more difficult to get burned out.

McKinsey recently did a study on burnout in companies post-COVID, and their research showed that participants who indicated they are "living their purpose" at work are much more likely to sustain or improve their levels of work effectiveness than those not aligned with their purpose. Those living with purpose had four times higher engagement and five times higher well-being.[3]

So what can we do about burnout? Maslach makes a key distinction between coping and prevention when it comes to facing burnout. Coping is a Band-Aid approach, like feeling some relief by taking a vacation, spending a few hours engaging in an activity you enjoy, or taking time off from work. But it doesn't get to the root of the problem. Instead, it presses pause. When you go back, those stressors are still going to be there and there are still going to be the problems that were leading to the burnout in the first place.[4]

Dynamic Drive pushes us to focus on what matters most in a different way—and that reenergizes the soul. Often when people experience burnout they focus on the problems and all that is going wrong when really they should ask themselves: "Does it align with my values?"

Burnout is about the expectations you set for yourself. Burnout starts way before you feel the exhaustion and disconnection. It starts in the beginning, with the expectations. External pressures including societal expectations, family demands, or workplace cultures that prioritize constant productivity can be sources of stress. When people feel compelled to meet these external expectations at the expense of their well-being, burnout becomes more likely. By aligning yourself with your core values—the ones that you hold for yourself, not others—you can work at combating those external expectations.

Now, purpose isn't a single silver bullet to solve for burnout—but it is a leading contributing factor.

Chapter 13

The Work Is Never Done

With a strong sense of Dynamic Drive, you'll find yourself more excited, prepared, and motivated to pursue your goals and dreams. You'll have a clear purpose and direction, which can push you to take action even in the face of challenges. You'll be less prone to distractions and more inclined to prioritize tasks that align with your objectives. Pursuing your ambitions and continuously striving for improvement will lead to personal growth. You'll learn new skills, gain knowledge, and develop a deeper understanding of yourself.

Challenges and setbacks are a natural part of life, but with Dynamic Drive, you'll be better equipped to bounce back from adversity. Instead of shying away from challenges, you'll be more likely to embrace them as opportunities for growth and learning. Your determination will help you persevere through tough times and come out stronger.

As you build the skills of discipline, resilience, and curiosity, and as you work on maximizing your energy and mindset, the work itself will get easier over time. That's when it's crucial to reengage with your purpose and goals and push yourself to improve. The pursuit of improvement and growth should be ongoing. Even when things become easier due to increased discipline, resilience, and energy, it's important to avoid complacency. Complacency can lead to stagnation and missed opportunities for development. Continuously seeking ways to improve yourself and your work is essential for long-term success. Without that, you're susceptible to drifting right into complacency. Reconnecting with your purpose and goals can reignite your motivation and enthusiasm for your work. It reminds you of why you started your journey and what you hope to accomplish.

A dear friend of mine, who is married with children, worked hard to become a successful salesperson in the medical device space. His customers loved him, and he built a robust client base. He talks to them often, sees them consistently, and anticipates their needs well. But then he got too comfortable. His boss told me that he took his relationships for granted. You'd rarely see him in the hospital early in the morning after his workouts (because he stopped going to the gym) like he used to do. He started to coast. And he started losing market share—fast. His phone was ringing, and it wasn't his customers. It was his boss. He was complacent, and needed to level up his Dynamic Drive.

Here's what he did:

Mindset: He tapped into his purpose, which was to positively impact the lives of the patients and their families with the products he sells.

Energy: He went into his calendar and protected thirty minutes on Monday, Wednesday, and Friday before his kids got up to do a workout at home. He set his Bible by his coffee machine and started reading it, with the goal of just five minutes in the morning while the coffee was brewing.

Discipline: Whenever he wanted to stop—in anything, his workouts, another sales call—he did one more. Just one more, but every time. Those "one mores" often turned into deals and sales. In fact, a "one more" got him back at the top of the sales leaderboard.

Curiosity: He had always loved to listen to podcasts between sales calls in the car, but that had slipped. He cued up his favorites and would listen to them during his morning and evening drive home.

Resilience: He put his purpose statement in his wallet alongside a picture of his family. After he heard "no" from a doctor, he would look at it before driving to the next appointment to help him recover fast.

Connection: He protected Friday nights for date night with his wife and called his parents every Sunday afternoon.

Confidence: He connected with his friends, family, and colleagues who can provide encouragement and positive feedback. Having a strong support system can make a significant difference in reigniting your confidence.

This is a lifelong process to better yourself and your skills. You must constantly reset and assess, even if you've worked the Seven Keys and feel like your work with Dynamic Drive is firing on all cylinders. Various keys will require more focus—some will be lit up all the time, and some will fade away.

Drive Dynamic Check-In Model

Complacency can sneak up on you, so it's essential to recognize the signs so you can take steps to address it and continue growing. Ask yourself these questions to assess and adjust, so that when you lose your spark—and you will—you know what to do.

	If you say . . .	Go and . . .
Mindset	"I can't do it."	Do a Total Mindset Reset.
Energy	"I don't have enough time."	Do the Energy Audit and update your calendar.

Discipline	"I've worked hard, so I can skip today."	Step back onto your Discipline Bridge to remember where you're heading.
Curiosity	"I know what I need to know."	Cold call people who are where you want to be and ask them questions.
Resilience	"I'll never recover."	Pull out your Smile File and revisit your purpose statement.
Connection	"I don't feel close to many people in my life."	Identify your most important relationships and map out a path for connection using the six-step process.
Confidence	"I'm not good enough."	Rewind the tape and revisit your successes.

Use Failure as Fuel

You aren't living in Dynamic Drive if you aren't failing. The pursuit of better means that we'll miss and fail. Of course we will! Failure is inevitable when you're pushing yourself to operate at a higher level. Accept that, and use it as fuel to DRIVE forward.

Here are some strategies to harness failure and turn it into a driving force. Cultivate the belief that failure is not a dead end, but an opportunity for learning and improvement.

Understand that abilities and intelligence can be developed through dedication and hard work. Take the time to reflect on what went wrong and why. Identify the mistakes you made, the decisions that led to the failure, and the lessons you can extract from the experience.

Engage your resilience. Failure can be discouraging, but it's essential to persevere through tough times. Keep pushing forward, knowing that failure is a natural part of the process, and success often requires multiple attempts.

Our societal narrative is that failure is negative, it means that you came up short by definition. People want to avoid it. But when you avoid the kinds of challenges that push you out of your comfort zone, you suffocate your drive. In a world where so much is visible, with one click, criticism of others is rampant. The easy path is to do what you know how to do, ask only what you already know the answer to—because that feels safe. We have to push hard against our inherent tendency here, against society's low tolerance of failure.

People with drive respond to failure differently. Those with Dynamic Drive take their failures as fuel. No one who has done anything interesting in life has let failure stop them. Instead, use failure as motivation to set clear and realistic goals. Create a new plan that takes into account the lessons learned from past failures. Instead of seeing failure as a personal attack or indictment of your abilities, view it as feedback on what didn't work in a particular situation. This can help you refine your approach and make better decisions in the future.

Each time you experience failure and bounce back from it, you build resilience. Over time, this resilience will help you face future challenges with a more positive and determined outlook. I know firsthand the power of using failure as fuel. I wrote a book to help people find tough jobs. I wanted to help the hundreds of young people who would reach out to me every year about how to get into the sports agent space whom I couldn't meet with one on one.

I went to a coffee shop by my house every day for a year to write. I wanted to help these eager young people pursue their dreams. I was pregnant with my oldest daughter, Emma, when I first started writing. After she was born, I'd run across to the coffee shop during her nap times and write. When I finally finished the manuscript, I knew my next step was reaching out to publishers. I sent letters and a copy of the manuscript to over thirty publishers—yes, letters; these were the days before email. I checked the mail every day, eagerly awaiting a response. And when I began to hear back, it wasn't what I hoped. I could have wallpapered my apartment with the rejection letters from publishers big and small. Even friends of friends said "no thanks." When I was in New York for a work trip, I managed to secure an in-person meeting with a publisher. It lasted ten minutes. It was just so that they could tell me no to my face.

I wrote more letters, and sent more queries out to publishers, until finally a small publisher in Indianapolis was willing to give me twenty minutes in their office to pitch the team on my book. With much preparation and excitement, I went to Indianapolis for what was, at this point, my single best option. They bit. I had a publisher!

Failure is integral to succeeding at what you most want. That's what I observed over and over with the athletes and coaches that I represented. Baseball players who fail 70 percent of the time at the plate might find themselves in the Hall of Fame. Coaches make the wrong call, football players miss tackles, golfers bogey holes, basketball players miss open shots, I didn't get every client I tried to sign. Here's the difference between good and great: how quickly you learn from it and recover.

Most great teams are solidified in moments of adversity. Clemson football coach Dabo Swinney has led his team to two national championships, but before they got their first title, they suffered a heartbreaking defeat. After an undefeated regular season in 2015 (perfection!), Clemson lost to Alabama in the national championship game. Dabo made sure that it was going to be a teachable moment. In the locker room, he stood in front of his players and gave them this message: "Don't let failure define you; let it develop you." He assured them they would be back the next season if they could do that. And in a storybook ending, that's exactly what happened. A year later, Clemson again faced Alabama with a national championship on the line. This time, it ended in a victory for Dabo and his team.

When you're focused on perfection, you're not doing the work of becoming resilient. Embracing imperfection allows you to take on more risk. This is the way we grow. A popular TED Talk by Reshma Saujani, the founder of Girls Who Code, makes the point that when we raise children to be perfect, we're not encouraging them to be brave. Taking risks is the soul of innovation. "We have to begin to undo the socialization of perfection," Reshma says.

Humans aren't perfect, and we aren't meant to be. If we're going to try to change in life, if we are going to be curious to evolve, along that journey we will miss, we will fail, we will fall. It's okay. Be gentle on yourself. Speak to yourself like you would speak to someone you love and respect. Expect the unexpected, and know the journey is real because it is imperfect, and it is imperfect because it is real. Trust the process, and don't let perfection stifle your progress.

And most importantly: keep going.

Dynamic Drive DNA

When you live with Dynamic Drive, it becomes a part of who you are. It's a badge of honor and symbol of freedom from complacency as you navigate the world around you. Your goals become opportunities to lean into hard work, engage your discipline and resilience, and expand your mindset.

Imagine a world in which you operate at the highest level of Dynamic Drive:

You are clear and committed to your purpose. You know why you are working hard. The results aren't the focus, the process is. When things get hard, you expect them. You welcome them. You glance at your purpose, swallow it whole again, and keep going. You say no and you know why. You say yes and know why. It's not an accident where you focus your time and energy; it's on purpose for a purpose.

Some people might question you, but their questioning holds no space in your head or heart unless they are part of your trusted, no-agenda tribe. You ask questions, to everyone from the Amazon delivery person to the leader of your company. You know that questions can inspire other people, and they might just unlock new ideas and opportunities for you. Questions create connections and bring your interests to life. You ask questions with the curiosity of a toddler and wrap it with safety that inspires the same back.

You are consistent and committed to what you want most, not what might be in front of you. You do the hard things repeatedly and reap the benefit of it. It inspires others around you to do the same. Failure is fuel to you. You welcome it because you know it means you are pushing your limits. The difference with your Dynamic Drive DNA is that you recover fast when you fall, really fast. You don't stay down, and here's what's cool: you come back better. You hear "no" and you see a starting line, not the red tape.

You embody confidence and humility all in one, walking that tightrope with ease. Your schedule protects your energy and your deepest priorities. You show up for the people and the moments in your life that matter most. You are fully present in your relationships. You are fulfilled and ambitious. Your daily efforts feel meaningful, and you feel like you are making an impact. People are encouraged by your optimism. They admire your confidence and curiosity. They watch you stumble and come back stronger.

You are content, but not complacent.

You're changed now. Dynamic Drive has become your identity.

Acknowledgments

My husband, Fred, who has supported the writing process of a book six times now very patiently for over two decades of our marriage. Thank you for your consistent love and support. I love you!

My mom and dad and my twin brothers. You were the first to help inspire Dynamic Drive in me. I love you!

Meg Fletcher, my daughter, who spent part of her summer supporting me in capturing stories, research, and perspective that made this book better. I love you, angel.

Sprague Paynter, thank you for your brilliance and unwavering commitment to this book and our mission. You are a gift to me and our entire team. I appreciate you.

Piper Neblett, thank you for always being eager to roll up your sleeves and unleash your marketing genius. This book is the in the hands of more people because of you, thank you.

Anne Reich, thank you for tapping into your Dynamic Drive with your curiosity, positive energy and supporting us with connecting this book to so many of the people and companies we serve. I am so grateful for you!

Jen Schuster, you captured my words, stories, and the research so seamlessly, and we had fun along the way. Thank you for your relentless commitment.

Acknowledgments

Nena Madonia Oshman, my literary agent, your belief, relationships and Dynamic Drive made this book possible. Thank you my friend.

Lauren Marino, my editor, and the team at Hachette, thank you for your belief in this book and Dynamic Drive. Thank you!

To discover more tools for Dynamic Drive,
visit www.getdynamicdrive.com/resources

Notes

Chapter 1

1. Kendall Cotton Bronk et al., "Purpose, Hope, and Life Satisfaction in Three Age Groups," *Journal of Positive Psychology* 4, no. 6 (2009): 500–510, https://doi.org/10.1080/17439760903271439.

2. Jim Baker, "The Story of Three Bricklayers—A Parable About the Power of Purpose," Sacred Structures by Jim Baker, September 10, 2021, https://sacredstructures.org/mission/the-story-of-three-bricklayers-a-parable-about-the-power-of-purpose/.

Chapter 2

1. Sharon Lipinski, "Biological Basis of Complacency," Habit Mastery Consulting, accessed August 16, 2023, https://habitmasteryconsulting.com/complacency-report/.

2. Lipinski, "Biological Basis."

3. AFFIDAVIT OF JEFFERY J. STEGENGA, In re Blockbuster, Inc., Case No. 1:10-bk-14977 (Bankr. S.D.N.Y. 2010) (No. 4).

4. Minda Zetlin, "Blockbuster Could Have Bought Netflix for $50 Million, but the CEO . . . ," accessed August 24, 2023, https://www.inc.com/minda-zetlin/netflix-blockbuster-meeting-marc-randolph-reed-hastings-john-antioco.html.

5. Todd Davis and John Higgins, "A Blockbuster Failure: How an Outdated Business Model Destroyed a Giant," accessed August 24, 2023, https://ir.law.utk.edu/cgi/viewcontent.cgi?article=1010&context=utk_studlawbankruptcy.

Chapter 3

1. Shosuke Suzuki et al., "Distinct Regions of the Striatum Underlying Effort, Movement Initiation and Effort Discounting," *Nature Human Behaviour* 5, no. 3 (2020): 378–388, https://doi.org/10.1038/s41562-020-00972-y.

2. Richard Sima, "The Brain Loves a Challenge. Here's Why," *Washington Post*, November 25, 2022, https://www.washingtonpost.com/wellness/2022/09/29/train-brain -for-hard-things/.

3. Georgia Clay et al., "Rewarding Cognitive Effort Increases the Intrinsic Value of Mental Labor," *Proceedings of the National Academy of Sciences* 119, no. 5 (2022), https://doi .org/10.1073/pnas.2111785119.

4. "Mark Lepper: Intrinsic Motivation, Extrinsic Motivation and the Process of Learning," Bing Nursery School, September 1, 2003, https://bingschool.stanford.edu /news/mark-lepper-intrinsic-motivation-extrinsic-motivation-and-process-learning.

5. Eric—Education Resources Information Center, accessed August 24, 2023, https:// files.eric.ed.gov/fulltext/ED556901.pdf.

6. Mark R. Lepper, David Greene, and Richard E. Nisbett, "Undermining Children's Intrinsic Interest with Extrinsic Reward: A Test of the 'Overjustification' Hypothesis," *Journal of Personality and Social Psychology* 28, no. 1 (1973): 129–137, https://doi .org/10.1037/h0035519.

7. Andrew Huberman, "Controlling Your Dopamine for Motivation, Focus & Satisfaction," Huberman Lab, July 17, 2022, https://hubermanlab.com/controlling-your -dopamine-for-motivation-focus-and-satisfaction/.

8. Huberman, "Controlling Your Dopamine."

9. Huberman, "Controlling Your Dopamine."

10. Matt Fuchs, "How to Get Healthier Dopamine Highs," *Time*, March 7, 2022, https://time.com/6155109/healthier-dopamine-highs/.

11. "Dopamine Deficiency: Symptoms, Causes & Treatment," Cleveland Clinic, accessed August 23, 2023, https://my.clevelandclinic.org/health/articles/22588-dopamine -deficiency.

12. Ian Connole, "Expect the Expected—Vision Pursue," Vision Pursue, May 25, 2020, https://visionpursue.com/expect-the-expected/.

13. Stephanie Watson, "Dopamine: The Pathway to Pleasure," *Harvard Health*, July 20, 2021, https://www.health.harvard.edu/mind-and-mood/dopamine-the-pathway -to-pleasure.

14. Michael Gervais, PhD, *The First Rule of Mastery: Stop Worrying About What People Think of You* (Harvard Business Review Press, 2023).

15. Lisa Evans, "The Positive Effects of Competition at Work," *Fast Company*, accessed August 24, 2023, https://www.fastcompany.com/90240826/this-is-how -competition-affects-your-brain-motivation-and-productivity.

16. Gavin J. Kilduff, Hillary Anger Elfenbein, and Barry M. Staw, "The Psychology of Rivalry: A Relationally Dependent Analysis of Competition," *Academy of Management Journal* 53, no. 5 (2010): 943–969, https://doi.org/10.5465/amj.2010.54533171.

17. W. E. Scott and David J. Cherrington, "Effects of Competitive, Cooperative, and Individualistic Reinforcement Contingencies," *Journal of Personality and Social Psychology* 30, no. 6 (1974): 748–758, https://doi.org/10.1037/h0037534.

18. Po Bronson and Ashley Merryman, *Top Dog: The Science of Winning and Losing* (Twelve, 2014).

19. Paolo Fulghieri and Merih Sevilir, "Mergers, Spin-Offs, and Employee Incentives," SSRN, November 17, 2010, https://papers.ssrn.com/sol3/papers.cfm?abstract_id=1710230.

20. Brynne C. DiMenici and Elizabeth Tricomi, "The Power of Competition: Effects of Social Motivation on Attention, Sustained Physical Effort, and Learning," *Frontiers in Psychology*, accessed August 23, 2023, https://pubmed.ncbi.nlm.nih.gov/26388801/.

Chapter 4

1. Kevin Baxter, "Carli Lloyd Is Mentally 'Stronger Than Ever' Thanks to Motivational Mentor," *Los Angeles Times*, June 17, 2019, https://www.latimes.com/sports/soccer/la-sp-carli-lloyd-james-galanis-world-cup-20190617-story.html.

2. Mike Jensen, "Mental Toughness Key to Carli Lloyd's Success," *Philadelphia Inquirer*, July 1, 2015, https://www.inquirer.com/philly/sports/soccer/worldcup/20150702_Carli_Lloyd_tells_The_Inquirer_how_she_stays_focused.html.

3. Carli Lloyd, "It's So Hard to Say Goodbye," *The Player's Tribune*, October 26, 2021, https://www.theplayerstribune.com/posts/carli-lloyd-uswnt-soccer-retirement.

4. Ethan Kross and Gretchen Rubin, *Chatter: The Voice in Our Head, Why It Matters, and How to Harness It* (Crown, 2021).

5. Albert Bandura, "Self-Efficacy: Toward a Unifying Theory of Behavioral Change," *Psychological Review* 84, no. 2 (1977): 191–215, https://doi.org/10.1037/0033-295x.84.2.191.

6. Richard Gregory Cowden, "Mental Toughness and Success in Sport: A Review and Prospect," *The Open Sports Sciences Journal* 10, no. 1 (2017): 1–14, accessed August 24, 2023, https://www.researchgate.net/publication/314286944_Mental_Toughness_and_Success_in_Sport_A_Review_and_Prospect.

7. A. W. Blanchfield et al., "Talking Yourself Out of Exhaustion: The Effects of Self-talk on Endurance Performance," *Medicine & Science in Sports & Exercise* 46, no. 5 (2014): 998–1007, accessed August 24, 2023, https://doi.org/10.1249/MSS.0000000000000184.

8. Carol S. Dweck, *Mindset: The New Psychology of Success* (Ballantine Books, 2006).

9. Mariana Brandman, "Biography: Serena Williams," National Women's History Museum, accessed August 23, 2023, http://www.womenshistory.org/education-resources/biographies/serena-williams.

10. Dweck, *Mindset*, ch. 1.

11. Tony Morris, Peter Terry, and Sandy Gordon, *Sport and Exercise Psychology: International Perspectives* (Fitness Information Technology, 2007).

12. Dweck, *Mindset*, ch. 2.

13. John Tayler, "Marlins' Jeff Francoeur Stays Positive Despite . . .," *Sports Illustrated*, accessed August 24, 2023, https://www.si.com/mlb/2016/09/01/jeff-francoeur-marlins-braves-career-sports-illustrated.

14. Tayler, "Marlins' Jeff Francoeur."

15. Joe Morgan, "The Meteoric Rise and Fall of Jeff Francoeur," Bleacher Report,

September 22, 2017, https://bleacherreport.com/articles/209182-the-meteoric-rise-and-fall-of-jeff-francoeur-and-how-he-will-bounce-back.

16. "Brian McCann Stats, Fantasy & News," MLB.com, accessed August 23, 2023, https://www.mlb.com/player/brian-mccann-435263.

17. "Brain Facts," Healthy Brains by Cleveland Clinic, May 11, 2020, https://healthybrains.org/brain-facts/.

Chapter 5

1. Leslie A. Perlow, "The Time Famine: Toward a Sociology of Work Time," *Administrative Science Quarterly* 44, no. 1 (1999): 57–81, https://doi.org/10.2307/2667031.

2. Toby Schwartz and Catherine McCarthy, "Manage Your Energy, Not Your Time," *Harvard Business Review*, February 8, 2023, https://hbr.org/2007/10/manage-your-energy-not-your-time.

3. James E. Loehr, *The Power of Full Engagement: Managing Energy, Not Time, Is the Key to High Performance and Personal Renewal* (Simon and Schuster, 2005).

4. Greg McKeown, *Essentialism: The Disciplined Pursuit of Less* (Currency, 2021).

5. Cal Newport, *Deep Work: Rules for Focused Success in a Distracted World* (Grand Central Publishing, 2016).

6. Earl Miller, "Here's Why You Shouldn't Multitask, According to a MIT Neuroscientist," *Fortune*, December 9, 2016, https://fortune.com/2016/12/07/why-you-shouldnt-multitask/.

7. Kevin P. Magore and Anthony D. Wagner, "Multicosts of Multitasking," *Cerebrum: The Dana Forum on Brain Science*, accessed August 23, 2023, https://pubmed.ncbi.nlm.nih.gov/32206165/.

8. Daniel Levitin, "How Multitasking Depletes Your Brain's Resources—And How to Restore Concentration," Big Think, September 30, 2021, https://bigthink.com/videos/daniel-levitin-on-multitasking-and-brain-evolution/.

9. UCLA Newsroom, "Don't Talk to a Friend While Reading This; Multi-Tasking Adversely Affects the Brain's Learning Systems, UCLA Scientists Report," https://www.Newmediawire.Com/News/Dont-talk-to-a-friend-while-reading-this;-multi-tasking-adversely-affects-the-brains-learning-systems-ucla-scientists-report-3072195.

10. Zameena Mejia, "How to Time Your Day for Peak Performance, Based on Your Chronotype," CNBC, April 30, 2018, https://www.cnbc.com/2018/04/30/daniel-pink-how-to-time-your-day-for-peak-performance.html.

11. Sooyeol Kim, Young Ah Park, and Lucille Headrick, "Daily Micro-Breaks and Job Performance: General Work Engagement as a Cross-Level Moderator," *Journal of Applied Psychology* 103, no. 7 (2018): 772–786, accessed August 23, 2023, https://pubmed.ncbi.nlm.nih.gov/29595289/.

Chapter 6

1. Stephania Bell, "Redskins QB Alex Smith 'Very Much Lucky to Be Alive' After Broken Leg," ESPN, accessed August 23, 2023, https://www.espn.com/espn/otl/story/_/id/28612793/redskins-qb-alex-smith-very-much-lucky-alive-broken-leg.

2. Billy Heyen, "What Happened to Alex Smith? The Story of His Broken Leg and a 'Miracle' NFL Comeback Two Years Later," *Sporting News*, September 18, 2021, https://www.sportingnews.com/us/nfl/news/alex-smith-broken-leg-injury-comeback-story/wikuf6ojjfsq131mepdrcuanb.

3. Alex Smith, "An NFL Quarterback on Overcoming Setbacks and Self-Doubt," TED Talk, accessed August 23, 2023, https://www.ted.com/talks/alex_smith_an_nfl_quarterback_on_overcoming_setbacks_and_self_doubt.

4. Angela L. Duckworth and Martin E. P. Seligman, "Self-Discipline Outdoes IQ in Predicting Academic Performance of Adolescents," *Psychological Science* 16, no. 12 (2005): 939–944, accessed August 23, 2023, https://pubmed.ncbi.nlm.nih.gov/16313657/.

5. Mark Manson, "How to 80/20 Your Life," March 15, 2023, https://markmanson.net/80-20-your-life.

6. Matthieu Ricard, "Neuroscience Reveals the Secrets of Meditation's Benefits," *Scientific American*, November 1, 2014, https://doi.org/10.1038/scientificamerican1114-38.

7. Madhav Goyal et al., "Meditation Programs for Psychological Stress and Well-Being: A Systematic Review and Meta-Analysis," *JAMA Internal Medicine* 174, no. 2 (2014): 357–368, accessed August 23, 2023, https://pubmed.ncbi.nlm.nih.gov/24395196/.

8. Elizabeth A. Hoge et al., "Randomized Controlled Trial of Mindfulness Meditation for Generalized Anxiety Disorder: Effects on Anxiety and Stress Reactivity," *Journal of Clinical Psychiatry* 74, no. 8 (2013): 786–792, accessed August 23, 2023, https://pubmed.ncbi.nlm.nih.gov/23541163/.

9. Brooke Lefferts, "Interview: Tom Brady on His Full Plate and What's Bringing Him Joy," NBC Boston, June 9, 2023, https://www.nbcboston.com/news/local/interview-tom-brady-on-his-full-plate-and-whats-bringing-him-joy/3064623/.

10. Sally Jenkins, "Beneath the Mystery of Tom Brady's Greatness Is a Modest Secret: Self-Discipline," *Washington Post*, November 12, 2021, https://www.washingtonpost.com/sports/2021/11/12/tom-brady-age-longevity-discipline/.

11. Sally Jenkins, "Intentionally Grounded," *Washington Post*, January 16, 2005, https://www.washingtonpost.com/archive/sports/2005/01/16/intentionally-grounded/75ba0d61-4f9d-42d1-ab79-810b1f49dd09/.

12. Greg Magliocetti, "Patriots Legend Julian Edelman: Tom Brady Promised 'Go for Jordan!,'" accessed August 24, 2023, https://www.si.com/nfl/patriots/news/new-england-patriots-julian-edelman-tom-brady-super-bowl-xlix-michael-jordan-go-for-jordan-promise.

13. "Steve Nash Career Stats—NBA," ESPN, accessed August 24, 2023, https://www.espn.com/nba/player/stats/_/id/592/steve-nash.

14. Kathleen Elkins, "How David Goggins Went from an Exterminator Living Paycheck-to-Paycheck to a Navy SEAL," CNBC, May 15, 2019, https://www.cnbc.com/2019/05/15/how-david-goggins-went-from-broke-exterminator-to-navy-seal.html.

15. Tom Bilyeu, "David Goggins on How He Became Unstoppable and Doing the Unthinkable | Impact Theory," YouTube, May 11, 2021, https://www.youtube.com/watch?v=Swj8GIIivXs.

16. Bilyeu, "David Goggins."

17. David Goggins, *Can't Hurt Me: Master Your Mind and Defy the Odds* (Lioncrest Publishing, 2021).

18. Elliot T. Berkman, "The Neuroscience of Goals and Behavior Change," *Consulting Psychology Journal: Practice and Research* 70, no. 1 (2018): 28–44, https://doi.org/10.1037/cpb0000094.

Chapter 7

1. Andy Raine and M. Pandya, "Three Keys to Entrepreneurial Success: Curiosity, Creativity, and Commitment," *Entrepreneurship Education* 2, no. 3 (2019): 189–198, https://doi.org/10.1007/s41959-019-00019-y.

2. Celeste Kidd and Benjamin Y. Hayden, "The Psychology and Neuroscience of Curiosity,"*Neuron* 88, no. 3 (2015): 449–460, https://doi.org/10.1016/j.neuron.2015.09.010.

3. Tomas Chamorro-Premuzic, "Curiosity Is as Important as Intelligence," *Harvard Business Review*, November 5, 2014, https://hbr.org/2014/08/curiosity-is-as-important-as-intelligence.

4. Matthias J Gruber, Bernard D Gelman, and Charan Ranganath, "States of Curiosity Modulate Hippocampus-Dependent Learning via the Dopaminergic Circuit," *Neuron* 84, no. 2 (2014): 486–496, https://doi.org/10.1016/j.neuron.2014.08.060.

5. William James, *The Principles of Psychology*, vol. 1, Henry Holt, 1890, https://doi.org/10.1037/10538-000.

6. Spencer Harrison, Jon Cohen, and Erin Pinkus, "Research: 83% of Executives Say They Encourage Curiosity. Just 52% of Employees Agree," *Harvard Business Review*, January 20, 2021, https://hbr.org/2018/09/research-83-of-executives-say-they-encourage-curiosity-just-52-of-employees-agree.

7. Spencer Harrison and Jon Cohen, "Curiosity Is Your Super Power," TED Talk, accessed August 24, 2023, https://www.ted.com/talks/spencer_harrison_jon_cohen_curiosity_is_your_super_power.

8. Gruber et al., "States of Curiosity."

9. CellPressNews, "How Curiosity Changes the Brain to Enhance Learning," Eurek Alert!, accessed August 24, 2023, https://www.eurekalert.org/news-releases/500062.

10. Rachit Dubey, Thomas L Griffiths, and Tania Lombrozo, "If It's Important, Then I'm Curious: Increasing Perceived Usefulness Stimulates Curiosity," *Cognition* 226 (2022), https://doi.org/10.1016/j.cognition.2022.105193.

11. Christopher Peterson and Martin E.P. Seligman, *Character Strengths and Virtues: A Handbook and Classification*, vol. 1, Oxford University Press, 2004.

12. Workstream, "Kat Cole's 3 Drivers for Career Growth," accessed August 24, 2023, https://www.workstream.us/blog/kat-coles-3-drivers-for-career-growth.

13. Maura Brannigan, "In Building Allbirds, Less Has Always Been More," Ideas, April 17, 2020, https://www.wework.com/ideas/research-insights/expert-insights/in-building-allbirds-less-has-always-been-more.

14. Simon Mainwaring, "Purpose at Work: How Allbirds Is Redefining Progress,"

Forbes, February 8, 2021, https://www.forbes.com/sites/simonmainwaring/2021/02/08/purpose-at-work-how-allbirds-is-redefining-progress/?sh=363986406128.

15. Lauren Debter, "Allbirds Valued at over $4 Billion After Stock Surges in IPO," *Forbes*, November 8, 2021, https://www.forbes.com/sites/laurendebter/2021/11/03/allbirds-shares-soar-after-shoemaker-raises-over-300-million-in-ipo/?sh=1630f72a6902.

16. "Sunrise Speaker Spotlight: Tim Brown, Allbirds," Blackbird, accessed August 24, 2023, https://www.blackbird.vc/blog/sunrise-speaker-spotlight-tim-brown-allbirds.

17. Sarah Austin, "Cultivating Curiosity Is What Drives Innovation," Entrepreneur, June 10, 2020, https://www.entrepreneur.com/leadership/cultivating-curiosity-is-what-drives-innovation/351487.

18. James Clear, "Shoshin: A Remarkable Zen Concept Used to Let Go of Old Assumptions," James Clear, June 12, 2018, https://jamesclear.com/shoshin.

19. Lattice, "How Defining Values and Culture Helped Airbnb Achieve Worldwide Success," Medium, October 30, 2017, https://medium.com/resources-for-humans/how-defining-values-and-culture-helped-airbnb-achieve-worldwide-success-ff7adef06092.

20. Alex Davies. "Inside X, the Moonshot Factory Racing to Build the Next Google," *Wired Magazine*, July 11, 2018, https://www.wired.comstory/alphabet-google-x-innovation-loon-wing-graduation/.

Chapter 8

1. Andrew Zolli and Ann Marie Healy, *Resilience: Why Things Bounce Back* (Simon & Schuster Paperbacks, 2013).

2. "Kobe Bryant—This Is Such BS! All the Training and . . . ," Facebook, accessed August 24, 2023, https://www.facebook.com/Kobe/posts/this-is-such-bs-all-the-training-and-sacrifice-just-flew-out-the-window-with-one/10151563315250419/.

3. John Jefferson Tan, "'It Started as Just a Hashtag That Came to Me One Day'—Kobe Bryant Revealed the Story Behind the Creation of 'Mamba Mentality,'" accessed August 24, 2023, https://www.basketballnetwork.net/old-school/kobe-bryant-revealed-the-story-behind-the-creation-of-mamba-mentality.

4. Marianne Cumella Reddan, Tor Dessart Wager, and Daniela Schiller, "Attenuating Neural Threat Expression with Imagination," *Neuron* 100, no. 4 (2018): 994–1005.e4, https://doi.org/10.1016/j.neuron.2018.10.047.

5. David Fletcher and Mustafa Sarkar, "A Grounded Theory of Psychological Resilience in Olympic Champions," *Psychology of Sport and Exercise* 13, no. 5 (2012): 669–678, https://doi.org/10.1016/j.psychsport.2012.04.007.

6. Francesca Gino, "The Business Case for Curiosity," *Harvard Business Review*, July 8, 2021, https://hbr.org/2018/09/the-business-case-for-curiosity.

7. Sibel Kaya and Dilan Karakoc, "Math Mindsets and Academic Grit: How Are They Related to Primary Math Achievement?," *European Journal of Science and Mathematics Education* 10, no. 3 (2022): 298–309, https://doi.org/10.30935/scimath/11881.

8. Yian Yin et al., "Quantifying the Dynamics of Failure Across Science, Startups and Security," *Nature* 575, no. 7781 (2019): 190–194, https://doi.org/10.1038s41586-019-1725-y.

9. Jean-Charles Lebeau et al., "Is Failing the Key to Success? A Randomized Experiment Investigating Goal Attainment Effects on Cognitions, Emotions, and Subsequent Performance," *Psychology of Sport and Exercise* 38 (2018): 1–9, https://doi.org/10.1016/j.psychsport.2018.05.005.

10. Kelly McGonigal, *The Upside of Stress: Why Stress Is Good for You, and How to Get Good at It* (New York: Penguin, 2016).

11. Chris Loftis, "Mental Flexibility," *Encyclopedia of Clinical Neuropsychology*, 2016, https://doi.org/10.1007/978-3-319-56782-2_2123-2.

12. Lena Rademacher, et al. "Individual Differences in Resilience to Stress Are Associated with Affective Flexibility," *Psychology Research* 87, no. 6 (2023): 1862–1879, doi: 10.1007/s00426-022-01779-4.

13. Tiziana Ramaci et al., "Psychological Flexibility and Mindfulness as Predictors of Individual Outcomes in Hospital Health Workers," *Frontiers in Psychology* 10 (2019): 1302, https://doi.org/10.3389/fpsyg.2019.01302.

Chapter 9

1. Scott Edinger, "Three Elements of Great Communication, According to Aristotle," *Harvard Business Review*, August 7, 2014, https://hbr.org/2013/01/three-elements-of-great-communication-according.

2. Mark Mabry, "Gregory Walton on Social Connectedness and Motivation," Bing Nursery School, October 1, 2010, https://bingschool.stanford.edu/news/gregory-walton-social-connectedness-and-motivation.

3. Gregory M. Walton et al., "Mere Belonging: The Power of Social Connections," *Journal of Personality and Social Psychology* 102, no. 3 (2012): 513–532, https://doi.org/10.1037/a0025731.

4. Mabry, "Gregory Walton."

5. James H. Fowler and Nicholas A. Christakis, "Dynamic Spread of Happiness in a Large Social Network: Longitudinal Analysis over 20 Years in the Framingham Heart Study," *BMJ* 337, no. dec04 2 (2008), https://doi.org/10.1136/bmj.a2338.

6. William Park, "How Your Friends Change Your Habits—For Better and Worse—BBC Future," BBC News, March 14, 2023, https://www.bbc.com/future/article/20190520-how-your-friends-change-your-habits—for-better-and-worse.

7. Paul J. Zak, "The Neuroscience of Trust," *Harvard Business Review*, August 31, 2021, https://hbr.org/2017/01/the-neuroscience-of-trust.

Chapter 10

1. Daniel Druckman and Robert A. Bjork, "Learning, Remembering, Believing: Enhancing Human Performance," National Academies Press, accessed August 24, 2023, https://nap.nationalacademies.org/catalog/2303/learning-remembering-believing-enhancing-human-performance.

2. Druckman et al., "Learning, Remembering."

3. Roy F. Baumeister et al., "Does High Self-Esteem Cause Better Performance,

Interpersonal Success, Happiness, or Healthier Lifestyles?," *Psychological Science in the Public Interest* 4, no. 1 (2003): 1–44, https://doi.org/10.1111/1529-1006.01431.

4. Carol S. Dweck, *Mindset: The New Psychology of Success* (Ballantine Books, 2006).

5. Margie Warrell, "Use It or Lose It: The Science Behind Self-Confidence," *Forbes*, October 12, 2022, https://www.forbes.com/sites/margiewarrell/2015/02/26/build-self-confidence-5strategies/.

6. Jim Kwik and Lisa Bilyeu, "Bring out Your Radical Confidence | Jim Kwik & Lisa Bilyeu," YouTube, May 9, 2022, https://www.youtube.com/watch?v=5W3WPuw0z1k.

7. Alan Henry, "The Science of Breaking out of Your Comfort Zone (and Why You Should)," Lifehacker, September 26, 2019, https://lifehacker.com/the-science-of-breaking-out-of-your-comfort-zone-and-w-656426705.

Chapter 11

1. Kendall Cotton Bronk et al., "Purpose, Hope, and Life Satisfaction in Three Age Groups," *Journal of Positive Psychology* 4, no. 6 (2009): 500–510, https://doi.org/10.1080/17439760903271439.

2. Naina Dhingra and Bill Schaninger, "The Search for Purpose at Work," McKinsey & Company, June 3, 2021, https://www.mckinsey.com/capabilities/people-and-organizational-performance/our-insights/the-search-for-purpose-at-work.

3. Patrick L. Hill et al., "Sense of Purpose Moderates the Associations Between Daily Stressors and Daily Well-Being," *Annals of Behavioral Medicine* 52, no. 8 (2018): 724–729, https://doi.org/10.1093/abm/kax039.

4. Gabrielle Pfund and P. L. Hill, "The Multifaceted Benefits of Purpose in Life," Researchgate, accessed August 24, 2023, https://www.researchgate.net/publication/330565076_The_Multifaceted_Benefits_of_Purpose_in_Life.

5. Emily B. Falk et al., "Self-Affirmation Alters the Brain's Response to Health Messages and Subsequent Behavior Change," *Proceedings of the National Academy of Sciences* 112, no. 7 (2015): 1977–1982, https://www.pnas.org /doi/10.1073/pnas.1500247112.

6. Allyson Felix et al., "Allyson Felix: My Own Nike Pregnancy Story," *New York Times*, May 22, 2019, https://www.nytimes.com/2019/05/22/opinion/allyson-felix-pregnancy-nike.html.

Chapter 12

1. Wilmar Schaufeli and Hans De Witte, "Burnout Assessment Tool," Een onderzoeksproject door KU Leuven, August 7, 2023, https://burnoutassessmenttool.be/.

2. Christina Maslach, "Speaking of Psychology: Why We're Burned Out and What to Do About It," American Psychological Association, accessed August 24, 2023, https://www.apa.org/news/podcasts/speaking-of-psychology/burnout.

3. Jonathan Emmett et al., "Covid-19 and the Employee Experience: How Leaders Can Seize the Moment," McKinsey & Company, June 29, 2020, https://www.mckinsey.com /capabilities/people-and-organizational-performance/our-insights/covid-19-and-the -employee-experience-how-leaders-can-seize-the-moment#/.

4. Maslach, "Speaking of Psychology."